Lecture Notes in Artificial Intelligence 7099

Subseries of Lecture Notes in Computer Science

Iris Hendrickx   Sobha Lalitha Devi
António Branco   Ruslan Mitkov (Eds.)

Anaphora Processing and Applications

8th Discourse Anaphora
and Anaphor Resolution Colloquium, DAARC 2011
Faro, Portugal, October 6-7, 2011
Revised Selected Papers

Springer

Volume Editors

Iris Hendrickx
Centro de Linguística da Universidade de Lisboa
Lisboa, Portugal
E-mail: iris@clul.ul.pt

Sobha Lalitha Devi
Anna University - K. B. Chandrasekhar Research Centre
Chennai, India
E-mail: sobha@au-kbc.org

António Branco
Universidade de Lisboa, Faculdade de Ciências
Lisboa, Portugal
E-mail: antonio.branco@di.fc.ul.pt

Ruslan Mitkov
University of Wolverhampton, School of Humanities
Wolverhampton, UK
E-mail: r.mitkov@wlv.ac.uk

ISSN 0302-9743 e-ISSN 1611-3349
ISBN 978-3-642-25916-6 ISBN 978-3-642-25917-3 (eBook)
DOI 10.1007/978-3-642-25917-3
Springer Heidelberg Dordrecht London New York

Library of Congress Control Number: 2011942993

CR Subject Classification (1998): I.2.7, I.2, I.7, F.4.3, I.5, H.3-4

LNCS Sublibrary: SL 7 – Artificial Intelligence

Typesetting: Camera-ready by author, data conversion by Scientific Publishing Services, Chennai, India

Printed on acid-free paper

Springer is part of Springer Science+Business Media (www.springer.com)

Preface

Anaphora has been studied from different perspectives and these studies have given new insights into resolving this complex language phenomenon both at discourse and sentence level. As the resolution of anaphora is vital for the interpretation of language, new advances from multi- and inter-disciplinary areas such as cognitive science, artificial intelligence and human language technology, theoretical and applied linguistics and philosophy of language are urgently needed to account for the better understanding of this phenomenon and to provide a better basis for its modelling.

The ever-growing importance of this topic in different disciplines made this a frontier area of research. This is seen from the high-quality submissions received for the 8th Discourse Anaphora and Anaphora Resolution Colloquium (DAARC). This colloquium is unique in that it covers the research area in anaphora within the gamut of multidisciplinary research ranging from theoretical linguistic approaches through psycholinguistic and cognitive science to corpus studies and computational treatment. It also keeps a strong focus on automatic anaphora resolution and its applications.

Since its inception in 1996 at Lancaster University and subsequent move to the University of Lisbon in 2002, DAARC remained in Europe until its sixth edition. It moved out of Europe for the first time in 2009 to Goa, India, hosted by Anna University and in 2011 it moved back to the University of Lisbon for the eighth edition which was held at Faro, Portugal. DAARC has established itself as a specialised and competitive forum for the presentation of the latest results on anaphora processing.

The program of the eighth edition of DAARC was selected from 45 initial submissions. It included 27 oral presentations, and 5 posters from over 60 authors coming from 16 countries: Belgium, Czech Republic, Denmark, France, Germany, India, Italy, The Netherlands, Poland, Portugal, Romania, Russia, Switzerland, Spain, UK and USA. The 16 best rated papers according to the reviews among the 27 selected were considered for this volume. These are the regular papers presented at DAARC. As a whole the accepted papers provide a unique overview of cutting-edge research in the field of anaphora resolution conducted at present. The submissions were anonymised and submitted to a selection process in which each received three evaluation reports by experts from the Programme Committee listed here.

The eighth edition of DAARC2011 lasted for two days, with invited talks, two parallel paper sessions and a poster session. These were further complemented with a tutorial on an open source anaphora resolution system. This edition of DAARC was honoured to have two invited speakers: Maria Mercedez Piñango, from Yale University, USA, and Emiel Krahmer, from Tilburg University, The Netherlands.

We would like to thank all the authors of submitted papers for choosing DAARC2011 for the presentation of their research results. Due to the high quality of the submitted papers, selecting the 32 papers was a very difficult task. We are deeply indebted to all the Programme Committee members for their conscientious and impartial judgment in the reviewing process of DAARC, and in particular of the papers included in the present volume. Without them neither this colloquium nor the present volume would have been possible.

October 2011

Iris Hendrickx
Sobha Lalitha Devi
António Branco
Ruslan Mitkov

Organisation

The 8th DAARC colloquium was organized by the University of Lisbon.

Organising Committee

António Branco	University of Lisbon, Portugal
Iris Hendrickx	University of Lisbon, CLUL, Portugal
Sobha Lalitha Devi	Anna University Chennai, India
Ruslan Mitkov	University of Wolverhampton, UK

Programme Committee

Sergey Avrutin	University of Utrecht, The Netherlands
Sivaji Bandopadhyaya	Jadavpur University, India
Patricio Martinez Barco	University of Alicante, Spain
Peter Bosch	University of Osnabrück, Germany
António Branco	University of Lisbon, Portugal
Francis Cornish	University Toulouse-Le Mirail, France
Dan Cristea	Alexandru Ioan Cuza University of Iaşi, Romania
Robert Dale	Macquarie University, Australia
Jeanette Gundel	University Minnesota, USA
Laura Hasler	University of Strathclyde, UK
Lars Hellan	Norwegian University of Science and Technology, Norway
Iris Hendrickx	University of Lisbon, Portugal
Graeme Hirst	University Toronto, Canada
Anke Holler	University of Göttingen, Germany
Véronique Hoste	University College Ghent, Belgium
Elsi Kaiser	University of Southern California, USA
Andrew Kehler	University of California, San Diego, USA
Roger Kibble	Goldsmiths University of London, UK
Andrej Kibrik	Russian Academy of Sciences, Russia
Sobha Lalitha Devi	AU-KBC Research Centre, India
José Leitão	University of Coimbra, Portugal
Fons Maes	Tilburg University, The Netherlands
Ruslan Mitkov	University of Wolverhampton, UK

Kavi Narayana Murthy	University of Hyderabad, India
Costanza Navarretta	University of Copenhagen, Denmark
Vincent Ng	University of Texas at Dallas, USA
Constantin Orasan	University of Wolverhampton, UK
Maria Mercedes Piñango	Yale University, USA
Massimo Poesio	University of Essex, UK
Georgiana Puscasu	University of Wolverhampton, UK
Marta Recasens	University of Barcelona, Spain
Eric Reuland	University of Utrecht, The Netherlands
Jeffrey Runner	University of Rochester, USA
Petra Schumacher	University of Mainz, Germany
Veselin Stoyanov	Johns Hopkins University, USA
Roland Stuckardt	University of Frankfurt am Main, Germany
Joel Tetreault	Educational Testing Service, Princeton, USA
Renata Vieira	Pontifícia Universidade do Rio Grande do Sul, Brazil
Jos van Berkum	University of Utrecht, The Netherlands
Klaus von Heusinger	University of Stuttgart, Germany

Table of Contents

Computational Resolution Methodology and Systems

Language Analysis and Representation

Human Processing and Performance

Analysis and Reference Resolution of Bridge Anaphora across Different Text Genres

Iris Hendrickx[1], Orphée De Clercq[2], and Veronique Hoste[2,3]

[1] Centro de Linguística da Universidade de Lisboa, Lisboa, Portugal
iris@clul.ul.pt
[2] LT3, School of Translation Studies, University College Ghent, Belgium
{orphee.declercq,veronique.hoste}@hogent.be
[3] Faculty of Linguistics, Ghent University, Ghent, Belgium

Abstract. We discuss bridge relations in Dutch between two textual referents across six different text genres. After briefly presenting the annotation guidelines and inter-annotation agreement results, we conduct an in-depth manual analysis of the different types of bridge relations found in our data sets. This analysis reveals that for all genres bridging references stand mostly in a class relationship, which is exactly the kind of information represented in a WordNet hierarchy. This inspired us to investigate to what extent a standard coreference resolution system for Dutch is capable of resolving bridge relations across different text genres and study the effect of adding semantic features encoding WordNet information. Our results reveal modest improvements when using Dutch WordNet LCS information for all but one genre.

Keywords: coreference resolution, bridging, Dutch, cross-genre, WordNet.

1 Introduction

Automatic coreference resolution systems are defined as systems that automatically detect references to discourse entities in a text. Often the same entity is mentioned multiple times in a text and it is the task of the resolution system to determine which mentions refer to the same entity (we will denote these as "identity" relations) and which ones introduce a new entity in the discourse. Besides these clear cases of direct references to previously mentioned entities, texts can also contain indirect, or more vague relations between two mentions. One of the earlier studies to introduce the term *bridging* for these instances was conducted by Clark [2]. He documents several scenarios in which an inference step is needed to grasp the meaning intended by the speaker. An important conclusion Clark draws about bridge relations is that the language or text itself does not offer the solution to resolve this inference relation, the listener or reader needs to use its world knowledge about the anaphor and antecedent to make the correct interpretation. Moreover, Clark also lists several types of bridging such as set-membership, part-whole relations, roles, reasons and consequences.

I. Hendrickx et al. (Eds.): DAARC 2011, LNAI 7099, pp. 1–11, 2011.

In this paper we discuss the annotation and resolution of bridge relations in Dutch across six different text genres: administrative texts (ADM) such as notes from political meetings or official speeches, texts used for external communication (EXT) such as commercial brochures, instructive texts (INST) for example instruction manuals of domestic products, newspaper text (JOUR), medical encyclopedic texts (MED) and wikipedia text (WIKI).

The broad definition for annotating bridge relations in the guidelines followed [1], and low inter-annotator agreement results necessitated an in-depth analysis of what had exactly been annotated as *bridge* in our data. In order to do so we decided to manually analyze 50 examples of each genre following a recently developed typology suited for bridging relation annotation [20].

Based on this analysis and previous studies on resolving bridge relations (e.g. [15,14,9]), we also present a first version of an automatic resolution system for Dutch bridge relations. We wish to investigate to what extent a standard mention-pair coreference resolver is applicable to the task, how it behaves across different genres, and study the usefulness of WordNet (WN) for resolving bridge relations in our data sets since computing semantic distance based on WN has proven a useful feature in previous work [14].

2 Related Work

Bridging anaphora have been extensively investigated by Poesio et al. [16,15,24,14]. Both the typology of bridging references and different information sources to improve automatic resolution were studied. Since bridging reference resolution often requires some form of world knowledge – or at least information that is not explicitly represented in the textual context of the reference – several investigations were conducted to measure the usefulness of WordNet as an external resource to resolve bridge relations. It was shown, however, that information extracted from WordNet does not necessarily help resolving bridge relations [24]. Another method is to use syntactic patterns that are able to express part-whole relations such as "the x of the y". If such patterns of a potential antecedent and anaphor are found with a high frequency in a corpus [13] or on the web [14,9], this provides a strong clue that they could stand in a bridge relation. Besides the above-mentioned features, in [14] features expressing salience, such as utterance distance and first-mention were also studied. Here, WordNet and Google were employed to compute lexical distances between referents and the study revealed that using the hypernym relations in WordNet gives comparable performance to using Google. [19] and [18] study bridge relations from a more theoretical viewpoint and focus on how to distinguish bridge relations from identity relations in the annotation task. This will be discussed in closer detail in Section 3.1.

Table 1. Statistics on the 6 different data sets and the type of annotated referential relations

genre	#texts	#tokens	IDENT	BRIDGE	PRED	BOUND
ADM	41	49,335	3,547	80	242	5
EXT	129	149,501	11,066	383	519	31
INST	26	38,001	3,869	92	1,566	2
JOUR	172	127,040	10,463	318	495	67
MED	499	74,445	4,924	1,779	289	19
WIKI	66	177,766	16,533	504	1,007	6

3 Annotation of Bridge Relations

For this study we use bridge relations that have been annotated during two Dutch corpus projects: SoNaR [22][1] and COREA [1][2]. In both projects different text types were annotated with coreferential relations. In the present study we decided not to use all available annotated data, more informal text genres such as blogs or spoken texts were excluded since these are difficult to process automatically. Six different text genres were selected, more information and some data statistics are presented in Table 1. Besides bridge relations, who are at the subject of this study, the coreference annotation includes identity, predicative and bound (e.g. '*every man* has *his* problems') relations. The data sets differ widely in size, document length and annotated relations: INST is the smallest genre, both in the number of documents and tokens. In comparison to the other genres, the MED data set contains a remarkably high amount of annotated bridge relations, which can be explained by this genre's explanatory nature. The data consists of short encyclopedic descriptions; a human body part or a disease, for example, is first described in general terms followed by more specific features.

In both projects coreference was annotated according to the same COREA guidelines [1]. In these guidelines a bridge relation is vaguely defined as 'a partial coreference relation exists when reference is made to a subpart of an object that has already been mentioned in the discourse', after which some Dutch examples are presented demonstrating two types of bridge relations: part-whole and subset-superset.

Here are some examples of how bridge relations have been annotated. Example 1 is taken from the JOUR data set and illustrates a superset -subset relation in which the antecedent expresses a rather general class whereas the anaphoric element is more specific. Example 2, also taken from a newspaper article, represents a part-whole relation and Example 3 (WIKI) shows two entities almost referring to the same thing. The first referent focuses on a published series whereas the second one refers to the physical albums.

[1] SoNaR is currently still under development.

[2] These data sets are available at: `http://www.inl.nl/tst-centrale`

Example 1. **Natuurlijke therapieën** zoals **voedingstherapie**, toepassingen van warmte, lucht, licht en water. (*Eng:* **Natural therapies** *such as* **nutritional therapy**, *application of heat, air, light and water.*)

Example 2. Voor **de website** hebben we de laatste tijd veel inspanningen gedaan. Van op **de Engelstalige homepage** kan je nu bijvoorbeeld met één klik naar een volledig aanbod van de Engelstalige masterprogramma's. (*Eng: A lot of effort has been put into* **the website** *lately. With only one click you can, for example, go from* **the English homepage** *to the full range of English Master's programs.*)

Example 3. De eerste verhalen werden gepubliceerd in wat **de Rode reeks** wordt genoemd (zo genoemd omdat **de albums** een helrode omslag hadden, die de reeks heel herkenbaar maakte). (*Eng: The first stories were published in what is called* **the Red series** *(given this name because* **the albums** *had a bright red color which made the series easily recognizable).*)

Other projects involving bridge annotation usually use a more fine-grained typology to label different types of bridge relations. In the GNOME corpus [12] bridge relations like set membership, subset, and generalized possession (i.e. part-whole) are annotated. The Prague Treebank [10] includes extended coreference annotation of bridge relations: part-whole, subset, functional, but two additional groups ("contrast" and "other") are also annotated in order to capture all other types of bridge relations, such as people-location or event-argument relations. The Copenhagen Dependency Treebank [7] has a very detailed annotation scheme for associative anaphora based on Pustejovsky's qualias and general semantic roles. It includes, for example, annotation of agent relations between two phrases like "the operation" and "the surgeon".

Since the COREA guidelines are not very specific nor detailed in their description of bridge relations and marking bridging references is a difficult task (cf. [17]), we can expect low inter-annotator agreement (IAA). In order to test this, two linguists annotated a set of ten randomly selected texts, containing 13,813 tokens in total. Since the COREA and SoNaR corpora comprise texts from six different domains at least one text of each genre was annotated. As evaluation metric we computed F-scores ($\beta = 1$) by each time taking one linguist as gold standard and scoring the annotations of the other for precision and recall. The results per genre can be found in Table 2, in which token counts, the total number of bridges annotated by either one of the annotators and the number of bridges on which both annotators agree are also included.

As expected, the results reveal low agreement scores for all genres, on average 46%, and most notably instructive texts with an IAA of 24% F-score. The level of complexity of the INST texts, containing many technical terms, is one of the main causes for this low agreement. When we compare this with other IAA scores on this type of task, for example [15] and [17], we find similar low agreement scores. Having a closer look at those bridging references on which both

Table 2. Inter-annotator agreement scores for bridge relations using the COREA-guidelines

genre	#tokens	#bridges total	match	$F_{\beta=1}$
ADM	1548	17	3	31.25
EXT	1134	24	13	71.57
INST	3631	40	5	24.24
JOUR	2796	46	10	39.28
MED	2260	112	44	60.08
WIKI	2444	79	22	51.42
Total	13813	318	97	46.30

annotators do agree we note that these stand mostly in a subset-superset relation and disagreements are mostly due to interpretation differences and inconsistent annotation.

Example 4 (from the JOUR data set) aptly illustrates how difficult the annotation task can be. Determining the meaning of this sentence requires very detailed and specific world knowledge. First of all, you need to know that a "V-twin" is a specific type of engine. Making the correct interpretation requires information about whether all Harley Davidson motors are equipped with this type of engine or not. Two possible interpretations exist here: if each Harley has this engine, the example expresses a metaphoric relation is which "V-twin" refers to all Harleys in general. However, it could also be the case that the writer merely sketches an image by referring to a specific type of Harley, a heavy V-twin, in that case there would be a bridge relation between Harley and V-twin[3].

Example 4. Maar het beeld van **de Harley** beklijft wel: onderuitgezakt zitten op **een zware "V-twin"**, met scènes uit de film "Easy Rider" in je hoofd. *Eng: But the image of* **the Harley** *is enthralling: slouched on* **a heavy "V-twin"**, *with scenes from the movie "Easy Rider" going through your head.*

3.1 Analysis

Since the guidelines followed do not accurately define bridge relations and the IAA results are rather low, we decided to analyse the annotations in detail. With this analysis we aimed to gain better insights into our data, i.e. to know what was exactly denoted as a bridge relation and to better understand what type of information is needed to resolve them automatically. To this purpose 50 Dutch examples were randomly selected from each of the different domains after which we tried to categorize them into the more fine-grained typology proposed by Recasens et al. [19]. They discuss a typology of *near-identity* relations closely resembling bridge relations and divide this type of relation into four broad classes: metonymy, meronymy, class type and spatio-temporal functions, each containing several subtypes. In [18] an even broader definition of bridge relation is

[3] In fact, all Harley-Davidson motors have a V-twin engine.

Table 3. Manual analysis according to the typology for Near Identity

Type	subtype	MED	WIKI	JOUR	ADM	EXT	INST
Meronymy	Part-Whole	6	9	13	1	3	2
Meronymy	Stuff-Object	0	0	0	0	2	0
Meronymy	Set-Set	5	11	11	7	12	2
Class	More specific	32	24	18	20	32	40
Class	More general	2	2	5	14	2	3
Other		4	4	3	4	0	3

presented, here referential relations are perceived as a continuum between identity and non-identity relations. Two different types of near-identity operations are identified: *neutralization* captures cases in which referents are considered to be equal and where distinctive attributes are ignored as one concentrates on what is in common. The other operation is *refocusing* which applies to referents that have a more specific or different attribute in focus than its antecedent. As the division in [19] offers a systematic annotation scheme, we decided to adopt this typology for our analysis. As far as the near-identity typology is concerned, we are mostly interested in the meronymy and class types since these match our definition of bridge relations in the COREA guidelines. In Example 1 we see a typical class type bridge relation in which the anaphor *voedingstherapie* is clearly a case of *Natuurlijke therapieën*. We were unable to completely follow the proposed typology completely because it also includes some additional classes that were not annotated as bridge-identity in our data; we chose to annotate metonymy as identity relations and we have special separate markers to denote different spatio-temporal references and modality and negation.

The left side of Table 3 lists the types and subtypes of the typology that we did use. The broad class meronymy is divided into part-whole relations where one entity is a functional part of the whole entity, stuff-object relations that cover the "is made of" relations and set-set relations that denote two (vaguely defined) overlapping sets. An example of a set-set relation can be found in Example 3.

We would like to stress that this type of annotation is highly subjective because language usage can lead to creative entity descriptions that are difficult to classify into nicely organized, predefined separate labels. This is also in line with the findings presented in [17] where 6 annotators were asked to classify difficult cases into the typology categories: for many sentences the annotators made different choices. For this reason, we added one additional type to the typology: all cases that do not fit the typology, that are erroneously labeled or that are highly ambiguous were labeled as "Other".

The results of our manual analysis of 50 annotated bridge relations for each of the 6 different text genres can be found in Table 3. The most frequent type of bridge relation found for all genres is a class relationship in which the anaphor provides a more specific description than the antecedent (such as Example 1). These more-spec class relations make up 50 to 70% of the cases. This implies that people tend to first introduce a general class, and then introduce a more specific entity referring back to this group. This tendency is particularly strong in the medical data, which can be explained by the explanatory content of these texts. For the ADM data set, however, we observe a remarkably high number of relations going in the opposite direction, i.e. a specific entity is introduced first, and later a reference to a larger class. This data set contains transcribed speeches and in Example 5, taken from a transcription of a discussion in the Belgian Senate, this relation is illustrated. We suspect that this might be a rhetorical method to draw the audience's attention.

Example 5. In het artikel 556 van hetzelfde wetboek worden zij " die (....) gestraft met **een geldboete van 10 tot 20 frank**. (....) **De straffen** waarin voorzien wordt lijken bovendien uiterst licht.
(*Eng: In article 446 from the same Code they who (...) will be punished with* **a fine of 10 to 20 francs**. *(...)* **The punishments** *provided seem extraordinarily light.*)

The second most common relation are overlapping sets (cf. Example 3), ranging from 10 to 25% for the different data sets. Part-whole relations seem rather scarce as they only occur in 1-10 % of the cases. This analysis thus reveals that although the annotated bridge relations do cover a quite diverse group of relations, the majority of the bridge relations concerns class type relations. Since this is exactly the type of information that can be extracted from the WordNet hierarchy, we decided to add additional WordNet features to our automatic coreference resolution system as will be explained in the next section.

4 Experiments

For our experiments we adopt a standard pairwise machine learning approach of Soon et al [23]. We view bridge relations, however, as a different kind of relations than the typical 'identity' relations. A common approach to automatically resolve coreferential identity relations is to first detect all referents in the text and make pairwise decisions between a potential anaphor and antecedent. As noted in Ng's survey on coreference resolution [11] this approach has the limitation that classifications are made independent from each other and that an additional clustering step is always needed to resolve overlapping and contradicting individual pair-predictions. In a bridge relation this is not the case: elements are not equal and do not all refer to the same entity, moreover, each element has a clear-cut role in the relation. One referent, for instance, expresses a more generic concept than the other, or one referent is a functional part of the other referent. This implies that the pairwise approach is well suited to accommodate this type of relation.

Since bridge relations occur less frequently than identity relations, making negative instances for all other NP pairs leads to a very sparse data set even when our search space is restricted to the 20 previous sentences. Consequently, we decided to use a sampling approach in order to reduce the number of negative instances to a ratio of 1: 3 positive/negative instances which was also done by

Poesio et al. in their study of bridge relations [14][4]. Because of this sampling approach the size of the different data sets ranges from only 68 positive instances for the ADM data set to 1698 for the MED data (this is represented in the second column of Table 4). When we compare this with the actual amount of bridge relations available in our annotated data (see Table 1), we see that the counts are slightly lower which can be explained by the limited search space. For some bridge relations the anaphor and antecedent are more than 20 sentences apart. We did manage, however, to retrieve 78% of all bridges annotated in WIKI and up to 95% in the MED data set.

We run two experiments: one with a standard feature set largely following the feature set of Soon et al, and one in which 4 additional features representing WN information were added. The coreference system and the features are described in more detail in [5,4]. Since our manual analysis revealed that most bridge relations express some kind of general/specific relation between both referents which is well expressed in the WordNet hierarchy, we chose to focus on *least common subsumer* (LCS) information of WN hyperonym relations. To determine the LCS of two words, you follow their edges upwards with the shortest possible path in the WordNet hierarchy until you reach a concept (a common subsumer) that both words share. The LCS is represented as the number of edges (distance) between the two lemmas of the head words of the two candidate referents. We also used LCS to compute three different similarity metrics: Resnik's similarity measure [21], Jiang & Conrath's similarity measure [6] and Lin's similarity measure [8]. As wordnet we use the Cornetto database[5], a lexical-semantic database for Dutch which combines EuroWordNet for Dutch and Referentiebestand Nederlands (RBN).

As our ML classifier we use Timbl [3], a k-nearest neighbor algorithm with default parameter settings. We each time perform 10-fold cross validation experiments and compute overall accuracy, and precision, recall and F-score for the bridge relations.

5 Results

Results are presented in Table 4, on the left side the results from the standard coreference resolution system are shown and on the right side the version that uses four additional WN features. In general the referential resolution system is able to correctly predict bridge relations with an F-score between 42.18% for the ADM data (without WN) and 65.69% for the JOUR data set (with WN). In general we observe that recall scores are clearly higher than precision and notable differences in performance can be observed between the data sets individually - JOUR, WIKI and MED score better than ADM, EXT and INST. This can be partly explained by the higher number of annotated unambiguous bridge relations in the training data. When we compare the performance of the

[4] We would like to stress that this is a preliminary experimental set-up and are aware of the methodological issues that arise when both train and test data are sampled.

[5] Available at `http://www.inl.nl/nl/lexica/cornetto`

Table 4. Results on bridge relation resolution

genre	# bridges	without WN				with WN			
		acc	recall	prec	$F_{\beta=1}$	acc	recall	prec	$F_{\beta=1}$
ADM	68	41.54	85.29	34.79	42.18	54.41	86.76	33.91	48.76
EXT	347	58.43	75.79	34.79	47.69	60.73	74.35	36.13	48.63
INST	86	62.21	76.74	37.50	50.38	62.50	73.26	37.28	49.41
JOUR	290	75.69	87.93	50.80	64.39	77.84	84.83	53.59	65.69
MED	1698	71.52	76.27	45.86	57.28	72.67	74.79	47.11	57.81
WIKI	398	79.75	71.90	58.98	64.81	80.12	71.32	60.00	65.17

system with and without the WN features, we see that these features do increase performance, most noticeably for the ADM data set (+ 6.58%). We also observe that in general the recall scores drops and precision goes up when WN features are added. Only for the INST data set no improvement was perceived at all (- 0.97%). We inspected the errors made by the system for these two outlier genres. For the ADM data set, containing the lowest number of bridge relations in training, we see that especially the recognition of true negatives increases because no similarity measures are found between two NPs which makes these features decisive. Looking at the INST data we notice that especially the type of bridge relations are far more complicated and therefore performance does not rise when adding WordNet features. A more fine-grained annotation is necessary to better understand these differences and to allow for a more in-depth error analysis.

6 Conclusion

We reported on the annotation and resolution of bridge relations in Dutch across six different text genres. In accordance with earlier research on bridging for other languages, we show low inter-annotator agreement scores, but also a great variability in the scores for the different genres, ranging from 24.2 % (INST) to 71.6% (EXT). A shallow analysis of these scores suggests that the complexity of the INST texts is the cause for the low agreement scores. Motivated by a more fine-grained annotation analysis which revealed that class relationships represent up to 70% of the annotated relations, we investigated whether adding WordNet LCS information improved the performance of an existing mention-pair model in revolving bridge relations. We showed modest performance improvements for five out of six text types when adding semantic information.

This first attempt to resolve bridging relations in Dutch texts revealed some shortcomings with respect to the experimental setup and the vagueness of the existing annotation guidelines. Future work will include a more in-depth annotation of the data per bridge type, in order to determine which features aid the resolution of bridge relations and to allow for a fine-grained error analysis.

Acknowledgments. This work is funded by the STEVIN programme of the Dutch Language Union within the framework of the SoNaR project under grant number STE 07014 and the National Foundation for Science and Technology (FCT) under the project "PEst-OE/LIN/UI0214/2011." Researcher under the Scientific Program *Ciência 2008.*

References

1. Bouma, G., Daelemans, W., Hendrickx, I., Hoste, V., Mineur, A.M.: The COREA-project, manual for the annotation of coreference in Dutch texts. Technical report, University Groningen (2007)
2. Clark, H.: Bridging. In: The Conference on Theoretical Issues in NLP, pp. 169–174 (1975)
3. Daelemans, W., Zavrel, J., van der Sloot, K., van den Bosch, A.: TiMBL: Tilburg Memory Based Learner, version 6.3, Reference Guide. Technical Report ILK Research Group Technical Report Series no. 10-01, Tilburg University (2010)
4. Hendrickx, I., Hoste, V., Daelemans, W.: Evaluating Hybrid Versus Data-Driven Coreference Resolution. In: Branco, A. (ed.) DAARC 2007. LNCS (LNAI), vol. 4410, pp. 137–150. Springer, Heidelberg (2007)
5. Hoste, V.: Optimization Issues in Machine Learning of Coreference Resolution. PhD thesis, Antwerp University (2005)
6. Jiang, J., Conrath, D.: Semantic similarity based on corpus statistics and lexical taxonomy. In: International Conference on Research in Computational Linguistics, Taiwan, vol. 33 (1997)
7. Korzen, I., Buch-Kromann, M.: Anaphoric relations in the copenhagen dependency treebanks. In: Beyond Semantics: Corpus-based Investigations of Pragmatic and Discourse Phenomena. DGfS Workshop, pp. 83–98 (2011)
8. Lin, D.: Automatic retrieval and clustering of similar words. In: 17th International Conference on Computational Linguistics, Montreal, Quebec, Canada, pp. 768–774 (1998)
9. Markert, K., Nissim, M., Modjeska, N.N.: Using the web for nominal anaphora resolution. In: EACL Workshop on the Computational Treatment of Anaphora, pp. 39–46 (2003)
10. Nedoluzhko, A., Mírovský, J., Pajas, P.: The coding scheme for annotating extended nominal coreference and bridging anaphora in the prague dependency treebank. In: LAW III, pp. 108–111. ACL, Suntec (2009)
11. Ng, V.: Supervised Noun Phrase Coreference Research: The First Fifteen Years. In: 48th Annual Meeting of the Association for Computational Linguistics, pp. 1396–1411 (2010)
12. Poesio, M.: Discourse annotation and semantic annotation in the gnome corpus. In: ACL Workshop on Discourse Annotation (2004)
13. Poesio, M., Ishikawa, T., im Walde, S.S., Vieira, R.: Acquiring lexical knowledge for anaphora resolution. In: 3rd Conference on Language Resources and Evaluation (LREC), pp. 1220–1224 (2002)
14. Poesio, M., Mehta, R., Maroudas, A., Hitzeman, J.: Learning to resolve bridging references. In: 42nd Meeting of the Association for Computational Linguistics (ACL 2004), pp. 143–150 (2004)
15. Poesio, M., Vieira, R.: A corpus-based investigation of definite description use. Computational Linguistics 24(2), 183–216 (1998)

16. Poesio, M., Vieira, R., Teufel, S.: Resolving bridging references in unrestricted text. In: ACL Workshop on Robust Anaphora Resolution, pp. 1–6 (1997)
17. Recasens, M.: Coreference: Theory, Annotation, Resolution and Evaluation. PhD thesis, Department of Linguistics, University of Barcelona, Barcelona, Spain (September 2010)
18. Recasens, M., Hovy, E., Marti, M.: Identity, non-identity, and near-identity: Addressing the complexity of coreference. Lingua 121(6), 1138–1152 (2011)
19. Recasens, M., Hovy, E., Mart, M.A.: A typology of near-identity relations for coreference (NIDENT). In: Seventh Conference on International Language Resources and Evaluation (LREC 2010), ELRA, Valletta, Malta (2010)
20. Recasens, M., Màrquez, L., Sapena, E., Martí, M.A., Tauleé, M., Hoste, V., Poesio, M., Versley, Y.: SemEval-2010 Task 1: Coreference resolution in multiple languages. In: 5th International Workshop on Semantic Evaluations (SemEval 2010), Uppsala, Sweden, pp. 1–8 (2010)
21. Resnik, P.: Using Information Content to Evaluate Semantic Similarity in a Taxonomy. In: International Joint Conference on Artificial Intelligence, Montreal, Canada, vol. 14, pp. 448–453 (1995)
22. Schuurman, I., Hoste, V., Monachesi, P.: Interacting Semantic Layers of Annotation in SoNaR, a Reference Corpus of Contemporary Written Dutch. In: LREC 2010, Valletta, Malta, pp. 2471–2477 (2010)
23. Soon, W.M., Ng, H.T., Lim, D.C.Y.: A machine learning approach to coreference resolution of noun phrases. Computational Linguistics 27(4), 521–544 (2001)
24. Vieira, R., Poesio, M.: An empirically based system for processing definite descriptions. Computational Linguistics 26, 539–593 (2000)

NADA: A Robust System for Non-referential Pronoun Detection

Shane Bergsma and David Yarowsky

Dept. of Computer Science and Human Language Technology Center of Excellence
Johns Hopkins University
sbergsma@jhu.edu, yarowsky@cs.jhu.edu

Abstract. We present NADA: the Non-Anaphoric Detection Algorithm. NADA is a novel, publicly-available program that accurately distinguishes between the referential and non-referential pronoun *it* in raw English text. Like recent state-of-the-art approaches, NADA uses very large-scale web N-gram features, but NADA makes these features practical by compressing the N-gram counts so they can fit into computer memory. NADA therefore operates as a fast, stand-alone system. NADA also improves over previous web-scale systems by considering the entire sentence, rather than narrow context windows, via long-distance lexical features. NADA very substantially outperforms other state-of-the-art systems in non-referential detection accuracy.

Keywords: non-referential pronoun identification, pleonastic pronoun, non-referential pronoun, non-anaphoric pronoun, dummy pronoun, expletive pronoun, pronoun resolution, anaphoricity, coreference resolution, anaphoric, referential, nominal pronoun, lexical disambiguation.

1 Introduction

Virtually all anaphora resolution systems search for the referents of an anaphor among the preceding noun phrases (NPs). However, not every expression that looks like an anaphor actually has an NP antecedent. In English, the pronoun *it* can refer both to NPs and also to more abstract entities, such as discourse segments [6,31]. *It* can also be used as a syntactic placeholder, as in −ref below:

+**ref** *It* is able to maintain a stable price.
−**ref** *It* is important to maintain a stable price.

The pronoun *It* in +ref is a *nominal* pronoun; it refers back to some previously-mentioned entity. *It* in −ref is a *pleonastic* or *expletive* pronoun, a dummy subject without an antecedent. For the purposes of information extraction or retrieval, we would like to know *who* is able to maintain a stable price in +ref, and might apply a pronoun resolution system to find the antecedent. On the other hand, we need to know that there is no antecedent for *It* in −ref; it would be wasteful and potentially harmful to try to find one.

I. Hendrickx et al. (Eds.): DAARC 2011, LNAI 7099, pp. 12–23, 2011.

In this paper, we investigate detectors that distinguish nominal *it* from both pleonastic *it* and from *it* referring to abstract entities, such as discourse segments. We call the latter cases *non-referential it*, following convention. This is the pragmatic division since, as mentioned, virtually all anaphora resolution systems only attempt to resolve pronouns with NP antecedents (but see [6]).

The referential/non-referential ambiguity is quite common in text. For example, there are over 7000 instances of *it* in the (one-million-token) Wall Street Journal portion of the Penn Treebank, of which 26% are non-referential (§4). Unfortunately, non-referential detection is not performed terribly well by today's coreference resolution systems. In experiments on a portion of the Treebank, the state-of-the-art Charniak and Elsner pronoun resolution system [7] achieves 73% accuracy in deciding if an *it* is non-referential, only marginally above the majority-class baseline. Thus there is need for attention to this problem.

Non-referential pronoun detection is structurally similar to other lexical disambiguation problems like word-sense disambiguation and spelling correction [2]; and, as in these tasks, supervised machine learning approaches have been adopted. We aimed to build a machine-learned non-referential detector that incorporates many of the features used in prior machine learning approaches to this problem [12,4,25]. However, the ±ref examples show why non-referential detection is a difficult disambiguation task: the decision depends on specific lexical items (i.e. *able* vs. *important*) rather than parts of speech. Hence, the information needed for robust detection cannot be derived from limited hand-annotated data. We thus look to leverage unlabeled data to improve non-referential detection, in particularly building on the use of web-scale N-gram data by Bergsma et al. [1].

We present a fast, freely-available non-referential detector for English that very substantially outperforms other state-of-the-art approaches. We call our system NADA (Non-Anaphoric Detection Algorithm). The NADA system and source code are available for download online through Google Code at:

`http://code.google.com/p/nada-nonref-pronoun-detector/`

To maximize adoption of NADA, we ensured: (1) it does not require parsed/tagged input, rather raw (tokenized) text, (2) it is fast, classifying *it* at speeds up to 20K sentences/sec., and (3) it works well out-of-domain.

2 Related Work

While the issue of non-referential pronouns has long been acknowledged [18,17], the problem has been side-stepped in various ways in past pronoun resolution research. Ge et al. [14] report that non-referentials "are excluded from computing the precision." Kehler et al. [19] only consider pronouns that were "ACE markables," so that "certain problems... such as non-referential pronouns and pronouns that refer to eventualities, did not have to be dealt with."[1] Yang et al. [33] only evaluate on "pronouns with non-empty candidate sets." Systems that do detect non-referentials as part of a fully-automatic pronoun resolution system include [24,8,7].

Early attempts to handle non-referentials were rule-based, and focused on English *it* [27,21]. While these approaches performed well in their original domains, later work has found these systems to perform poorly on new data [12,4,1]. Recent work has focused on training non-referential classifiers using machine learning [12,4,25,1]. Instances of *it* are classified on the basis of various features, with feature weights learned from a labeled training set. A recent departure from this approach is by Charniak and Elsner [7] who perform non-referential *it* detection jointly with pronoun resolution via inference in an unsupervised generative model. Recent work has also moved to identify non-referential pronouns in other languages, including French [10], Arabic [16] and Spanish [29].

A related line of work aims to identify all noun phrases that have an antecedent in text, but these systems typically classify all pronouns as referential and ignore non-referential *it* [26,11].

Bergsma et al. [1] detect non-referential pronouns using counts from web-scale N-gram data (we describe this approach in detail in §3.2). NADA improves on the Bergsma et al. work in several ways. First, we integrate their web count features with lexical (indicator) features that are inspired by previous non-referential classifiers. Secondly, because the original Bergsma et al. approach relies on the very large Google N-gram corpus, their approach cannot easily be made into a stand-alone, publicly-available system. For example, Miltsakaki [23] used the Bergsma et al. approach to detect non-referential *it* in the *Antelogue* pronoun resolution system, but usage of *Antelogue* therefore required separate access to the huge Google corpus. Since our objective is to develop a publicly-available, stand-alone system that works on a variety of texts, we adapt the Bergsma et al. approach to ensure the needed counts can fit into computer memory.

To our knowledge, up until now there have been no publicly-available, state-of-the-art non-referential pronoun detectors. Potential users of non-referential technology usually re-implement systems when needed, often adopting the simpler rule-based approaches as baselines. The Charniak and Elsner [7] system is publicly-available (and we compare to it), but requires (expensive) syntactic parses of entire documents as input. Since NADA is simpler, faster, and more accurate, we expect it to be adopted both as a component of larger coreference resolution systems and as a competitive comparison system for future non-referential detection research.

---

[1] ACE (Automatic Content Extraction) is a NIST program that conducted a series of evaluations on information extraction systems. These evaluations resulted in the availability of new coreference data for researchers, but, unfortunately, this data only includes coreference annotations for a subset of entity types, including people, organizations, and facilities. Furthermore, assuming the availability of the ACE markables "unrealistically simplifies the coreference resolution task" [30].

3 Supervised Non-referential Detection

We build on previous supervised approaches to detecting non-referential pronouns [12,4,25,1]. For each instance of the pronoun *it*, we create a feature vector, $\bar{x}$, to encode information about the pronoun's context. Our feature vector consists of two types of features: (1) *Lexical features*: binary-valued features that indicate the presence or absence of a particular string at a given position in the input (§3.1) and (2) *Web count features*: real-valued features that give the log-count of relevant N-grams derived from the input, with the counts taken from an auxiliary web-scale N-gram corpus (§3.2). The feature vector is given as input to a classifier and the output is a decision, y, as to whether the instance is referential or not. We take 'y=1' to denote the non-referential class and 'y=0' to denote the referential class.

We use a (regularized) logistic regression model as our supervised classifier. Logistic regression has been shown to perform well on a range of NLP tasks. In binary logistic regression, the features are weighted with a set of learned weight parameters, $\bar{w}$. The probability of a positive class is the logistic function:

$$\Pr(y = 1) = \frac{e^{\bar{w}\cdot\bar{x}}}{1 + e^{\bar{w}\cdot\bar{x}}}$$

We predict non-referential if $\Pr(y = 1) > 0.5$ (equivalently, $\bar{w} \cdot \bar{x} > 0$), otherwise we predict referential.

We assume N labeled training examples $\{(y^1, \bar{x}^1), ..., (y^N, \bar{x}^N)\}$ are available to train the classifier. The weight parameters $\bar{w}$ are set at training time in order to maximize performance on the training corpus.

While the supervised learning paradigm has been very successful in NLP, there are some important caveats. First of all, adding new features only improves classification accuracy if there's sufficient training data from which to learn good feature weights; the more features one uses, the more training data one needs. Secondly, many supervised systems perform poorly when used outside of their training domain. However, recent work has shown that the use of web N-gram features in supervised classifiers can alleviate both problems: systems combining lexical and count features tend to do better than using lexical features alone, especially with less training data and when operating on new domains [3].

3.1 Lexical Features

The optimum amount of context to encode in a feature representation remains an open question for this task. In [12], the "vectors convey information obtained from the paragraph in which the instance appears," while Bergsma et al. [1] use "context patterns that together span from four-[tokens]-to-the-left to four-[tokens]-to-the-right of the pronoun." We therefore tested how humans perform with varying amounts of context, comparing their decisions to the labels in the BBN Pronoun Coreference Corpus [32]. Given only four tokens on either side of the *it* pronoun, our subject achieved 85% accuracy on 200 instances.

When subsequently given the entire sentence, the subject achieved 95%, which is broadly similar to inter-annotator agreement given the full discourse [1]. We therefore extract our lexical features from the entire sentence.

Consider the referential example "*The EU team says* **it** *was able to address its concerns in full.*" We first normalize the text by converting all digits to '0' and replacing multi-character capitalized words with special named-entity tokens (e.g. *EU* → *NE*). Lexical features then encode the following specific attributes of the pronoun's normalized context, via binary indicator features:

1. All 3-grams to 5-grams that span the confusable pronoun, e.g. *team-says-***it**, *says-***it***-was*, **it***-was-able*, *NE-team-says-***it**, etc.
2. Tokens conjoined with their positions, from two tokens before, to 5 tokens after the pronoun, e.g. $team_{-2}$, $says_{-1}$, was_{+1}, ..., its_{+5}.
3. Any token within the 20 tokens on the right, e.g. was_{right}, $able_{right}$, to_{right}, $address_{right}$, its_{right}, $concerns_{right}$, in_{right}, $full_{right}$.
4. Any token within 10 tokens on the left that is on the list {*that, this, and, said, says,* NE, *it, It, its, itself*}, e.g. NE_{left}, $says_{left}$.

These specific features were developed over the course of extensive development experiments on BBN data. We aimed to encapsulate many of the features used in prior machine learning approaches to this problem [12,4,25], but omitted those that did not prove effective in development experiments.[2] Given sufficient training data, such lexical features provide excellent discriminators for this task. For example, the system learns the presence of other forms of the third-person-neutral pronoun (e.g. *its/itself*) are associated with referential *it*: the *it*-to-classify is likely part of this coreference chain. The presence of preceding *NE* tags also indicates referential; these entities are often the antecedents of referential *it*. Prepositions immediately preceding the pronoun are also indicative of referential, as noted by Paice and Husk [27], while following complementizers such as *that* or *to* are indicative of non-referential, even when they occur many tokens after the pronoun.

3.2 Web Count Features

We also use features derived from web-scale unlabeled data following Bergsma et al. [1]. The Bergsma et al. approach first converts the context around *it* into patterns, e.g. "*it is able to*" → "*_ is able to.*" Then, the Google N-gram data [5] is queried to determine which words fill the patterns. For referential cases, fillers like "**he** is able to" or "**China** is able to" are common, while for non-referentials (e.g., "*_ is important to*"), the word *it* is usually the most common filler. Rather than using a single pattern, Bergsma et al. gather fillers for all 4-and-5-gram patterns spanning the *it* token. The patterns are generalized using

[2] Notably, we did not observe a performance improvement using part-of-speech tags, and thus only use lexical features in the final system. One benefit is that our system can operate on raw sentences; it thus runs as a convenient, stand-alone program.

Table 1. Steps taken to compress the huge Google N-gram corpus (33 GB just for 4-grams) by several orders of magnitude to a small file that can be quickly loaded into NADA's memory (44 MB without zipping)

Sequence of Steps in Compression	Resulting Size
1. All N-grams in the Google N-gram corpus (unzipped)	93 GB
2. Extract N-grams of length-4 only	33 GB
3. Extract N-grams containing *it*, *they*, *them* only	500 MB
4. Lower-case, truncate tokens to four characters, replace special tokens (e.g. named entities, pronouns, digits) with symbols, etc.	189 MB
5. Encode tokens and values, store only changes from previous line	44 MB
6. `gzip` resulting file	33 MB

both stemming and various rules for irregular verbs and common contractions. Features are created with the counts of different filler classes (e.g., count(*word-it*)-in-pattern, count(*they/them*), count(*all-pronouns*), etc.). Each count feature is associated with a feature dimension (i.e., a particular element of the $\bar{x}$ vector) depending on the count's filler class, its pattern length, and the position of the filler slot in the pattern. Since each feature dimension has a corresponding weight (i.e., the corresponding element in the $\bar{w}$ vector), counts are ultimately weighted depending on their filler-class, pattern length, and filler-position.

Since these counts were shown to be effective, we want to use them in our own system, but the Google N-gram corpus is too large to include directly in a stand-alone system. We therefore took steps to compress the counts so they could be quickly loaded and accessed in a computer program's working memory.

Recent work has proposed ways to compress the Google N-gram corpus to fit it into memory for language modeling tasks [15,28]. We could have potentially used these approaches to retrieve counts for our task, however, there are properties of our problem that will allow us to use significantly less memory than, e.g., the compression to 10 GB achieved in the recent Pauls and Klein paper [28]. Nevertheless, some of our lossless compression steps below (token/value encoding, trie-like compression) were inspired by recent work in this area.

Steps in Data Compression. Table 1 shows the sequence of steps and their effect on the data size. The first steps are *lossy* compression steps in that they might result in loss of information. Note that, as in [1], we sum the counts of any N-grams that map to the same tokens as a result of our processing. Only using 4-grams (Step 2) and also truncating tokens to four characters (Step 4) were motivated by the analysis in [1], which showed only a small impact on accuracyr after these steps. The largest reduction is achieved by Step 3: only keeping N-grams that contain the words *it*, *they*, or *them* (regardless of capitalization); this filters 98% of the 4-grams. Unfortunately, as a result of this filtering we can now only make use of two of the five original filler classes used as features in [1]; however there is precedent for this in the SUMLM system in [2] and in Antelogue [23]. During development, we found that overall accuracy degrades by roughly 1% with these steps compared to the original Bergsma et al. system, which seems a reasonable price to pay for a practical system. Finally, Step 5 (and, of course, Step 6) is a *lossless* compression of the remaining N-gram data; we describe this step in more detail below. The following details are likely not relevant to all readers of this paper, however they might provide some insight for others trying to incorporate large-scale statistics into small-scale programs.

More Detailed Steps in Lossless Compression. After Step 4, our N-grams are roughly 9.5 million lines that look like this:

```
make _ clea that 659127 0
make _ clea the 8500 152
make _ clea then 105 0
make _ clea ther 2224 0
make _ clea thes 427 0
make _ clea this 3194 42
make _ clea thor 118 0
make _ clea thos 89 0
make _ clea thou 392 0
make _ clea thro 827 0
```

Each line begins with the 4-gram (with the filler-position marked by a '_'), followed by the count of *it* and then the count of *they/them*.[3]

Our first step was to replace the tokens in each N-gram with a fixed numerical encoding (converting from a text file to a binary file). After the Step 4 processing, we found there were only 28047 unique tokens (types) in our data. These 28047 types can be stored in a separate list (the *token list*), and looked up when needed using a 15-bit index (since $2^{15} > 28047$). Furthermore, rather than storing the filler '_' in the same way as the other tokens, we instead add another flag bit to each encoded token to indicate whether or not that token is preceded-by-the-filler. In this way we replace the four original tokens with three 16-bit (2-byte) integers. Clearly, we now don't require any delimiters as in the original text file. Also, the 2-byte encoding aligns nicely with the 2-byte types native to C/C++, the language in which we coded NADA.

A slightly-more-complicated trick works to replace the values (i.e. the counts of the *it* and *they/them* fillers). To reduce the value space further, we only keep the two most significant digits in each value (e.g. 3194 42 is mapped to 3200 42).[4] After this quantization, we found there were only 65354 unique **pairs** of values, which could together be stored in a separate list (the *values list*) and looked up, when needed with a 16-bit integer index ($2^{16} > 65354$). So we can replace every pair of values with a single 2-byte integer.

For those keeping track, each N-gram needs six bytes for tokens, two bytes for values, and since there are 9.5 million N-grams in our data, we can store the whole shebang in $8 * 9.5 = 76$ MB. This is indeed how we store things in NADA's

[3] Although it may not seem so based on this sample, this is indeed more compact than storing these two counts separately.

[4] Actually, this step is *lossy* but the resulting effect on NADA is negligible.

memory. We hash the 2-byte encoded-value as the hash value and look it up with the 6-byte encoded-tokens as the hash key. As we run NADA on text, we have separate, small and very fast hashes for the token list (TL) and values list (VL). We use the TL to encode the input text (as hash keys). We look up the encoded token keys in our big hash of encoded values, and then use the VL to decode the retrieved values back to pairs of counts, which of course provide the feature values in our classifier.

However, this is still wasteful, since one can observe from the sample above that most tokens in the N-grams don't change from line-to-line. So, to make the data even smaller in our final file *on disk* (which makes it faster to load from disk into memory) for each N-gram we only store the changes from the previous N-gram (having special flags to indicate when changes happen and which tokens have changed). This is broadly similar to the idea behind the *trie* data structure: essentially, we re-use the space for some tokens among many different N-grams.

This processing results in a 44 MB file (uncompressed) of pattern counts, which easily fits into computer memory. Thus our system ships and operates with all the data it needs.[5]

4 Experimental Details

We evaluate NADA in comprehensive experiments on news and other domains (§5). The NADA classifier is trained using L2-regularized logistic regression via the LIBLINEAR package [13]. We optimize the classifier's regularization parameter for development accuracy (the percentage of examples classified correctly). As a logistic regression classifier, NADA returns a probability of an instance being non-referential. To turn this probability into classification decisions, we threshold the probability at 0.5, predicting *non-referential* if the probability exceeds this threshold, referential otherwise. We report final accuracy, precision, recall, and F-score (F1) for classifications on held-out test data.

Unlabeled N-gram Data: All N-gram counts are taken from the web-scale Google N-gram Corpus [5]. The feature values are the logarithm of the counts. We add one to all counts for smoothing. If a count is unavailable, or if a context pattern spans beyond the sentence, we indicate so with binary indicator features.

Labeled Data: We use a much more extensive set of labeled data for our experiments than has been used in past research, namely, the BBN Pronoun Coreference Corpus [32]. The BBN corpus provides the antecedents of all *referential* pronouns in the Wall Street Journal (WSJ) portion of the Penn Treebank [22]. If a pronoun is labeled with an antecedent, we mark the instance as referential, otherwise as non-referential. There are 7195 instances of *it* in this corpus, of which 26% are non-referential. We train all classifiers on the first 3195 instances

[5] Note it would have been possible, but of dubious additional value here, to use variable-length encoding of the token and value indices to save even more space [9].

Table 2. Accuracy (%) on various datasets of majority-class (referential) and classifiers with different features. Web count features are better, especially out-of-domain, but **lexical and count-based features can be combined effectively on this task**

Features	BBN	WSJ-2	ItBank
Majority Class	72.5	74.9	67.7
Lexical	82.9	82.5	78.7
Web Counts	83.3	85.6	83.1
Lexical+Counts (final NADA system)	**86.0**	**86.2**	**85.1**

of *it*. We use another 1000 BBN examples as development data, and the last 3000 BBN examples as a final held-out test set.

We also evaluate on data from the publicly-available ItBank corpus [1]. We use the 709 instances from (separate) WSJ data as another in-domain dataset, called 'WSJ-2.' We also use another 1928 instances from ItBank as an out-of-domain set, called 'ItBank.' This set includes *it* instances from both Science News articles and articles from the Slate portion of the American National Corpus. Taking a system trained on the WSJ and testing it on this out-of-domain data is a good test of the robustness of our proposed detector.

5 Results

We first evaluate the speed of NADA, and find it to be very fast. It takes NADA just over two minutes to identify non-referential pronouns in 1.7 million English sentences in Europarl [20] (a speed of approximately 12 thousand sentences per second). On news text, NADA is even faster, tagging the 49 thousand sentences in the WSJ portion of the Treebank in 2.5 seconds, at a speed of roughly 20 thousand sentences per second. Of course, many of these sentences are passed unmodified if they do not contain an instance of *it*; on the 6511 WSJ sentences containing an *it*, NADA tags around 3900 sentences per second.

We then assess the value of the different features, alone and in combination, on the three test sets (Table 2). The system with *Lexical* features can be regarded as a reasonable approximation of a range of previous supervised approaches [12,4,25] (but trained and evaluated on more data), while the *Web Counts* system is a reasonable (but practical) approximation of the Bergsma et al. [1] approach. On the BBN data, the system with lexical features performs almost as well as the system with count features. On out-of-domain data, however, the lexical features perform 3-4% worse (confirming the trend observed in [3] on a range of other tasks). The classifier using both lexical and count features is best, performing between 85.1% and 86.2% on all data. This shows, for the first time, that the two dominant machine learning paradigms for this task (i.e., indicator features and count features) can be integrated effectively into a single system.

Our integrated approach is also superior to competing approaches in the literature. We reimplemented the rule-based approach of Paice and Husk [27].

Table 3. Classification performance of several comparison systems. NADA achieves superior classification results (%) on BBN, yielding a 47% error-rate-reduction relative to Charniak and Elsner [7].

System	Prec.	Rec.	F1	Acc.
Paice-Husk	56.9	40.8	47.5	75.2
Charniak-Elsner	51.2	**64.9**	57.3	73.4
NADA	**81.6**	63.4	**71.3**	**86.0**

We also tested the joint non-referential-detection/pronoun-resolution system of Charniak and Elsner [7]. This system is publicly available, so we compare directly to its output; we mark a pronoun as non-referential when the probability of being non-referential exceeds a fixed threshold (set by the system designers). Unlike NADA, the Charniak and Elsner system requires full parses of entire documents, so we charitably provide it with the gold-standard Treebank parses for the BBN test data. Our proposed system does a very substantially better job than both these approaches (Table 3).

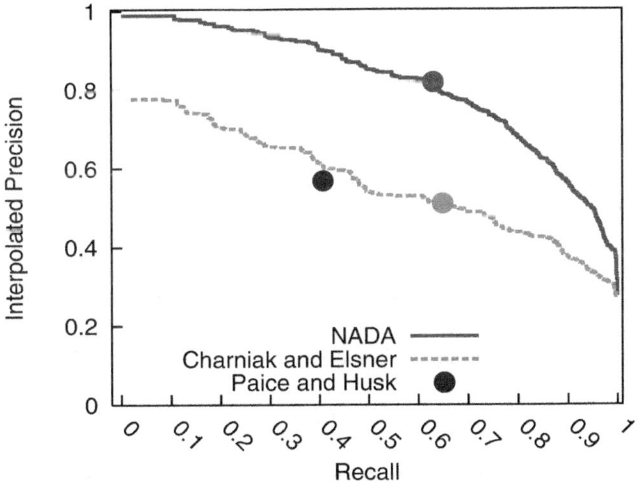

Fig. 1. Performance on BBN, showing superiority of NADA to Charniak-Elsner and Paice-Husk. NADA curve produced by thresholding output probability (• for $P>0.5$). Charniak-Elsner curve produced by thresholding probability of most probable antecedent (• where probability exceeds their (fixed) probability of being non-referential).

As mentioned, NADA returns a probability of an instance being non-referential, which we threshold at 0.5 to produce the above classification results. By lowering this threshold, we can increase the recall of NADA (at the expense of precision), while raising the threshold increases the precision (at the expense of recall). We can do the same for the Charniak and Elsner system, which also produces probabilistic output. Figure 1 provides a precision-recall curve for both detectors over a range of thresholds. For comparison, the plot also includes the fixed Paice and Husk performance. Note in particular that NADA obtains close to 100% precision on the 10-20% most-confident non-referentials. In fact, many of these instances are incorrectly 'resolved' by the Charniak-Elsner system, and this could be prevented by using our system as a reliable coreference preprocessor.

6 Conclusion

We presented NADA, a new system for detecting non-referential instances of the English pronoun *it*. NADA is a supervised system based on two kinds of features: lexical and web-scale N-gram counts. We showed how to compress the N-gram counts to make NADA an efficient, stand-alone program. An extensive empirical evaluation showed that NADA outperforms all previous similar systems. Furthermore, NADA offers a number of important additional advantages: (1) it is publicly-available, (2) it operates on raw (tokenized) text, without requiring any special preprocessing, (3) it is very fast, and (4) it performs well on different domains. We hope many other groups also find NADA useful in their work.

References

1. Bergsma, S., Lin, D., Goebel, R.: Distributional identification of non-referential pronouns. In: ACL 2008: HLT, pp. 10–18 (2008)
2. Bergsma, S., Lin, D., Goebel, R.: Web-scale N-gram models for lexical disambiguation. In: IJCAI, pp. 1507–1512 (2009)
3. Bergsma, S., Pitler, E., Lin, D.: Creating robust supervised classifiers via web-scale N-gram data. In: ACL, pp. 865–874 (2010)
4. Boyd, A., Gegg-Harrison, W., Byron, D.: Identifying non-referential *it*: A machine learning approach incorporating linguistically motivated patterns. In: ACL Workshop on Feature Engineering for Machine Learning in Natural Language Processing, pp. 40–47 (2005)
5. Brants, T., Alex Franz, A.: The Google Web 1T 5-gram Corpus Version 1.1. LDC2006T13 (2006)
6. Byron, D.: Resolving pronominal reference to abstract entities. In: ACL, pp. 80–87 (2002)
7. Charniak, E., Elsner, M.: EM works for pronoun anaphora resolution. In: EACL, pp. 148–156 (2009)
8. Cherry, C., Bergsma, S.: An Expectation Maximization approach to pronoun resolution. In: CoNLL, pp. 88–95 (2005)
9. Church, K., Hart, T., Gao, J.: Compressing trigram language models with Golomb coding. In: EMNLP-CoNLL, pp. 199–207 (2007)
10. Danlos, L.: Automatic recognition of French expletive pronoun occurrences. In: IJCNLP, pp. 73–78 (2005)
11. Denis, P., Baldridge, J.: Joint determination of anaphoricity and coreference using integer programming. In: NAACL-HLT, pp. 236–243 (2007)

12. Evans, R.: Applying machine learning toward an automatic classification of *it*. Literary and Linguistic Computing 16(1), 45–57 (2001)
13. Fan, R.-E., Chang, K.-W., Hsieh, C.-J., Wang, X.-R., Lin, C.-J.: LIBLINEAR: A library for large linear classification. Mach. Learn. Res. 9, 1871–1874 (2008)
14. Ge, N., Hale, J., Charniak, E.: A statistical approach to anaphora resolution. In: Proceedings of the Sixth Workshop on Very Large Corpora, pp. 161–170 (1998)
15. Guthrie, D., Hepple, M.: Storing the web in memory: Space efficient language models with constant time retrieval. In: EMNLP, pp. 262–272 (2010)
16. Hammami, S.M., Sallemi, R., Belguith, L.H.: A bayesian classifier for the identification of non-referential pronouns in Arabic. In: INFOS, Special Track On Natural Language Processing and Knowledge Mining (2010)
17. Hirst, G.: Anaphora in Natural Language Understanding: A Survey. Springer, Heidelberg (1981)
18. Hobbs, J.: Resolving pronoun references. Lingua 44(311), 339–352 (1978)
19. Kehler, A., Appelt, D., Taylor, L., Simma, A.: The (non)utility of predicate-argument frequencies for pronoun interpretation. In: HLT-NAACL, pp. 289–296 (2004)
20. Koehn, P.: Europarl: A parallel corpus for statistical machine translation. In: MT Summit X, pp. 79–86 (2005)
21. Lappin, S., Leass, H.J.: An algorithm for pronominal anaphora resolution. Computational Linguistics 20(4), 535–561 (1994)
22. Marcus, M.P., Santorini, B., Marcinkiewicz, M.: Building a large annotated corpus of English: The Penn Treebank. Computational Linguistics 19(2), 313–330 (1993)
23. Miltsakaki, E.: Antelogue: Pronoun resolution for text and dialogue. In: Coling 2010: Demonstrations, pp. 41–44 (2010)
24. Mitkov, R., Evans, R., Orasan, C.: A new, fully automatic version of Mitkov's knowledge-poor pronoun resolution method. In: CICLing, pp. 168–186 (2002)
25. Müller, C.: Automatic detection of nonreferential *It* in spoken multi-party dialog. In: EACL, pp. 49–56 (2006)
26. Ng, V., Cardie, C.: Identifying anaphoric and non-anaphoric noun phrases to improve coreference resolution. In: COLING, pp. 730–736 (2002)
27. Paice, C.D., Husk, G.D.: Towards the automatic recognition of anaphoric features in English text: the impersonal pronoun "it". Computer Speech and Language 2, 109–132 (1987)
28. Pauls, A., Klein, D.: Faster and smaller N-Gram language models. In: ACL, pp. 258–267 (2011)
29. Rello, L., Suárez, P., Mitkov, R.: A machine learning method for identifying impersonal constructions and zero pronouns in Spanish. In: Procesamiento del Lenguaje Natural, pp. 281–287 (2010)
30. Stoyanov, V., Gilbert, N., Cardie, C., Riloff, E.: Conundrums in noun phrase coreference resolution: making sense of the state-of-the-art. In: ACL-IJCNLP, pp. 656–664 (2009)
31. Webber, B.L.: Discourse deixis: reference to discourse segments. In: ACL, pp. 113–122 (1988)
32. Weischedel, R., Brunstein, A.: BBN pronoun coreference and entity type corpus. LDC2005T33 (2005)
33. Yang, X., Jian Su, J., Tan, C.L.: Improving pronoun resolution using statistics-based semantic compatibility information. In: ACL (2005)

Resolving Noun Phrase Coreference in Czech

Michal Novák and Zdeněk Žabokrtský

Charles University in Prague, Institute of Formal and Applied Linguistics
Malostranské nám. 25, Praha 1, CZ-118 00, Czech Republic
{mnovak,zabokrtsky}@ufal.mff.cuni.cz

Abstract. In this work, we present first results on noun phrase coreference resolution on Czech data. As the data resource for our experiments, we employed yet unfinished and unpublished extension of Prague Dependency Treebank 2.0, which captures noun phrase coreference and bridging relations. Incompleteness of the data influenced one of our motivations – to aid annotators with automatic pre-annotation of the data. Although we introduced several novel tree features and tried different machine learning approaches, results on a growing amount of data shows that the selected feature set and learning methods are not able to sufficiently exploit the data.

Keywords: coreference resolution, Czech, ranking, Prague Dependency Treebank.

1 Introduction

The task of coreference resolution (CR) attracts attention of many authors. They concentrate on analyzing coreference relations mainly in English, probably due to the availability of annotated data. This work attempts to advance in resolution of Czech coreference.

Motivation for research on CR comes from several directions. For instance, knowledge of coreference relations is central in Information Retrieval and in Question Answering. Our long-term objective is to use our CR system in Machine Translation. Specifically, we would like to incorporate it into the TectoMT system [18], which provides translations through a layer of deep syntax.

In this work, we make use of partial results coming from a project in progress that aims to supply an annotation of extended anaphoric relations into Prague Dependency Treeebank 2.0 [8]. Thus another motivation for our research was to help annotators to decide on coreference links with automatic pre-annotation of the data.

A substantial amount of newly annotated data is represented by so called noun phrase (NP) coreference, by which we mean coreference relations when the head of an expression in the later context – anaphor is a noun.[1] This work focuses only on this type of coreference relations.

[1] We borrow the broadly used term "NP coreference" even if there are no noun phrases (in the sense of phrase-structure grammar) annotated in the PDT.

I. Hendrickx et al. (Eds.): DAARC 2011, LNAI 7099, pp. 24–34, 2011.

In this work almost all of the proposed features comes from a gold standard annotation. This decision is acceptable, if the CR system serves as an aid for annotators. However, if it becomes a part of end-to-end Natural Language Processing system, these features will have to be replaced by their counterparts obtained from morphological and syntactical analysis.

2 Data

The Prague Dependency Treebank 2.0 (PDT) [8] is a large collection of manually linguistically annotated texts, based on the theory of Functional Generative Description [16]. Annotation of sentences in PDT is stratified into three layers:

Morphological (m-layer) – surface form of the sentence with morphological information included.

Analytical (a-layer) – the sentence is represented as a surface syntax dependency tree, where each node corresponds to one word of the m-layer.

Tectogrammatical (t-layer) – the layer of deep syntax represented again as a dependency tree. It contains only auto-semantic words. On the other hand there are reconstructed nodes which have no visible surface counterparts, e.g. due to prodrop.

Tectogrammatical layer captures also anaphoric relations. Their annotation has been carried out in two stages:

1. **Annotation in the published PDT** comprises grammatical and pronominal textual coreference. Arguments of grammatical coreference usually appear within the same sentence and they are determined by grammatical rules. For instance, reflexive pronouns mainly corefer with the subject in the same clause. Conversely, regarding textual pronominal coreference the anaphor is a personal or demonstrative pronoun, whose antecedent can be a noun phrase, clause or a larger utterance.
2. **Annotation of extended anaphoric relations in PDT** [14] is an ongoing project, which aims to enrich PDT with remaining coreference and bridging relations. The data resulting from this project are not yet published, since the process of annotation is not completed yet (extended anaphoric relations are planned to be a part of the next version of PDT).

Whereas in corpora MUC-7 [10] and ACE [13], which are extensively used for English CR, the coreference is annotated on the surface level between NP chunks

Table 1. Number of NP coreference links in data sets used during experiments. Reduced train set represents a data the final model was built from.

	train				dev		eval	
	complete		reduced					
all	98,053		16,384		25,784		21,467	
coreferential	13,790	14.1%	2,694	16.4%	3,781	14.7%	3,148	14.7%

of words, in PDT it is labeled on the t-layer between heads of subtrees (see Figure 1). An advantage of its annotation on the t-layer is in the presence of surface-dropped words and availability of rich linguistic features, with many of them being related to semantics. This provides more information to decide on coreference link.

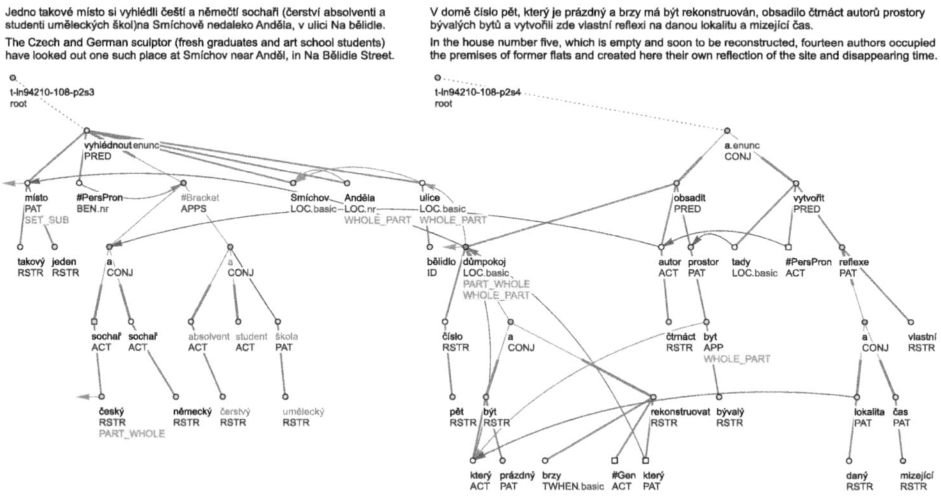

Fig. 1. Example of a tectogrammatical representation of two sentences interlinked with various types of anaphora

Although PDT is already divided into training, development and evaluation set, it is not completely covered with NP coreference annotation. Therefore, we had to make our own partitioning of available data. The number of instances and the proportion of coreferential links in the data is sketched in Table 1.

3 Related Work

Exploring the possibilities of the coreference resolution for Czech was until recently limited by the availability of annotated data. To our knowledge Prague Dependency Treebank 2.0 (PDT) [8] represented the only data source that contained coreference annotation, however it was constrained to more or less pronoun coreference.

This work is not the first one which attempts to exploit rich data in PDT to resolve coreference relations. PDT was utilized in the work [12], where the authors presented the resolver of Czech pronominal coreference with so far the highest performance – 79.43%, measured by pairwise F-measure.

We are not aware of any work prior to ours which conducted a research on NP CR for Czech. The main reason is the relative novelty of the PDT extension, the only corpus that captures NP coreference for Czech.

Our system relies on supervised machine learning approaches,[2] and is inspired by several recent advances in the field of CR.

Many authors handled the CR as a sequence of two separate subtasks: anaphor identification and antecedent selection. Rahman and Ng [15] joined these subtasks into a single step by training a common model for them, which boosted a success rate of their system.

Pascal and Denis [4] suggested to distinguish different types of anaphor. They improved their resolution system by training a separate model for coreference with 3rd person pronoun, speech pronoun, definite NP and proper noun anaphor.

For years, the coreference resolution task has been treated with classification approaches. Denis and Baldridge [3] showed that the task is more reasonable and even better in performance if it is cast as a ranking task. In such an approach, the competition between individual candidates is captured directly in the trained model, which does not hold for classification models.

In recent years unsupervised approaches made significant performance progress as well. Indeed, Haghighi and Klein [7] created an unsupervised system based on inference in Bayesian networks, which outperforms best known supervised resolvers.

4 Extracted Features

Features the resolver works with can be divided into following categories:

Grammatical: These features are extracted from m-layer and consist of morphological tags of the anaphor and the antecedent, agreement in number, gender and negation. In addition, the t-layer supplies semantic functions of dependency relations, information about the presence of a determiner 'tento' ('this') and also a technical feature of being an apposition member.

Distance: How far the antecedent lies from its anaphor is a key attribute in coreference resolution. We measure it by a word and sentence distance.

Lexical: The most important component for lexical features is a lemma. We utilized features which indicate whether lemmas of the anaphor and the antecedent candidate are equal, particularly the ranking feature based on this property.[3]

We incorporated a dictionary of synonyms from a translation model extracted from the Czech-English Parallel Corpus [1]. This dictionary served as a basis of synonymy feature.

Looking at the data, we noted that the entities which are frequent in a document are more likely to appear again. Hence we introduced a ranking feature denoting the number of occurrences of the particular word in the text.

[2] The progress in research on supervised NP coreference resolution is nicely summarized by Ng [11].

[3] Ranking features assign positive integers to candidates, which meet some condition (e.g. lemma equality), in a way that the antecedent candidate closest to the anaphor obtains 1, the second closest one gets 2, etc. If the condition does not hold, the feature is undefined.

Another set of lexical features relates to named entities. We introduced a simple feature indicating whether the first letter of the lemma is upper-cased. Apart from this, we exploited the information about possible named entity types stored on the m-layer of PDT. However, for future work, we see a possible improvement in complying the findings of Denis and Baldridge [4] and training a special model for coreference with a proper noun anaphor.

All features that we have introduced so far are describing only heads of either anaphor or antecedent candidates. They ignore dependent nodes of an NP. Therefore we suggested several tree features which involves all nodes becoming to the NP subtree. For instance, we included a ranking feature indicating the equality of whole phrases. We also designed features that compare the number of dependent nodes of both participants (if their head lemmas are identical), or the number of dependent nodes that are common for them.

It is necessary to emphasize that except for synonymy approximation, all features originate from PDT annotation which is manual gold standard.

From the list of weights, the learning method assigned to features, we noticed that some rarely distributed features obtained relatively high weights. From this reason we decided to incorporate feature pruning in this work. To what extent features are cut off is determined by a parameter σ. For each multi-value feature we sorted its values by the number of occurrences and merged those least frequent values which in sum account for proportion of at most σ.

5 Data Preparation for Machine Learning

As it is the dominating practice, we treat recognition of individual coreference links as separated task instances. One instance consists of an anaphor candidate a and a set of its antecedent candidates c_i, out of which exactly one antecedent should be chosen by a Machine Learning technique. For this purpose, a rich set of features is provided for each pair $\langle a, c_i \rangle$. Following [15], we join anaphoricity determination and antecedent selection into a single step. For this purpose, a is artificially included into the set of antecedent candidates. If a is non-coreferential, then a is supposed to be chosen from the antecedent candidate set, which is interpreted as absence of any coreference link from the given anaphor candidate.

Since we are interested merely in NP coreference, we constrained anaphors to be subtrees with a noun head. Because pronouns do not carry a sufficient amount of information to be matched with an NP anaphor, we restricted antecedent heads to be nouns as well.[4] After such filtering noun-to-pronoun links might be omitted. Hence, if the head of the closest true antecedent is not a noun, we follow the coreferential chain in order to find the noun antecedent. If such node is found, it is marked as a true antecedent, otherwise the anaphor candidate is assigned to be non-anaphoric.

Selecting the proper window size determines how many antecedent candidates will be under consideration. To avoid the computational complexity we decided

[4] Noun phrases account for 72% of antecedents.

to collect candidates for training from the sentence where the anaphor lies[5] and previous 10 sentences. Such choice covers 97% of antecedents. For the testing data there is no need for such restriction so we use much larger window: 200 previous sentences.

6 Training and Resolving

Data, preprocessed in the way described above, served as an input for modeling by means of various machine learning techniques. We decided to compare two ranking approaches based on different learning methods – maximum entropy (ME) and perceptron. Although in previous works it has been already shown that rankers are more suitable for CR than classifiers, we wanted to prove that a performance drop of classifiers appears also for our specific task of Czech NP coreference resolution.

In the following we briefly describe the learning methods that we incorporated.

6.1 Maximum Entropy Classifier

Having pairs of anaphor and antecedent candidate $\langle a, c_i \rangle$, classifiers tackle each pair separately. Every such pair carry a label, whether it is coreferential (COREF) or not. Coreference modeling is conceived as a learning how likely it is for the pair, described by a feature vector f_j, that a class COREF is assigned to it. These probabilities are modeled by maximum entropy and in the stage of resolution calculated for every anaphor a and corresponding candidates c_i with a following formula:

$$P\left(\text{COREF}\middle|\left\langle a,c_i\right\rangle\right)=\frac{\exp\left(\sum_{j=1}^{n}\lambda_j f_j\left(\left\langle a,c_i\right\rangle,\text{COREF}\right)\right)}{\sum_c\exp\left(\sum_{j=1}^{n}\lambda_j f_j\left(\left\langle a,c_i\right\rangle,c\right)\right)}$$

Among the candidates, whose probability of being coreferential is greater than 0.5, the one closest to the anaphor is picked as an antecedent (closest-first strategy [17]). For maximum entropy modeling we employed a Perl library from CPAN `AI::MaxEntropy`, specifically the L-BFGS algorithm [5] for estimating parameters.

6.2 Maximum Entropy Ranker

In contrast to the classifier, a ranker takes into account all candidates at once. In this case, the maximum entropy model itself includes a competition between individual candidates, thus there is no need for an additional step to single out an antecedent, as it is in the case of classification. That candidate is denoted as an antecedent, for which the following probability is maximum:

$$P\left(c_i|a\right)=\frac{\exp\left(\sum_{j=1}^{n}\lambda_j f_j\left(a,c_i\right)\right)}{\sum_k\exp\left(\sum_{j=1}^{n}\lambda_j f_j\left(a,c_i\right)\right)}$$

[5] Concerning just words that precede the anaphor.

We used an implementation of maximum entropy ranker from the Toolkit for Advanced Discriminative Modeling[6] [9], which was already employed for English pronominal CR in [3]. Parameters were estimated with a limited memory variable metric algorithm, closely resembling the L-BFGS algorithm, which we adopted for the classifier.

6.3 Perceptron Ranker

This method follows the ranking scenario as in the previous case. Nonetheless, instead of maximum entropy, it provides a modeling by a perceptron. In order to pick an antecedent, perceptron model does not work with probabilities, though maximizing of dot product of weights and a feature vector remains the same as in the case of ME ranker.

The main difference lies in the algorithm used for estimating parameters. We reused the perceptron ranker, which successfully served as a modeling method for the system for Czech pronominal CR [12]. Parameters were estimated using an averaged perceptron algorithm [2] with a modified loss function tailored to the ranking approach.

7 Evaluation and Model Analysis

During development experiments we discovered several facts. Although available training data contained almost 100,000 instances, in preliminary tests we noticed that the ME as well as perceptron ranking models built just from 16,384 instances perform superior to models trained on full number of instances. Due to better performance and also in order to compare learning methods on the same data, we adopted this training subset for creation of all computational models involved in final evaluation tests.

Moreover, training a model with the maximum entropy classifier turned out to be much more time-consuming than with the other methods. This time complexity led us to omit all additional experiments on this model except for the final evaluation, having left the pruning parameter σ equal to that used with the ME ranker.

Obviously, we had to find proper values of pruning parameter σ before we proceeded to the final evaluation. The tuning was performed on the development set. Figure 2 shows the highest F-scores for the ME ranker (44.11%) and the perceptron ranker (44.52%) were achieved by models pruned with $\sigma = 0.09$ and $\sigma = 0.15$, respectively. These values were used for final tests on the evaluation set.

We assessed the quality of the proposed NP coreference resolution system on the evaluation set described in Section 2. As a baseline we set the result of a simple resolver, which for each anaphor candidate picks as its antecedent the closest candidate from the window with a lemma equal to the anaphor‘s lemma.

[6] `http://tadm.sourceforge.net/`

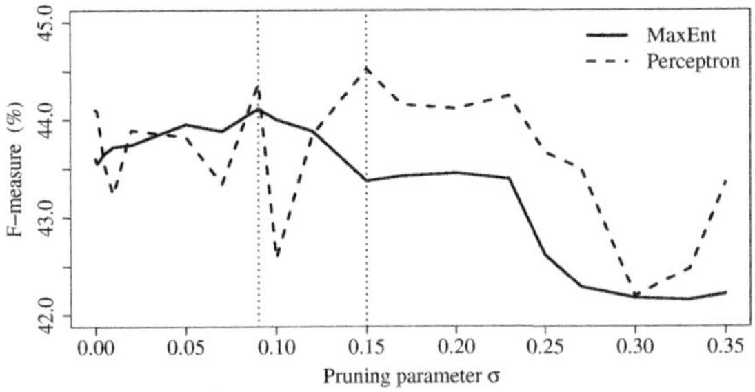

Fig. 2. Values of F-score on the development data while changing the pruning parameter σ

If there is none, it is non-coreferential. We specified the upper bound as an inter-annotator agreement measured in [14] on the subset from extended PDT similar to that we used. Performance of various models compared to lower and upper bound can be seen in Table 2.

Table 2. Performance of trained models compared with a baseline and inter-annotator agreement

Method	Precision	Recall	F-Measure
MaxEnt classifier	57.30%	33.54%	42.32%
MaxEnt ranker	58.55%	35.58%	44.26%
Perceptron ranker	42.39%	46.54%	44.37%
Baseline	26.29%	60.01%	36.56%
Inter-annotator agreement	—	—	68.00%

All three machine learning approaches outperformed the baseline. The ranking approach proved to be more suitable for the task of CR than the classification one. There is no significant difference between F-values of the two ranking approaches. However, if the CR system is to be used as an aid for annotators, high values of precision are preferred. From this point of view, maximum entropy ranker performs better than perceptron ranker.

Except for the final evaluation we were interested how models deal with quantitative and qualitative changes. Since annotation of the data we exploited is not finished, findings on the former can give us information, whether it is worth going on in annotation process. The latter will elaborate on how valuable are the novel features which exploit a tree structure of sentences in PDT.

To show the impact of changes in quantity we examined how model accuracy was changing, when built from different amounts of data. Sizes of the training data ranged along the logarithmic scale from 2^4 to the full size of training set.[7]

[7] It corresponds to less than 2^{17} as we can see in Table 1.

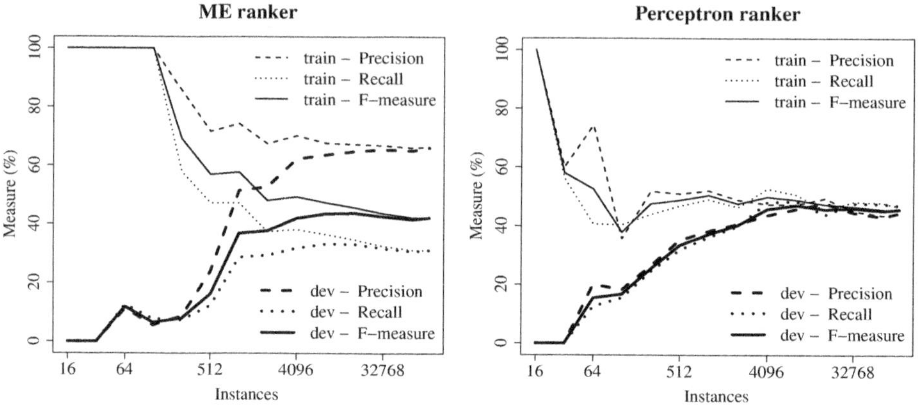

Fig. 3. Learning curves show how the ranking models perform on the training and development set with various sizes of training data

These models were tested on the data, whose size accounted for 1/8 of the training data size and the size of the complete development data for limited and full training sets, respectively. Furthermore, we carried out testing of models on the training data they were created from.

Resulting learning curves of the ME and perceptron rankers depicted in Figure 3 shows averaged values after performing 9-fold cross validation.[8] Looking at the graph, we can observe three trends. The first is a convergence of success rate performed on seen and unseen data. Second, with amount of the training data growing over 5000 instances the quality of the computational model remains more or less the same. Lastly, while two learning approaches we investigated exhibit comparable F-scores, precision and recall behaves in a different way. ME ranker achieves about 25% better values of precision than recall. Conversely, these statistics are bound around the same value for perceptron ranker.

To show qualitative influence of tree features we tweaked the final model by adding or leaving them out. If a feature was present in the final model, its removal would negatively affect the result. On the other hand, potential inclusion of a feature omitted from the final model would not improve the score. We analyzed the differences in F-score between the final and tweaked model.

In Table 3 we can see which features were included into and which excluded from the final model. We observe that influence of these features is up to 0.75%. The most valuable features are those, which capture an equality of the anaphor's and antecedent candidate's lemmas (`desc_self_equal_rank` and `desc_counts_equal`).

[8] N-fold cross validation requires the testing segments to be mutually disjoint for every two folds. In our case, this holds except for the full data, where we allowed overlapping. The reason is simple arithmetic that for $n = 9$ this condition cannot be fulfilled.

Table 3. List of tree features and their influence on the final model

Final feature set		44.11%
Included		
desc_self_equal_rank	ranking feature of desc_self_equal	+0.74%
desc_counts_equal	equality of numbers of dependent nodes for identical lemmas	+0.40%
anaph_this_attr	is the determiner 'tento' a descendant of the anaphor head	+0.29%
both_functors	concatenation of semantic functions	+0.28%
anaph_functor	semantic function of the anaphor	+0.04%
ante_functor	semantic function of the antecedent	+0.03%
Excluded		
desc_self_equal	equality of whole NPs	0.00%
desc_counts_zero	desc_counts_equal with zero dependent nodes	-0.05%
common_desc_lemmas_count	number of words in common between NPs	-0.17%

8 Conclusion and Future Work

In this paper we have presented first experiments on NP coreference resolution in Czech. Even though the created models have succeeded in surpassing the baseline, differences between their nature are substantial. We confirmed the worse performance of classifiers in the task of coreference resolution. ME ranker turned out to be a universal solution, providing the best F-measure as well as precision score. Nevertheless, its performance does not seem to achieve a success rate high enough to help in a practical usage. In spite of that we plan to incorporate it into TectoMT and evaluate this CR system as a component of the end-to-end Natural Language Processing pipeline.

A crucial finding comes from the analysis of the learning curves. The combination of presented feature sets and learning methods are not able to sufficiently exploit a growing amount of knowledge in a growing quantity of the annotated data.

We took advantage of the tree nature of the annotated data to design several novel features. Most of them affect the quality of resolution positively, though there is still a place for smarter involvement of dependent nodes of phrases.

Our future work should focus on feature engineering, mainly to investigate deeper lexical and semantic relations between phrases. To even partially accomplish this task we would like to incorporate manually designed language sources, such as EuroWordNet. It might help us to reveal hypero-/hyponymic relations, which are not covered by our system.

Furthermore we believe that lexical semantics can be to some extent exploited from unannotated texts. For instance, we would like to search huge data sources like Czech National Corpus or Czech Wikipedia for appositions and noun predicates in order to identify synonyms and potentially coreferential phrases, as reported in the work of Haghighi and Klein [6].

Acknowledgments. This research was supported by the following grants: GAUK 4226/2011, GAUK 4383/2009, Czech Science Foundation 201/09/H057, MSM 0021620838 and GA405/09/0729. We thank three anonymous reviewers for their useful comments.

References

1. Bojar, O., Žabokrtský, Z.: CzEng 0.9, Building a Large Czech-English Automatic Parallel Treebank. The Prague Bulletin of Mathematical Linguistics (92), 63–83 (2009)
2. Collins, M.: Discriminative Training Methods for Hidden Markov Models: Theory and Experiments with Perceptron Algorithms. In: EMNLP, vol. 10, pp. 1–8 (2002)
3. Denis, P., Baldridge, J.: A Ranking Approach to Pronoun Resolution. In: IJCAI, pp. 1588–1593 (2007)
4. Denis, P., Baldridge, J.: Specialized Models and Ranking for Coreference Resolution. In: EMNLP, pp. 660–669 (2008)
5. Liu, D.C., Nocedal, J.: On the Limited Memory BFGS Method for Large Scale Optimization. Mathematical Programming 45, 503–528 (1989)
6. Haghighi, A., Klein, D.: Simple Coreference Resolution with Rich Syntactic and Semantic Features. In: EMNLP, pp. 1152–1161 (2009)
7. Haghighi, A., Klein, D.: Coreference Resolution in a Modular, Entity-Centered Model. In: HLT-NAACL, pp. 385–393 (2010)
8. Hajič, J., et al.: Prague Dependency Treebank 2.0. CD-ROM, Linguistic Data Consortium, LDC Catalog No.: LDC2006T01, Philadelphia (2006)
9. Malouf, R.: A Comparison of Algorithms for Maximum Entropy Parameter Estimation. In: 6th Conference on Natural Language Learning, COLING 2002, vol. 20, pp. 1–7. Association for Computational Linguistics, Stroudsburg (2002)
10. MUC-7: Coreference Task Definition. In: Seventh Message Understanding Conference. Morgan Kaufmann, San Francisco, CA (1998)
11. Ng, V.: Supervised Noun Phrase Coreference Research: The First Fifteen Years. In: ACL, Uppsala, Sweden, pp. 1396–1411 (July 2010)
12. Nguy, G.L., Novák, V., Žabokrtský, Z.: Comparison of Classification and Ranking Approaches to Pronominal Anaphora Resolution in Czech. In: SIGDIAL 2009 Conference, pp. 276–285. ACL, London (2009)
13. NIST: ACE Evaluation Plan. Tech. rep. (2007), `http://www.itl.nist.gov/iad/mig/tests/ace/2007/`
14. Nědolužko, A., Mírovský, J., Ocelák, R., Pergler, J.: Extended Coreferential Relations and Bridging Anaphora in the Prague Dependency Treebank. In: DAARC 2009 (2009)
15. Rahman, A., Ng, V.: Supervised models for coreference resolution. In: EMNLP, pp. 968–977 (2009)
16. Sgall, P., Hajičová, E., Panevová, J.: The Meaning of the Sentence in Its Semantic and Pragmatic Aspects. D. Reidel Publishing Company, Dordrecht (1986)
17. Soon, W.M., Ng, H.T., Lim, C.Y.: A Machine Learning Approach to Coreference Resolution of Noun Phrases. Computational Linguistics 27(4), 521–544 (2001)
18. Žabokrtský, Z., Ptáček, J., Pajas, P.: TectoMT: Highly Modular MT System with Tectogrammatics Used as Transfer Layer. In: ACL 2008 WMT, pp. 167–170 (2008)

Leveraging Different Meronym Discovery Methods for Bridging Resolution in French

Emmanuel Lassalle and Pascal Denis

Alpage, INRIA & Univ. Paris Diderot
Sorbonne Paris Cité, F-75205 Paris, France
emmanuel.lassalle@ens-lyon.org, pascal.denis@inria.fr

Abstract. This paper presents a statistical system for resolving bridging descriptions in French, a language for which current lexical resources have a very low coverage. The system is similar to that developed for English by [22], but it was enriched to integrate meronymic information extracted automatically from both web queries and raw text using syntactic patterns. Through various experiments on the DEDE corpus [8], we show that although still mediocre the performance of our system compare favorably to those obtained by [22] for English. In addition, our evaluation indicates that the different meronym extraction methods have a cumulative effect but that the text pattern-based extraction method is more robust and leads to higher accuracy than the Web-based approach.

Keywords: bridging anaphora resolution, relation extraction, syntactic patterns.

1 Introduction

Bridging descriptions are a special kind of anaphora whose interpretation requires not only identifying an antecedent, but also inferring a specific relation linking it to the anaphor [6]. In this paper, we focus on *mereological* bridging anaphora (that is, cases wherein the inferred relation is a *part-whole* relation). An illustrative English example is given in (1):

(1) <u>The car</u> will not move. <u>The engine</u> is broken.

The resolution of bridging anaphora currently represents one of the most challenging tasks in discourse processing. It is considerably much harder than standard coreferential anaphora resolution for which shallow predictors (like distance, string matching, or morphosyntactic agreement) have been shown to be rather effective [15,25,18]. Part of the challenge is due to an important information bottle-neck. Lexical resources like *WordNet* are still too poor and uneven in coverage to provide a realistic solution [19]. In turn, more recent approaches to bridging resolution have turned to web-based extraction methods to fill this "knowledge gap"[4,22]. To date, the most complete and best-performing approach combines focus and lexical distance predictors using machine learning techniques [22].

I. Hendrickx et al. (Eds.): DAARC 2011, LNAI 7099, pp. 35–46, 2011.

While there has been a lot of research on resolving bridging anaphora in English [19,28,4,22], much fewer work exist for other languages (see [27] for an attempt on German). In this paper, we develop a system that performs bridging resolution in French; to our knowledge, this is first such system for this language. Note that languages other than English, the knowledge gap is even wider, since lexical resources are typically scarcer. Our system directly builds upon the system developed for English by [22], and enriches it in several ways. First, we refine the search engine queries to include a wider range of meronym-holonym extraction patterns (some of them specific to French). Second, and more substantially, we augment the system with an original iterative pattern-based relation extraction method from raw text.

Our system is evaluated on *DEDE* [8], a corpus of French definite descriptions annotated for bridging. Initial experiments indicate that our system achieves performance that compares favorably to those of [22] for English under the same simple evaluation protocols. We found that the two meronym discovery approaches have a cumulative effect for resolution accuracy, and further comparison between the two methods suggests extraction from raw text is less noisy. But we also show that, when tested in a more realistic setting, the system still has rather low accuracy (at least for French). Our analysis reveals that the current features are still not discriminative enough, which in turns suggests the need for acquiring additional relational data.

The rest of this paper is organized as follows. Section 2 briefly presents the corpus we used. In section 3, we first describe a free lexical database for French, as well as our two methods for extracting meronyms. Section 4 details various experiments wherein we use these different resources for bridging resolution. A detailed comparison of the two extraction methods is given in section 5. Finally, section 6 discusses related work and section 7 offers some conclusions and directions for future work.

2 DEDE: A French Corpus for Bridging Descriptions

For this study, we use *DEDE*[1], a French corpus annotated with definite descriptions [8], built from *Le Monde* articles in 1987. The corpus is not only the first of its kind in French with a high agreement rate between annotators, but it also introduces a fine-grained classification of definite descriptions.

The corpus contains 4,910 descriptions classified in 5 main categories (autonomous, coreferential, associative, situational and non-referential) themselves further divided into subcategories, so that the corpus provides an appropriate resource for evaluating a complete system for processing definite descriptions. As we are solely interested in bridging resolution for now, we only detail the"associative" class (that is bridging).

The "associative" class contains 530 anaphors of 4 different types (see [8]for details): 322 *MERO*(meronymy e.g. a *tree/the trunk*), 87 *CIRC*(modifier-modified

[1] `http://www.cnrtl.fr/corpus/dede/`

relation, e.g.*Paris/the region*), 97 *REL* (predicate-argument, e.g.*two robbers/the attack*), 24 *MOD* (relation introduced by a modifier e.g.*in July/the next month*). The *MERO* subclass involves 296 distinct holonym-meronym pairs.

It is worth noticing that the *MERO* subclass of *DEDE* collapses together several kinds of part-whole relation: it contains classical component-object relations (e.g.,*trunk/tree*), unnecessary parts (e.g.,*wine/diner*), and functions (e.g.,*mayor / city*).

Some of bridging relations involve a proper name as antecedent such as: *steering committee/La Société Générale.* That should be taken into account in resolution. For more details on part-whole relations, please refer to [30,11].

3 Methods for Meronymy Extraction

Having access to lexical and encyclopedic knowledge is an essential ingredient for resolving definite bridging, for it is precisely the existence of an inferable relation that permits bridging. Static databases like WordNet suffer from a low coverage impacting the performance in bridging resolution. In French, similar databases are even smaller than in English, which further motivates the need for automatic lexical relation extraction methods. Another point is that bridging relations do not always correspond to a lexical relation (e.g.*fragment/pot*, about archeology) so that we cannot expect to find some of those relations in a static lexicon, but perhaps in texts if their usage is frequent enough.

3.1 A Static Lexical Database

As there is no *free* equivalent to the *Princeton Wordnet*[2] for French, we use the *WOLF* database[3] [23], a resource built from *WordNet* and several multilingual resources. It has a total of 32,351 synsets, which is more than the *French Euro WordNet*(22,121 synsets), but much less than English WordNet (177,659 synsets). Crucially, *WOLF* only covers 2.7% of meronyms in *DEDE*, whereas *WordNet* covers 38.8% of the corpus used in [19]. We will see during the experiment that the contribution of this resource in bridging resolution is very small because of this low coverage. In particular, many lexical distance calculations will be impossible because of this low coverage.

3.2 Querying Meronyms from the Web

Recent approaches to bridging resolution compensate the lack of lexical data by using web-based methods [4,22] (see also [12,13] for related tasks). The idea is to query a search engine for syntactic patterns taken to instantiate a particular lexical relation, and use the number of hits returned as an estimate of the

[2] `http://wordnet.princeton.edu/`

[3] `https://gforge.inria.fr/projects/wolf/`

plausibility of that relation. In English, the pattern mostly used to instantiate meronymy is "*the X of the Y*'.

We also adopt this method (using *Yahoo!*[4]), with some modifications. In French, the equivalent of "*the X of the Y*" has different realizations depending on the grammatical genders and numbers of *X and Y* . Because we used lemmatized lexical heads, we only took singular *Xs* and *Ys*[5], which gives the three initial patterns: *"le X du/de/de la Y"*.

Because the first patterns are not in one-to-one correspondence with the meronymy relation, we defined another set of nine syntactical patterns, based on the possessive. Our purpose is to combine them to obtain less noisy results. Different settings can be applied to combine the patterns, whether we want a better coverage or a better precision: we set a threshold that corresponds to a minimum of nonzero matches among all the patterns required to accept a meronym candidate. In our experiments, meronym candidates are *(potential antecedent, anaphora)*pairs for the *MERO* class of *DEDE*. The Web-based method has a very high coverage: with a threshold set at value 1, 92.9% of all meronyms were positively identified (275/296 different meronyms in *DEDE*, or 292/322 annotated bridges). We will give more detailed results in section 5.

3.3 Extracting Meronyms from Raw Text

To further alleviate the "knowledge gap", we set up a system that iteratively extracts lexical relations and corresponding syntactic patterns from raw text. This type of approach has proven quite efficient on problems similar to bridging [13,2,9,24]. Although it was developed independently, our system is most similar to [1] in the sense that it alternatively extracts syntactic patterns and pairs. However, we enhance the system by considering two kinds of pattern: (i) linear patterns (i.e., a *n*-gram between 2 words) as well as (ii) dependency patterns (i.e., a path between 2 words in the dependency tree). In the latter case, we use two kinds of pattern (common ancestor or domination, see figure 1).

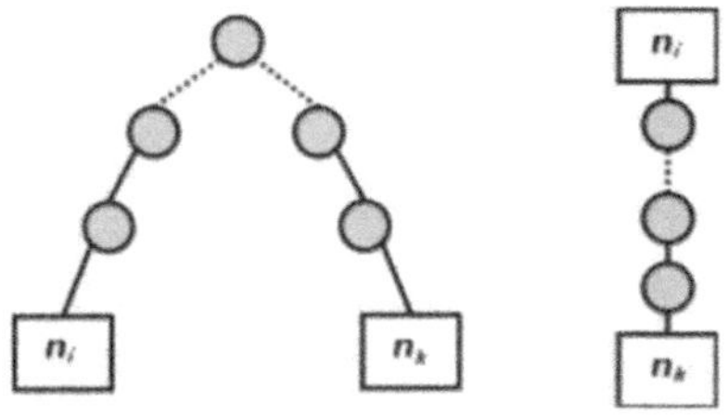

Fig. 1. Two types of dependency pattern

[4] http://developer.yahoo.com/search/boss/

[5] Another reason is the time it takes to query a search engine with meronym candidates: for all the patterns we used, it took more than a week.

We used a preprocessed corpus of 142M words from newspaper *L'Est Républicain*[6]. The system starts from a database of meronyms and syntactic patterns (linear or in dependencies) and iteratively extracts new pairs and patterns to enrich the initial database. To avoid to noisy results, we only retain pairs of nouns appearing within two patterns or more (about 50,000 pairs). We also discard all pairs of patterns occurring less than a threshold of 5 (an empiric value).

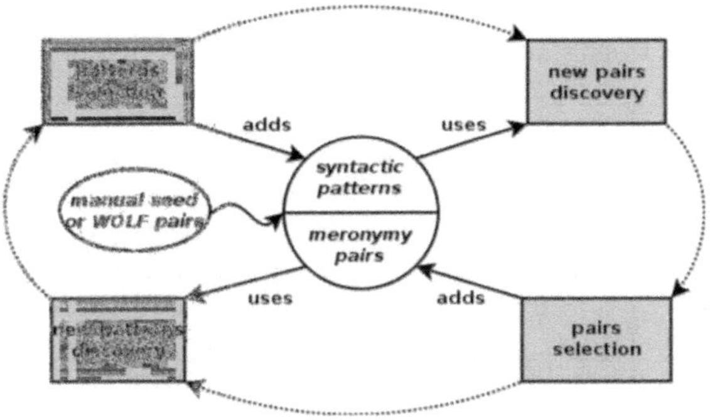

Fig. 2. Our system for extracting meronyms

The system was initialized with two different types of seed data. When starting with a small set of manually crafted pairs and patterns, it retrieved 0.5% (=54) of meronyms in *WOLF* and 11.5% (=34) of meronyms in *DEDE*. When launched with the known meronyms in *WOLF*(with no patterns), the system was able to retrieve up to 16.2% (=48/296) of *distinct* meronyms in *DEDE* (by extracting 135 linear patterns and 42 dependency patterns), a much better coverage than *WOLF* but well below the Web-based method. This will be the final setting for our resolution system. A more restrictive selection of extracted pairs (e.g. with a ranking method like in [1]) would have reduced that coverage (some of *DEDE* meronyms were not found frequently by the system). But our purpose was mainly to reach an acceptable coverage while still filtering noisy pairs. Section 5 provides further comparison between the two extraction methods.

4 Experiments on Bridging Resolution

4.1 Task and System Setup

Our system performs the following task: given a definite description known to be a meronymic bridging anaphora, find its correct antecedent among previously occurring NPs. We avoid the complete inference task on *DEDE*(jointly resolving bridging and coreference, finding the lexical relation, and the antecedent) to fully evaluate the performances of the system (and extraction methods) on meronymy.

[6] `http://www.cnrtl.fr/corpus/estrepublicain/`

Our system relies heavily on [22]. This system uses standard classification techniques to combine focus features (such utterance distance and first-mentionhood) and lexical features (scores calculated from *WordNet* and *Google* results). Our feature set (see Table 1) enriches that of [22] with new lexical features, and an extra salience feature (salience is enriched by the grammatical function of the antecedent). *WOLF* is used to calculate lexical similarity and directly as a meronymy database. Extracted relations are used as a database (with an associated *Yahoo!* score for the Web-based method).

Table 1. Feature set (a is the anaphora and p a potential antecedent)

group	feature	description	type
salience	utterance distance NPs distance "is first mention" grammatical function	# of sentences separating p and a # of NPs separating p and a p is the first mention of a sentence the function of p (sub, obj, dep)	num num bool class
known relations	*WOLF meronyms extracted meronyms*	(a,p) is a meronymy in WOLF (a,p) is an extracted meronymy	bool bool
lexical distance	*WOLF distance*	$\frac{L(ShortestPath(a,p))}{L(MaxLengthPath(a,p))}$ or 0 if no path	num
search engine	*Yahoo! score*	number of pages, on 12 patterns	*num/bool*

Like [22], we have experimented with a naive Bayes and multi-layer perceptron classifier, but we found no significant differences in performance. Results will therefore be reported only for the naive Bayes classifier (for which distances are modeled by exponential laws, and *Yahoo!* scores by a Gaussian).

4.2 Corpus Preprocessing

DEDE corpus was preprocessed in several ways. First, we recovered accentuations: these were absent from the released texts. We performed NPs chunking (with Tree Tagger[7]), as well as dependency parsing (using MSTParser[8]). We also separated texts in much finer and balanced documents than the originals (original documents contain several articles with non-related topics). All NP chunks that precede an anaphor in the text are considered as potential antecedents.

4.3 Evaluation and Results

We use two different types of evaluation procedures. For comparison, we first follow the evaluation protocol of [22] and first report accuracy figures for positive

[7] `http://www.ims.uni-stuttgart.de/projekte/corplex/TreeTagger/`

[8] We used the retrained version of the MSTParser [14] described in [5].

and negative instances classification (all results were obtained by doing 5-fold cross-validations). Under this evaluation we obtain from 88.12% (salience only) to 90.0% (all features)[9]. These high scores come in part from the rareness of the bridging relation, and in turn the overwhelming number of negative instances. Recall on positives was around 76% with salience features, and lexical features did not bring any significant improvement.

Table 2. Baselines comparison with [22]

baseline	accuracy	accuracy in [22]
random (previous) mention	1.7%	-
random mention, in first position of a sentence	1.7%	-
random mention in the previous 5 sentences	1.8%	4%
mention with best yahoo! score	1.9%	13.8%
mention in first position with best yahoo! score	2.0%	12%
random mention in the previous sentence	2.0%	19%
random in the previous 5 sentences, first position	2.0%	21.3%
best yahoo! score in the previous 5 sentences	3.9%	-

A second, more realistic evaluation consists in evaluating the accuracy in finding the correct antecedent for a given bridging anaphora. For comparison, we used various baselines similar to those in [22]. As shown in table 2, the accuracy rates are consistently much lower than for equivalent baselines on Poesio *et al.*'s corpus, suggesting that the number of potential antecedents is probably much higher in *DEDE* corpus than the corpus used in [22]. Note that the low score of the baseline based *Yahoo!* score suggests that the number of *hits* is not necessarily a good indicator.

Table 3. Overall resolution accuracy results

features	accuracy
salience	7.9%
+ WOLF (distance/meronyms)	12.6%
+ Yahoo! score	22.4%
+ extracted meronyms	23.6%

We tested our system by successively adding features to the classifier (see table 3). First, note that the salience features make the system better than the baselines. Lexical features increase performance, and the different lexical resources appear to have a cumulative effect on performance (suggesting that they are somehow complementary). Under this evaluation, our best system obtains an overall accuracy of 23.6%, which is significantly lower than the scores reported by

[9] The best score obtained in [22] among several classifier is 79.3%.

[22] on their corpus[10] but comparatively much better than the baselines[11]. The results were almost the same when ignoring *Yahoo!* scores and using extracted meronyms as a database (with a threshold on *Yahoo!* score to filter noisy pairs).

4.4 Error Analysis

Preliminary error analysis reveals that (i) the correct antecedent was in the top 10 candidates (out of 206 on average) in 66.5% of cases; (ii) many errors are due to selecting an antecedent with the same lexical head as the true one; (iii) the system fails in most cases where the antecedent is a proper name[12]; (iv) the system sometimes selects a meronym of the true antecedent (e.g.*room/first floor/hotel*).These results suggest that current features are still not discriminative enough, and point to a need for acquiring additional relational data using a more accurate model for selecting new pairs and patterns.

5 Web-Based Method vs. Extraction from Text

In order to gain a better understanding of the influence of the different meronym extraction methods on resolution, we perform some additional evaluation. When setting up the two methods, we were mainly concerned with maximizing coverage (to make up for the lack of coverage of *WOLF*). On that metric alone, the web-based extraction technique clearly outperforms both *WOLF* and the raw text extraction. Given that the two approaches produce noisy results, we also have to compare them on the basis of precision.

The evaluation protocol we propose is simple: all pairs (potential antecedent, anaphora) of *DEDE* are tested as meronym candidates (there are 45,605 different pairs). A pair is marked as positive if it has been extracted by the method, and negative otherwise. Only meronyms marked in *DEDE* are considered true positives, and all the other pairs are negatives. We aware that this evaluation clearly over-estimates the number of false positives, but the point is meronyms that are not marked in *DEDE* are a small portion of all possible pairs and the aim of this test is to compare the noise of our two methods.

Looking first at the web-based approach, we compared extracted pairs to *DEDE* meronyms. For this, we considered a pair to be extracted if its *Yahoo!* score was above an arbitrary threshold. First, we tested all patterns separately and grouped them by gender variation (results in table 4).

---

[10] They report an impressive 92.5%, but their evaluation protocol consists in finding the correct antecedent for 6 anaphora randomly chosen in the evaluation set, which is absolutely not significant if not repeated a large number of times (but in that case, cross-validations would be wiser).

[11] Baselines are the only point of comparison we can have with [22] on this task.

[12] Proper nouns antecedents require a two steps inference (e.g. identify *Technip* as a company identify the meronymy *employees/company*).

French translations of "*the X of the Y*" ("*X du/de l'/de la Y*") have the best coverage but one of the lowest precision. Patterns based on the possessive have a low coverage but they also less noisy. Finally, patterns obtaining the best F1-score are "*X et son/et sa Y*".

Table 4. Testing patterns independently on *DEDE*meronyms (best results were boldfaced

	TP	FP	Prec.	recall	F1-score
Y **d'** *X*	74	6904	1.06%	25.00%	2.03%
Y **de** *X*	245	29081	0.84%	82.77%	1.65%
comb.	248	29781	0.83%	83.78%	1.64%
Y **du** *X*	165	16159	1.01%	55.74%	1.99%
Y **de l'** *X*	69	6924	0.99%	23.31	1.89
Y **de la** *X*	135	13383	1.00%	45.61%	1.95%
comb.	252	28760	0.87%	**85.14%**	1.72%
Y **dont le** *X*	72	5749	1.24%	24.32%	2.35%
Y **dont l'** *X*	38	2949	1.27%	12.84%	2.31%
Y **dont la** *X*	47	3731	1.24%	15.88%	2.31%
comb.	144	12008	1.18%	48.65%	2.31%
Y **et son** *X*	100	7483	1.32%	33.78	2.54
Y **et sa** *X*	41	3569	1.14%	13.85%	2.10%
comb.	136	10858	**1.24%**	45.95	**2.41%**
Y **de son** *X*	98	7602	1.27%	33.11%	2.45%
Y **de sa** *X*	33	4175	0.78%	11.15%	1.47%
comb.	129	11189	1.14%	43.58%	2.22%

Next we defined a more restrictive criterion to classify meronyms: a pair is classified as a meronym if it has been observed by the search engine with strictly more than x patterns, x being a parameter that varies from 0 to 11[13]. From the precision, recall and F1 values given in 5 we see that combining the patterns leads to a better F1-score than using patterns separately: at $x = 7$, the F1-score has doubled (5.10%) compared to the best F1-score for isolated patterns. This motivates the use of several patterns with the web-based method.

Now turning to meronyms extracted from raw text (using the settings mentioned in section 3, we found 48 true positives and 1,096 false positives, which gives a precision of 4.20%, a recall of 16.22%, and reaches a F1 of 6.66%, which is better than the F1-score for all settings of the web based method (the comparison is acceptable because, as mentioned in section 4, *Yahoo!* scores do not have a strong influence on the performances of our resolution system compared to using a threshold on it and considering extracted pairs as a lexical database). Extracting meronyms from text seems not only less noisy than web-based methods, but it also has the advantage of being faster than web queries, and the possibility to exploit more information (e.g. dependency parses or contextual information).

[13] Value 0 corresponds to combining all 12 patterns by disjunction.

Table 5. Testing patterns combinations on *DEDE* meronyms(best results were boldfaced)

	TP	FP	prec.	recall	F1-score
# *patterns* >0	275	34319	0.79%	**92.91%**	1.58%
# *patterns* >1	246	27664	0.88%	83.11%	1.74%
# *patterns* >2	193	19661	0.97%	65.20%	1.92%
# *patterns* >3	150	12718	1.17%	50.68%	2.28%
# *patterns* >4	116	7569	1.51%	39.19%	2.91%
# *patterns* >5	72	3926	1.80%	24.32	3.35%
# *patterns* >6	36	1452	2.42%	12.16%	4.04%
# *patterns* >7	20	469	4.09%	6.76%	**5.10%**
# *patterns* >8	7	100	**6.54%**	2.36%	3.47%
# *patterns* >9	0	14	0 %	0 %	-
# *patterns* >10	0	4	0 %	0 %	-
# *patterns* >11	0	0	-	0 %	-

6 Related Work

Bridging anaphora resolution was investigated by [28,22,4,27], among others. Earlier systems were rule-based, while more recent ones use machine-learning techniques. We can find similar work (web-based methods) on similar problems such as nominal anaphora [12] and metonymy [16]. [21] points out the problem of lack of knowledge with static lexical resources on bridging anaphora resolution and examines the contribution of lexical extraction techniques on this task.

Pattern-based lexical relation extraction from raw text dates back to [9], but fully automatic methods have now become available [1]. Recently, many advances have been made in open information extraction [31,32,10] and can be also applied to discovering lexical relations.

Extraction of relations from the Web using patterns were used in bootstrapping methods for discovering named entities or relations [3,7] as well as directly in the resolution of problems requiring lexical knowledge [4,22,12,13].

7 Conclusion and Perspectives

We have set up and compared two approaches for extracting meronyms. We have improved the web-based method for French by using several patterns and combining them, and we have developed an original method pattern-based extraction method from raw text. We have then used the acquired lexical data as features in a system for resolving bridging anaphora in the case of a part-whole relation. In the system, salience is a very relevant feature to localize antecedent in a region (in restricting the antecedent space), while lexical features must provide a better precision in this region to find the actual antecedent. However, our results show that current methods for discovering meronyms are still not sufficient to get reach good results in the resolution process. Finally, we have shown that the web-based method, even when it combines several syntactic patterns, is more noisy that extraction from raw text although it provides a wider coverage.

Improving the resolution system will first require more accurate data, both lexical and encyclopedic. In fact, some of the required data, such as proper nouns classes, can be retrieved from Wikipedia, and some other data, like lexical relations between common nouns, might be inferred by relational learning. Then, transforming Wikipedia into an ontology (like in [26,17]) and relational learning become central issues for a proper treatment of bridging. While the improvement of web-based methods appears limited, there are more possible extensionsin relational learning that can be applied to text pattern-based methods. We now plan to extend these techniques and apply them to definite bridging processing.

Acknowledgments. We thank the DAARC 2011 anonymous reviewers for their helpful comments.

References

1. Agichtein, E., Gravano, L.: Snowball: extracting relations from large plain-text collections. In: DL, pp. 85–94 (2000)
2. Berland, M., Charniak, E.: Finding parts in very large corpora. In: ACL, pp. 57–64 (1999)
3. Brin, S.: Extracting patterns and relations from the world wide web. In: International Workshop on The World Wide Web and Databases, pp. 172–183 (1999)
4. Bunescu, R.: Associative anaphora resolution: A web-based approach. In: EACL Workshop on the Computational reatment of Anaphora (2003)
5. Candito, M., Nivre, J., Denis, P., Anguiano, E.H.: Benchmarking of statistical dependency parsers for french. In: COLING, pp. 108–116 (2010)
6. Clark, H.: Bridging, pp. 441–420. Cambridge University Press (1977)
7. Etzioni, O., Cafarella, M., Downey, D., Popescu, A.M., Shaked, T., Soderl, S., Weld, D.S., Yates, A.: Unsupervised named-entity extraction from the web: an experimental study. Artif.Intell 165 (2005)
8. Gardent, C., Manuélian, H.: Création d'un corpus annot pour le traitement des descriptions définies. Traitement Automatique des Langues 46-I (2005)
9. Hearst, M.A.: Automatic acquisition of hyponyms from large text corpora. In: COLING, pp. 539–545 (1992)
10. Hoffmann, R., Zhang, C., Weld, D.S.: Learning 5000 relational. In: ACL, pp. 286–295 (2010)
11. Kleiber, G.: L'anaphore associative. PUF (2001)
12. Markert, K., Nissim, M.: Using the web for nominal anaphora resolution. In: EACL Workshop on the Computational Treatment of Anaphora (2003)
13. Markert, K., Nissim, M.: Comparing knowledge sources for nominal anaphora resolution. Computational Linguistics 31(3), 367–402 (2005)
14. McDonald, R.T., Crammer, K., Pereira, F.C.N.: Online large-margin training of dependency parsers. In: ACL (2005)
15. Mitkov, R.: Anaphora resolution. Pearson Education (2002)

16. Nastase, V., Strube, M.: Combining collocations, lexical and encyclopedic. In: EMNLP, pp. 910–918 (2009)
17. Nastase, V., Strube, Boerschinger, M.B., Zirn, C., Elghafari, A.: Wikinet: A very large scale multi-lingual concept network. In: LREC, Valletta, Malta (2010)
18. Ng, V.: Supervised noun phrase coreference research: The first fifteen years. In: ACL, Uppsala, Sweden (July 2010)
19. Poesio, M., Vieira, R., Teufel, S.: Resolving bridging references in unrestricted text. In: Workshop on Operational Factors in Practical,Robust Anaphora Resolution for Unrestricted Texts, pp. 1–6. Association for Computational Linguistics (1997)
20. Poesio, M., Vieira, R.: A corpus-based investigation of definite description use. Computional Linguistics 24(2), 183–216 (1998)
21. Poesio, M., Ishikawa, T., Walde, S.S., Vieira, R.: Acquiring lexical knowledge for anaphora resolution. In: LREC, pp. 1220–1224 (2002)
22. Poesio, M., Mehta, R., Maroudas, A., Hitzeman, J.: Learning to resolve bridging references. In: ACL, page 143 (2004)
23. Sagot, B., Fišer, D.: Construction d'un wordnet libre du français à partir de ressources multilingues. In: TALN (2008)
24. Snow, R., Jurafsky, D., Ng, A.Y.: Learning Syntactic Patterns for Automatic Hypernym Discovery. In: Saul, L.K., Weiss, Y., Bottou, L. (eds.) NIPS, pp. 1297–1304. MIT Press (2005)
25. Soon, W.M., Ng, H.T., Lim, D.C.Y.: A machine learning approach to coreference resolution of noun phrases. Computional Linguistics 27(4), 522–544 (2001)
26. Strube, M., Ponzetto, S.P.: Wikirelate! computing semantic relatedness using wikipedia. In: AAAI, pp. 1419–1424 (2006)
27. Versley, Y.: Using the web to resolve coreferent bridging in german newspaper text. In: GLDV-Frühjahrstagung 2007 (2007)
28. Vieira, R., Poesio, M.: Corpus-based development and evaluation of a system for processing definite descriptions. In: COLING (2000)
29. Vieira, R., Salmon-Alt, S., Schang, E.: Multilingual corpora annotation for processing definite descriptions. In: ANLP, London, UK, pp. 249–258. Springer, Heidelberg (2002)
30. Winston, M.R., Chan, R., Herrmann, D.: A taxonomy of part-whole relations. Cognitive Science 11, 417–444 (1987)
31. Wu, F., Weld, D.S.: Open information extraction using wikipedia. In: ACL, pp. 118–127 (2010)
32. Zhu, J., Nie, Z., Liu, X., Zhang, B., Wen, J.: Statsnowball: a statistical approach to extracting entity relationships. In: WWW, pp. 101–110 (2009)

Multiobjective Simulated Annealing Based Approach for Feature Selection in Anaphora Resolution

Asif Ekbal[1], Sriparna Saha[1], Olga Uryupina[2], and Massimo Poesio[3]

[1] Department of Computer Science and Engineering, IIT Patna, India
{asif,sriparna}@iitp.ac.in
[2] University of Trento, Center for Mind/Brain Sciences
uryupina@gmail.com
[3] University of Essex, Language and Computation Group
poesio@essex.ac.uk

Abstract. In this paper we propose a multiobjective simulated annealing based technique for anaphora resolution. There is no generally accepted metric for measuring the performance of anaphora resolution systems, and the existing metrics–MUC, B^3 , CEAF, Blanc, among others–tend to reward significantly different behaviors. Systems optimized according to one metric tend to perform poorly with respect to other ones, making it very difficult to compare anaphora resolution systems, as clearly shown by the results of the SEMEVAL 2010 Task 1 on the Multilingual Coreference Resolution. One solution would be to find a single completely satisfactory metric, but its not clear whether this is possible and at any rate it is not going to happen any time soon. An alternative is to optimize models according to multiple metrics simultaneously. In this paper, we propose a multiobjective simulated annealing based technique to solve the feature selection problem of anaphora resolution by optimizing multiple objective functions. Experimental results show that the proposed approach performs superior in comparison to the previously developed multiobjective genetic algorithm based feature selection technique.

Keywords: Multiobjective Optimization, Simulated Annealing, Anaphora Resolution, Feature Selection.

1 Introduction

In anaphora resolution,[1] as in other Human Language Technology (HLT) tasks, optimization to a metric is essential to achieve good performance [7,21]. However, many evaluation metrics have been proposed for anaphora resolution, each capturing what seems to be a key intuition about the task: from MUC [24] to

[1] We use the term 'anaphora resolution' to refer to the task perhaps most commonly referred to as 'coreference resolution', which many including us find a misnomer. For the purposes of the present paper the two terms could be seen as interchangeable.

I. Hendrickx et al. (Eds.): DAARC 2011, LNAI 7099, pp. 47–58, 2011.

B^3 [1], from the ACE metric [6] to CEAF [9] to BLANC [16]. And unlike in other areas of HLT, none has really taken over. This would not matter so much if those metrics were to reward the same systems; but in fact, as dramatically demonstrated by the results of the Multilingual Coreference Resolution Task at SEMEVAL 2010 [17], the opposite is true–almost every system could come on top depending on which metric was chosen.

It seems unlikely that the field will converge on a single metric any time soon. This being the case, and given that many of the proposed metrics do capture what would seem to be plausible intuitions, it would seem desirable to develop methods to optimize systems according to more than one metric at once–in particular, according to at least one metric of what we might call the 'link-based cluster' of metrics (e.g., the MUC scorer) and at least one of what we will call the 'entity-based cluster' (e.g., CEAF).

As it happens, techniques for doing just that have been developed in the area of **multi-objective optimization** (MOO) [4]. In [18], we have developed a multiobjective genetic algorithm (GA) based technique which was used to optimize anaphora resolution models (we focused for the time being on feature selection) by looking for a solution in the space defined by a multiplicity of metrics (we used MUC and CEAF (in two variants) as the optimization functions). Perhaps the most interesting result of the work was the finding that by working in such a multi-metric space it is possible to find solutions that are better with respect to an individual metric than when trying to optimize for that metric alone–which arguably suggests that indeed both families of metrics capture some fundamental intuition about anaphora, and taking into account both intuitions we avoid local optima. In a recent work [2], it has been shown that multiobjective simulated annealing (SA) techniques perform better than the multiobjective genetic algorithm (GA) if there are more objective functions to be optimized. Here, we propose a multiobjective SA based technique for feature selection in anaphora resolution. This approach optimizes five different objective functions as used in the CoNLL-2011 shared task [14]. We compare the proposed approach with the previous technique [18]. Experimental results show the efficacy of the proposed technique.

2 Background: Optimizing for Anaphora Resolution

A great number of statistical approaches to anaphora resolution have been proposed in the past ten years. These approaches differ with respect to their underlying models, machine learners and their parameters, and with respect to feature sets used. There have been, however, only few attempts at explicit optimization of these aspects, and in those few cases, optimization tends to be done by hand.

An early step in this direction was the work by Ng and Cardie [12], who developed a rich feature set including 53 features, but reported no significant improvement over their baseline when all these features were used with the MUC6 and MUC7 corpora. They then proceeded to manually select a subset of features that did yield better results for the MUC-6/7 datasets. A much larger scale and very systematic effort of manual feature selection over the same dataset was carried out by Uryupina [20], who evaluated over600 features. Recasens and Hovy [15] carried out an investigation of feature selection for Spanish using the ANCORA corpus.

The first systematic attempt at automatic optimization of anaphora resolution we are aware of was carried out by Hoste [7], who investigated the possibility of using genetic algorithms for automatic optimization of both feature selection and of learning parameters, also considering two different machine learners,**TiMBL** and Ripper. Her results suggest that such techniques yield improvements on the MUC-6/7 data sets. There are two major differences between the approach of [7] and that followed in our study. First, the scope of [7] is restricted to *single-objective* optimization. As we have shown in [18], this might provide unstable solutions, that are too tailored to a particular scoring metric. Second, the feature set of [7] is relatively small and therefore does not provide an efficient test-bed for a feature selection approach. Not surprising, parameteroptimization shows a more consistent effect on the overall performance than feature selection in [7]s experiments. These approaches focused on a single metric; the one proposal simultaneously to consider multiple metrics, Zhao and Ng [25] still optimized for each metric individually.

The effect of optimization on anaphora resolution was dramatically demonstrated by Uryupina's contribution to SEMEVAL 2010 Multilingual Coreference Task [21].Uryupina directly optimizes two parameters of her system: the choice of a model (mention-pair vs. ILP with various constraints) and the definition of mention types for training separate classifiers. The optimization is done on the development data in a brute-force fashion, in order to maximize the performance according to a pre-defined metric (MUC,CEAF or BLANC). The results on the SEMEVAL-10 dataset clearly show that existing metrics of coreference rely on different intuitions and therefore a system, optimized for a particular metric, might show inferior results for the other ones. For example, the reported BLANC difference between the runs optimized for BLANC and CEAF is around 10 percentage points.

This highlights the importance of the multi-objective optimization (MOO) for coreference, that suggests a family of systems, showing reliable performance according to all the desired metrics. A form of multi-objective optimization was applied to coreference by Munson et al. [11]. Their general conclusion was negative, stating that "ensemble selection seems too unreliable for use in NLP", but they did see some improvements for coreference.

3 Optimization with Simulated Annealing

In this section, we review a recently developed multi-objective optimization (MOO) technique based on simulated annealing (SAs) [8], Archived multiobjective simulated annealing (AMOSA) [2].

3.1 Multi-objective Optimization

Multi-objective optimization (MOO) can be formally stated as follows [4]. Find the vectors $\overline{x}^* = [x_1{}^*, x_2{}^*, ..., x_n{}^*]^T$ of decision variables that simultaneously optimize the M objective values

$$\{f_1(\overline{x}), f_2(\overline{x}), ..., f_M(\overline{x})\}$$

while satisfying the constraints, if any.

An important concept in MOO is that of **domination.** In the context of a maximization problem, a solution $\overline{x}_i$ is said to dominate $\overline{x}_j$ if $\forall \kappa \in 1, 2, ..., M, f_k(\overline{x}_i) \geq f_k(\overline{x}_j)$ and $\exists \kappa \in 1, 2, ..., M$, such that $f_k(\overline{x}_i) > f_k(\overline{x}_j)$.

Among a set of solutions P , the nondominated set of solutions P' are those that are not dominated by any member of the set P . The nondominated set of the entire search space S is called the **globally Pareto-optimal set.** In general, a MOO algorithm usually admits a set of solutions not dominated by any solution encountered by it.

```
Begin
generate the initial state q
T = T_max
Let E(q,T) be the associated energy
while ( T ≥ T_min)
    for i = 1 to k
        Perturb q to yield s
        Let E(s,T) be the associated energy
        Set q ← s with probability 1/(1+e^(-(E(q,T)-E(s,T))/T))
    end for
    T = rT
end while
        Decode q to provide the solution of the problem.
End
```

Fig. 1. Steps of Simulated Annealing

3.2 The SA Based MOO Algorithm: AMOSA

Archived multiobjective simulated annealing (AMOSA) [2] is a generalized version of the simulated annealing (SA) algorithm based on multiobjective optimization (MOO). MOO is applied when dealing with the real-world problems where there are several objectives that should be optimized simultaneously. In general, a MOO algorithm usually admits a set of solutions that are not dominated by any solution it encountered, i.e.,non-dominated solutions [4]. During recent years, many multiobjective evolution algorithms, such as multiobjective EA (MOEA), have been suggested to solve the MOO problems [22].

Simulated annealing (SA) is a search technique for solving difficult optimization problems, which is based on the principles of statistical mechanics [10]. Recently,

SA has become very popular because not only can SA replace the exhaustive search to save time and resource, but also converge to the global optimum if annealed sufficiently slowly. The simulated annealing steps are shown in Figure 1.

Although the single objective version of SA is quite popular, its utility in the multi-objective case was limited because of its search-from-a-point nature. To overcome this limitation, recently an efficient multiobjective version of SA called as AMOSA was proposed in [2].

The AMOSA algorithm incorporates the concept of an archive where the non-dominated solutions seen so far are stored. Two limits are kept on the size of the archive:a hard or strict limit denoted by *HL*, and a soft limit denoted by *SL*. The algorithm begins with the initialization of a number $(\gamma \times SL, \gamma > 1)$ of solutions each of which represents a state in the search space. The multiple objective functions are computed. Each solution is refined by using simple hill-climbing and domination relation for a number of iterations. Thereafter the non-dominated solutions are stored in the archive until the size of the archive increases to *SL*. If the size of the archive exceeds *HL*, a single-linkage clustering scheme is used to reduce the size to *HL*. Then, one of the points is randomly selected from the archive. This is taken as the current-pt, or the initial solution, at temperature $T = Tmax$. The current-pt is perturbed to generate a new solution named new-pt, and its objective functions are computed. The domination status of the new-pt is checked with respect to the current-pt and the solutions in the archive.A new quantity called amount of domination, $\Delta dom(a, b)$ between two solutions a and b is defined as follows: $\Delta dom(a,b) = \prod_{i=1, f_i(a) \neq f_i(b)}^{M} \frac{f_i(a) - f_i(b)}{R_i}$, where $f_i(a)$ and $f_i(b)$ are the ith objective values of the two solutions and R_i is the corresponding range of the objective function. Based on domination status different cases may arise viz.,accept the (i) new-pt, (ii) current-pt, or, (iii) a solution from the archive. Again, in case of overflow of the archive, clustering is used to reduce its size to *HL*. The process is repeated *iter* times for each temperature that is annealed with a cooling rate of α (< 1)till the minimum temperature *Tmin* is attained. The process thereafter stops, and the archive contains the final non-dominated solutions.

It has been demonstrated in Ref.[2] that the performance of AMOSA is better than that of NSGA-II [5] and some other well-known MOO algorithms.

4 Algorithm for Feature Selection in Anaphora Resolution

In this section, we discuss how we use multi-objective simulated annealing based optimization technique for selecting appropriate features in the anaphora resolution task.

4.1 State Representation and Archive Initialization

If the total number of features is F , then the length of each state is F . If the ith position of a state is 0 then it represents that i^{th} feature does not participate in constructing the classifier. Else if it is 1 then the ith feature participates in constructing the classifier. The entries of each state are randomly initialized to either 0 or 1.

4.2 Fitness Computation

In this paper we follow the scoring strategy used in CoNLL-2011 [14]. We use the official CoNLL scorer [14] for this purpose. The following 5 metrics are used here: MUC, B-CUBED, $CEAF_m$, $CEAF_e$ and BLANC. For fitness computation, the following procedure is executed:

1. Suppose there are N number of features present in a particular state (i.e., there are total N number of 1's in that state).
2. Construct the coreference resolution system (i.e., BART) with only these N features.
3. This coreference system is evaluated on the development data. The recall, precision and F-measure values of five metrics are calculated using CoNLL scorer.

For MOO, the objective functions corresponding to a particular chromosome are F_{MUC} (for the MUC metric), F_{CUBED} , F_{CEAFm} , F_{CEAFe} and F_{BLANC} . These five objective functions are simultaneously optimized using the search capability of AMOSA.

4.3 Mutation Operation

A mutation operator is applied to each entry of the state with a mutation probability, μ_m , where the entry is randomly replaced by either 0 or 1. The solutions on the final Pareto optimal front provide the different solutions to the feature selection problem.

5 Methods

5.1 The BART System

For our experiments, we use BART [23], a modular toolkit for anaphora resolution that supports state-of-the-art statistical approaches to the task and enables efficient feature engineering. BART implements different models of anaphora resolution (mention-pair and entity-mention; best-first vs. ranking), has interfaces to different machine learn-ers (MaxEnt, SVM, decision trees) and provides a large set of linguistically motivated features, along with the possibility to design new ones. It is thus ideally suited for ex-perimenting with optimization and feature selection.

In this study, we specifically focus on feature selection.[2] The complete list of features currently implemented in BART is listed in Table 1; all were considered

[2] The choice of the best model and the best machine learner, along with its parameters, is the main direction of our future work.

Table 1. Features used by BART : each feature describes a pair of mentions $\{M_i, M_j\}$, $i < j$, where M_i is a candidate antecedent and M_j is a candidate anaphor

Mention types and subtypes	
Mention Type*	relevant types of M_i and M_j, as identified in Soon et al.
Mention Type_Ante_Salient	M_i is demonstrative; M_i is an NE
Mention Type_Ante_Extra	M_i is a pronoun
Mention Type_Ana	M_j is a definite, demonstrative or indefinite NP, or pronoun of a specific type
Mention Type2	relevant types of M_i and M_j, as identified in Soon et al.
Mention Type_Salience	combination of *MentionType* and *MentionType_Ana*
FirstSecondPerson	M_i is a pronoun of the 1st/second person, same for M_j
PronounLeftRight	4 possible values for < M_i is a pronoun >* < M_j is a pronoun >
PronounWordForm	lemma for M_i if it's a pronoun; same for M_j
SemClassValue	semantic class of M_i, and M_j and the pair
BothLocation	both M_i and M_j are locations or geo-political
Agreement	
GenderAgree*	M_i and M_j, agree in gender
NumberrAgree*	M_i and M_j, agree in number
AnimacyAgree*	M_i and M_j, agree in animacy
Aliasing	
Alias*	heuristical NE-matching
Betternames	heuristical matching for personal names
Syntax	
Appositive*	M_i and M_j are in an apposition
Appositive2	M_i and M_j are adjacent
Coordination	M_i is a coordination ; same for M_j
HeadPartofSpeech	POS of M_i's head; same for M_j and the pair
SynPos	depth of M_i's node in the parse tree
Attributres	M_i and M_j have incompatible premodifiers
Relations	M_i and M_j have incompatible postmodifiers
Matching	
StringMatch*	M_i and M_j have the same surface form after stripping off the determiners
NonPro_StringMatch	both M_i and M_j are non-pronominal and *Stringmatch(M_i and M_j)* == 1
Pro_StringMatch	both M_i and M_j are pronominal and *Stringmatch(M_i and M_j)* == 1
NE_StringMatch	both M_i and M_j are NE and *Stringmatch(M_i and M_j)* == 1
HeadMatch	M_i and M_j have the same head
MinSame	M_i and M_j have the same minimal span
LeftRightMatch	M_j is a prefix or suffix substring of M_i or vice versa
StringMatchExtra	extra string-matching for bare plurals
StringKernel	approximate matching
Salience	
First_Mension	M_i is the first mention in its sentence
Corefchain	Size of the coreference chaing suggested for M_i so far (with a threshold)
First_Mension	for non-pronominal M_i number of preceding mentions with the same head lemma
Web	
Wiki	M_i and M_j have the same wikipedia entry
Yago	M_i and M_j are linked in Yago via means of typeof relation
WebPatterns	specific contexts for co-reference extracted from the web
Proximity	
DistanceMarkable	distance in mentions between M_i and M_j
DistanceSentenceInt*	distance in sentences between M_i and M_j
DistanceSentence	log-distance in sentences between M_i and M_j
DistanceSentence2	log-distance in sentences between M_i and M_j, different formula
DistDiscrete	distance in sentences between M_i and M_j discretized into {0,1, >= 2}
Miscellaneous	
Speech	M_i is in quoted speech; same for M_j and the pair

in the present experiments. We used a simple mention-pair model without ranking as in [19].In the mention-pair model, anaphora resolution is recast as a binary classification problem. Each classification instance consists of two mentions, i.e. an anaphor Mj and its potential antecedent Mi $(i < j)$. Instances are modeled as feature vectors (cf. Table 1)and are handed over to a binary classifier that decides, whether the anaphor and its can-didate antecedent are mentions of the same entity or not. All the feature values are com-puted automatically. We train a maximum entropy classifier and follow the approach of [19] to partition mentions into coreference sets given the classifiers decisions.

5.2 The Data Sets

We evaluated our approach on the ACE-02 dataset, which is divided in three subsets:bnews, npaper, and nwire. We provide results for both gold (hand-annotated) versions ofthe datasets (gbnews, gnpaper, gnwire) and system mentions extracted with CARAFE[3] (cbnews, cnpaper, cnwire).

Table 2 compares the performance level obtained using all the features in Table 1 with that of a loose re-implementation of the system proposed by [19], commonly used as baseline and relying only on very shallow information. Our reimplementation of the Soon et al. model uses only a subset of features: those marked with an asterisk in Table 1 Table 2 also provides typical state-of-the-art figures on the ACE-02 dataset, as presented in an overview by [13].

The results clearly show that although even larger sets of features have been proposed [20,3], the set of features already included in BART is sufficient to achieve results well above the state of the art on the dataset we used.

Table 2. Baseline performance on the ACE-02 dataset

		F_{MUC}	F_{B3}	F_{CEAFm}	F_{CEAFe}	F_{BLANG}
		gold mentions				
gbnews	following [19]	71.43	74.29	68.15	71.42	69.66
	All features (Table 1)	73.70	73.16	68.29	72.49	69.75
	state-of-the-art	65-69	-	-	-	-
gnpaper	following [19]	71.05	71.43	65.45	68.58	73.85
	All features (Table 1)	71.65	69.15	63.62	65.46	74.02
	state-of-the-art	70-72	-	-	-	-
gnwire	following [19]	69.40	75.39	69.12	71.35	74.26
	All features (Table 1)	72.44	75.96	71.26	71.82	79.63
	state-of-the-art	54-67	-	-	-	-
		system mentions				
cbnews	following [19]	60.63	71.09	60.41	61.23	65.70
	All features (Table 1)	61.73	69.88	59.79	59.92	64.79
cnpaper	following [19]	65.56	70.18	61.68	61.29	72.93
	All features (Table 1)	64.62	66.45	55.97	56.38	68.00
cnwire	following [19]	61.33	72.19	62.74	64.29	70.03
	All features (Table 1)	63.41	70.62	61.18	62.17	70.20

[3] http://sourceforge.net/projects/carafe

The results in Table 2 confirm the intuition that, contrary to what is suggested by early papers working on smaller datasets [19, 12], linguistic factors do play a crucial role in anaphora resolution: rich feature sets may lead to performance improvements once larger datasets are considered (a similar result was obtained by [3]). Such im-provements, however, come at high costs, as both using larger datasets and larger sets of features, learning a model becomes slower and requires much more memory.

This suggests that automatic feature selection may be essential not just to improve performance but also to be able to train a modeli.e., that an efficient coreference resolution system should combine rich linguistic feature sets with automatic feature selection mechanisms.

5.3 Simulated Annealing Parameter Setting

We set the following parameters for AMOSA: $SL = 30$, $HL = 20$, $T_{\max} = 100$, $T_{\min} = 0.01$, $\alpha = 0.8$, $iter = 20$. Both approaches are executed on development data to determine the optimal feature vector(s). Final results are reported on the test data.

Table 3. Evaluation results of the proposed AMOSA based approach

DataSet	Features	F_{MUC}	F_{B3}	F_{CEAFm}	F_{CEAFe}	F_{BLANC}
gbnews	0011101100010101000011100000111001010100011000	77.21	76.73	71.86	74.86	75.15
	0011101100010111000011100110101101010100011000	77.36	76.61	71.63	75.02	74.83
	0011101110011111000000100011111111011100000100	76.19	76.66	71.88	74.45	74.71
gnpaper	101010100000001100001100110010011001 1 01 01111	73.43	72.15	67.36	69.65	78.29
	00101010000101101010111000001000000100 01 110	73.80	73.24	68.60	69.46	78.96
	101010110000000100001000111011011011101 00 001	73.25	72.46	68.30	70.00	78.28
	001001101000101011101110101011001101110 01 110	74.34	72.07	66.39	68.89	76.49
	001001001000001011001000101001001101100 11 010	73.19	72.66	67.92	68.27	79.84
	000101111111100010011010001100100110100 10 101	72.40	72.34	67.96	67.74	79.70
gnwire	101010010010000111111110100000110 001 10 100110	72.36	76.71	72.06	73.29	79.42
	101101101001111100101011100000110001010 00 001	72.96	76.89	71.78	72.77	79.52
	1111111100001111001010010000000011101011 11 001	73.86	77.25	72.39	73.57	78.88
	111110100001110010101010010010110101100 00 100	72.55	76.53	71.40	72.48	79.79
cbnews	111100001001011000110010001010100011100 10 000	64.43	72.22	62.99	63.36	67.76
	001111110011100100011101001100011100100 10 001	63.72	71.52	62.28	60.66	70.97
	010111101111000000111110111110110011001 01 010	63.97	72.49	61.97	61.70	68.39
	110111001111000100110110111110111011001 01 111	64.58	71.59	62.28	61.54	68.85
	110111101111001100110110110100010011010 01 011	64.35	72.37	62.59	61.71	69.56
	010110001010011010001011010011110000001 00 001	63.56	72.67	62.22	61.69	69.72
	000111001100100000101000000110110000101 01 101	63.36	72.83	62.48	62.62	68.69
	110000110011001100001011111001010011101 11 101	63.42	72.61	62.21	61.76	70.22
	010010011001110100001001111010101011111 10 101	63.84	72.51	62.88	61.98	70.48
	110111101101101100110110110100010101010 01 111	63.68	72.82	62.61	62.45	68.91
	001111101100010001101010101110110011001 10 101	63.97	72.37	61.87	61.83	67.89
cnpaper	011001110101011001101011011011001101100 00 111	66.23	71.16	63.45	61.79	76.20
	010101110101011001001011011010101000100 00 111	66.37	71.04	63.20	62.22	75.36
	110011010011011001111110010101101000100 01 111	66.80	70.35	62.07	62.17	73.50
	110011010011011000111110001101100010110 11 111	66.41	71.30	63.70	61.76	76.90
	011111100001111110100011010011101001110 01 101	67.16	70.74	63.06	61.86	75.30
	011101110101011001101011001011001001100 10 101	66.75	71.56	63.44	61.67	76.28
	101111010011011000011011011100001100100 00 101	65.56	70.03	62.66	61.00	76.91
cnwire	1111110010111101001111111011110101111011 11110	64.22	73.20	64.40	64.18	71.94
	101101110011110101001010101111111110001 11010	64.32	73.25	64.47	63.54	73.78
	101011101001111001101101010100011001110 01101	63.84	73.34	64.38	64.67	72.23
	111011101001111001101101011101010001110 01101	63.73	73.29	64.93	65.07	73.43
	001001101101111101100010110001011110100 10101	62.95	73.67	64.53	64.57	72.56

6 Results

AMOSA based feature selection technique was executed on the six data sets to deter-mine the appropriate set of features. For each data set the experiments were carried out by optimizing the F-measure values of the five different evaluation metrics. The MOO approach provides a set of non-dominated solutions on the final Pareto optimal front. All the solutions are equally important from the algorithmic point of view. In Table 3,we show the final solutions obtained by the MOO based approach for all the data sets. The order of the features in the vector corresponds to their order in Table 1; the values of 0's and 1's represent the absence and presence of the corresponding features. These results show that for all the datasets, the proposed multi objective AMOSA- based feature selection technique performs better than the baseline approach of using all features–in fact, they achieve results comparable to the state-of-the-art on these data sets, as discussed in [13].

In order to compare the performance of our proposed approach with that of previously developed multiobjective GA based technique [18] the later is also executed on the above mentioned six data sets with the modified CoNLL-2011 scorer [14]. Thus the modified version of NSGA-II based feature selection technique also optimizes 5 objec-tive functions rather than 3 objective functions. The corresponding results are shown in Table 4. The results in Table 3 and Table 4 indicate that the AMOSA based technique achieves higher performance than NSGA-II based approach. For the gbnews data set,AMOSA achieves 2.37, 1.29, 1.68, 1.56, and, 3.05 F-measure points increments for five metrics, respectively, over the NSGA-II based technique. For the gnpaper data set,there are

Table 4. Evaluation results of the NSGA-II based approach

DataSet	Features	F_{MUC}	F_{B3}	F_{CEAFm}	F_{CEAFe}	F_{BLANG}
gbnews	00001111011011101001101111011000111010011001	74.99	74.09	69.22	71.85	72.00
	01111011000100011010100100000101001011111010	74.82	75.44	70.20	73.46	71.59
	01101110111010000111101111111100011101001100	73.29	74.58	69.12	71.87	72.10
gnpaper	10001100000110101111100110000100010011001010	71.31	70.31	64.85	67.33	75.90
	01110101010101000011010111000010101111001111	71.22	69.70	64.76	68.54	74.79
	01100101000111100011100010011100010101101100	70.90	69.87	65.25	67.76	74.66
	00001111011011101001101111011000111010011001	71.86	69.29	63.97	66.80	73.16
gnwire	00110000101100001111110111111000001110100000	70.54	73.58	68.82	69.35	77.01
	10101010101011101010011101110110111100111010	70.06	74.28	69.57	72.16	75.62
	11101001100011011010010100110111101010111001	71.28	74.47	68.85	72.35	74.91
	01111011000100011010100100000101001011111010	71.62	75.53	69.77	71.99	76.35
	11010110011111100011111000011000111011010011	72.14	73.88	68.96	71.61	74.38
	00110000101100001111110111111000001110100000	70.54	73.58	68.82	69.35	77.01
cbnews	00110101000110111010001000111110010001111011	62.21	72.05	61.20	61.27	67.60
	00001111011011101001101111011000111010011001	62.52	70.83	60.86	60.19	68.79
	11010110011111100011111000011000111011010011	62.93	69.95	60.00	59.72	67.13
	01111011000100011010100100000101001011111010	61.76	71.46	61.11	61.38	67.05
cnpaper	00110101000110111010001000111110010001111011	66.28	69.64	60.78	60.48	73.45
	01100101000111100011100010011100010101101100	64.54	69.09	61.11	61.52	72.05
	01110100010010110110110110111111110001110101	65.33	69.54	60.91	59.64	75.38
cnwire	10001100000110101111100110000100010011001010	62.38	72.62	62.90	63.98	71.42
	10110110001000111100001100101100010100101101	63.44	71.39	62.24	62.91	70.37
	10110110001000111100001100101100010100101101	62.39	72.38	62.73	63.25	72.56
	10001100000110101111100110000100010011001010	62.38	72.62	62.90	63.98	71.42
	11010110011111100011111000011000111011010011	63.44	71.3	62.24	62.91	70.37

increments of 2.48 F-measure points on first metric, 2.93 F-measure points on second metric, 3.35 F-measure points on third metric, 1.46 F-measure points on fourth metric and 3.94 F-measure point on fifth metric over the corresponding NSGA-II based technique. For the gnwire data set, improvements attained by AMOSA based approach are 2.24, 1.72, 2.62, 1.22 and 2.79 F-measure points, respectively. Similarly,for all other datasets the AMOSA based approach attains superior performance over the NSGA-II-based approach.

7 Discussion and Conclusions

In this paper we advocate a simulated annealing-based approach to optimizing a coreference resolution system according to several metrics. We show that it may not be necessary to choose one among the existing metricsin fact, developing systems attempting to optimize according to a combination of them may lead to better results. We also show that multiobjective SA based approach performs better in comparison to the multiobjective GA based approach for feature selection in anaphora resolution.

In subsequent work, we plan to expand the optimization technique to consider also learning parameters optimization, classifier selection, and learning model selection.

References

1. Bagga, A., Baldwin, B.: Algorithms for scoring coreference chains. In: LREC Workshop on Linguistic Coreference, pp. 563–566 (1998)
2. Bandyopadhyay, S., Saha, S., Maulik, U., Deb, K.: A simulated annealing based multi-objective optimization algorithm: AMOSA. IEEE Transactions on Evolutionary Computation 12(3), 269–283 (2008)
3. Bengtson, E., Roth, D.: Understanding the value of features for coreference resolution. In: EMNLP (2008)
4. Deb, K.: Multi-objective Optimization Using Evolutionary Algorithms. John Wiley and Sons, Ltd., England (2001)
5. Deb, K., Pratap, A., Agarwal, S., Meyarivan, T.: A fast and elitist multiobjective genetic algorithm: NSGA-II. IEEE Transactions on Evolutionary Computation 6(2), 181–197 (2002)
6. Doddington, G., Mitchell, A., Przybocki, M., Ramshaw, L., Strassell, S., Weischedel, R.: The automatic content extraction (ACE) program-tasks, data, and evaluation. In: LREC (2000)
7. Hoste, V.: Optimization Issues in Machine Learning of Coreference Resolution. Ph.D. thesis, Antwerp University (2005)
8. Kirkpatrick, S., Gelatt, C.D., Vecchi, M.P.: Optimization by simulated annealing. Science 220, 671–680 (1983)
9. Luo, X.: On coreference resolution performance metrics. In: NAACL / EMNLP, Van-couver (2005)
10. Metropolis, N., Rosenbluth, A.W., Rosenbloth, M.N., Teller, A.H., Teller, E.: Equation of state calculation by fast computing machines. J. Chemical Physics 21(6), 1087–1092 (1953)

11. Munson, A., Cardie, C., Caruana, R.: Optimizing to arbitrary NLP metrics using ensembleselection. In: HLT/EMNLP, pp. 539–546 (2005)
12. Ng, V., Cardie, C.: Improving machine learning approaches to coreference resolution. In: ACL, pp. 104–111 (2002)
13. Poon, H., Domingos, P.: Joint unsupervised coreference resolution with Markov logic. In: EMNLP (2008)
14. Pradhan, S., Marcus, M., Palmer, M., Ramshaw, L., Weischedel, R., Xue, N.: Conll-2011:Shared task on modeling unrestricted coreference in ontonotes, Portland, Oregon, USA, June23-24 (2011), `http://www.cnts.ua.ac.be/conll/`
15. Recasens, M., Hovy, E.: A Deeper Look into Features for Coreference Resolution. In: Lalitha Devi, S., Branco, A., Mitkov, R. (eds.) DAARC 2009. LNCS, vol. 5847, pp. 29–42. Springer, Heidelberg (2009)
16. Recasens, M., Hovy, E.: Blanc: Implementing the rand index for coreference evaluation. Natural Language Engineering (2011)
17. Recasens, M., Márquez, L., Sapena, E., Mart, M.A., Taul, M., Hoste, V., Poesio, M., Ver-rsley, Y.: Semeval-2010 task 1: Coreference resolution in multiple languages. In: SE-MEVAL 2010, Uppsala (2010)
18. Saha, S., Ekbal, A., Uryupina, O., Poesio, M.: Single and multi-objective optimization forfeature selection in anaphora resolution. In: IJCNLP (2011)
19. Soon, W.M., Ng, H.T., Lim, D.C.Y.: A machine learning approach to coreference resolution of noun phrases. Computational Linguistics 27(4), 521–544 (2001)
20. Uryupina, O.: Knowledge Acquisition for Coreference Resolution. Ph.D. thesis, University of the Saarland (2007)
21. Uryupina, O.: Corry: a system for coreference resolution. In: SemEval (2010)
22. Veldhuizen, D.V., Lamont, G.: Multiobjective evolutionary algorithms: Analyzing the state-of-the-art. Evolutionary Computations 2, 125–1473 (2000)
23. Versley, Y., Ponzetto, S.P., Poesio, M., Eidelman, V., Jern, A., Smith, J., Yang, X., Moschitti, A.: BART: a modular toolkit for coreference resolution. In: ACL/HLT, pp. 9–12 (2008)
24. Vilain, M., Burger, J., Aberdeen, J., Connolly, D., Hirschman, L.: A model-theoretic coreference scoring scheme. MUC 6, 45–52 (1995)
25. Zhao, S., Ng, H.T.: Maximum metric score training for coreference resolution. In: COLING 2010 (2010)

Can Projected Chains in Parallel Corpora Help Coreference Resolution?

José Guilherme Camargo de Souza and Constantin Orăsan

Research Group in Computational Linguistics,
University of Wolverhampton,
Wolverhampton, UK
jose.camargo.souza@gmail.com, C.Orasan@wlv.ac.uk

Abstract. The majority of current coreference resolution systems rely on annotated corpora to train classifiers for this task. However, this is possible only for languages for which annotated corpora are available. This paper presents a system that automatically extracts coreference chains from texts in Portuguese without the need for Portuguese corpora manually annotated with coreferential information. To achieve this, an English coreference resolver is run on the English part of an English-Portuguese parallel corpus. The coreference pairs identified by the resolver are projected to the Portuguese part of the corpus using automatic word alignment. These projected pairs are then used to train the coreference resolver for Portuguese. Evaluation of the system reveals that it does not outperform a head match baseline. This is due to the fact that most of the projected pairs have the same head, which is learnt by the Portuguese classifier. This suggests that a more accurate English coreference resolver is necessary. A better projection algorithm is also likely to improve the performance of the system.

Keywords: coreference resolution, parallel corpus, machine learning.

1 Introduction

Coreference resolution is "the problem of identifying which noun phrases (NPs) or mentions refer to the same real-world entity in a text or dialogue" [16]. This is a very important task for many NLP fields including information extraction, question answering, automatic summarisation and machine translation. The task has been extensively researched for English (see [17] for an overview), but has received less attention for other languages. This is largely due to the fact that most methods require corpora annotated with coreferential information which are not available for many languages.

This paper presents a system that automatically extracts coreference chains from texts in Portuguese without the need for Portuguese corpora manually annotated with coreferential information. In order to achieve this, a method is developed for automatically producing training data for a supervised machine learning coreference resolver for Portuguese. This is done by using an English-Portuguese parallel corpus in which the coreference chains annotated in the

I. Hendrickx et al. (Eds.): DAARC 2011, LNAI 7099, pp. 59–69, 2011.

English part are projected to the Portuguese part in a similar way to that proposed by [21] for projecting coreference chains from English to Romanian. In contrast to the method developed by [21], the goal of our method is not to create an annotated resource, but to implement a fully functional coreference resolver for Portuguese. It should be pointed out that there is nothing in the overall idea that makes it specific to the English-Portuguese language pair. The method can be applied to other language pairs as long as there is a parallel corpus available and the components that deal with Portuguese are replaced with the corresponding components for the target language.

The remainder of this paper presents and evaluates the system and is structured as follows: A brief overview of related research is presented in Section 2, followed by Section 3 which describes the approach proposed in this work. Evaluation results are presented and discussed in Section 4. The paper finishes with conclusions in Section 5.

2 Related Work

As in many other NLP fields, two main approaches are used in coreference resolution: knowledge engineering methods and machine learning methods. The knowledge engineering methods generally require humans to manually create rules which determine whether two noun phrases are coreferential or not. These methods usually exploit regularities of the documents they process and are designed for specific applications [12]. Given the difficulty of creating rules manually, the vast majority of existing systems use machine learning approaches for this task [17]. The most common model used for this is the *mention-pair* model where the system is first trained to classify whether pairs of noun phrases are coreferential or not [1,14]. In the second step, a clustering algorithm is used to group entities into coreferential chains. For the classification stage, but sometimes also for the clustering stage, positive and negative instances are extracted from an annotated corpus and used to train the machine learning algorithm. Even for the other models used in coreference resolution, an annotated corpus is necessary. In light of this, it becomes obvious that the lack of availability of annotated data is the main bottleneck in the development of machine-learning based coreference resolution systems.

Some languages have enough annotated data to allow training of machine learning methods. For example for English, the MUC[1] and ACE[2] corpora have been successfully used by many researchers. In recent years, corpora annotated with coreference containing Spanish and Catalan [23], and Dutch [11] texts were also released, in this way facilitating the development of coreference resolution systems for these languages. Unfortunately, for many other languages such corpora are either not available or are rather small to allow training of robust methods.

[1] `http://www.itl.nist.gov/iaui/894.02/related_projects/muc/muc_data/muc_data_index.html`

[2] `http://projects.ldc.upenn.edu/ace/data/`

One such language is Portuguese, for which, to the best of our knowledge, the only available corpus annotated with coreferential data is the Summ-It corpus [7] and the only study that uses it to develop a supervised machine learning approach for coreference resolution is [25]. The small size of the corpus imposes some limits on the kind of machine learning that can be used. So far, most of the work for Portuguese has focused on certain types of pronominal anaphora ([20], [5] and [9]) or problems related to coreference and anaphora resolution such as anaphoricity classification [8]. This was the main motivation for developing the proposed method.

As mentioned before, our research was inspired by [21] but it goes several steps further. The goal of the work presented there is to provide a bootstrapping method for creating coreferentially annotated data. For this reason, several manual operations are envisaged in the process. The starting point is an English-Romanian parallel corpus in which the English texts were manually annotated with coreference information. In contrast, we assume no annotation available for English and use an English coreference resolver to obtain coreference pairs. The annotation is transferred to Romanian using an automatic aligner, but it is not used to train a system. Instead it is foreseen that it is given to human annotators for post-editing. In this paper, we intend to use the transferred information to train a coreference resolver for Portuguese.

Several researchers have used parallel corpora and projection of information across languages before. [29] project part-of-speech tags onto English-French and English-Chinese corpora; [15] improve the performance of anaphora resolvers for English and French using an English-French parallel corpus; [2] project word senses onto an English-Italian parallel corpus; and [19] use projection to reduce the effort on annotation of semantic roles and presents evaluation on an English-German parallel corpus for both automatically and manually annotated English data.

3 Methodology

The aim of our research is to extract coreference chains automatically from Portuguese texts without the need for an annotated corpus for Portuguese. To achieve this, the system presented in Figure 1 is used.

The system is composed of several components that can be roughly grouped into three main modules: automatic corpus annotation (English coreference resolution and Portuguese parsing and noun phrase extraction), alignment (word alignment of the parallel corpus), and coreference resolution for Portuguese (instance and feature generation, and coreference resolution). This section gives a brief overview of the system. More details about the architecture used can be found in [10]. The section finishes with some observations about adapting the system to other language pairs.

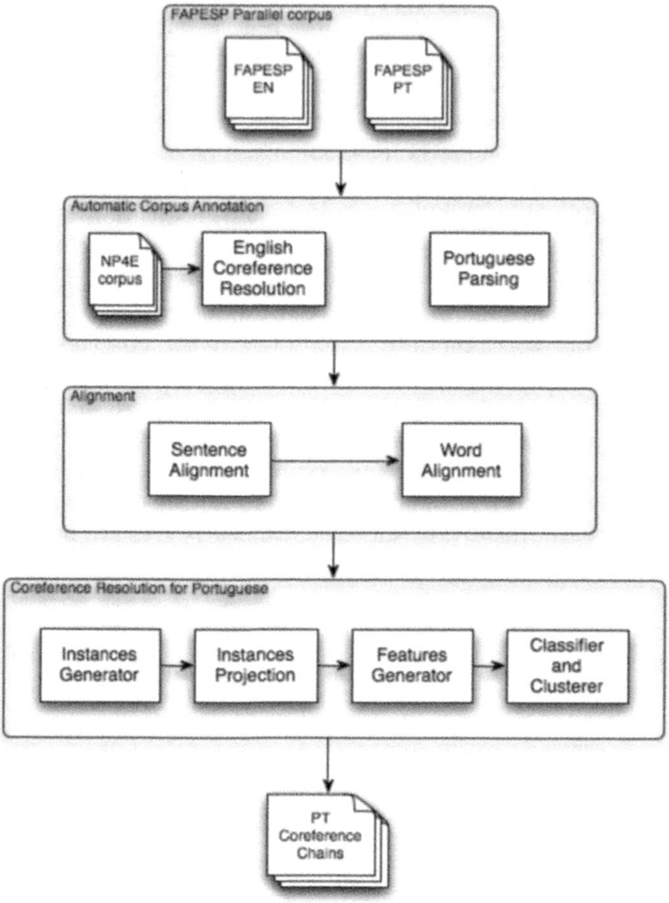

Fig. 1. The overview of the system's architecture

3.1 Automatic Corpus Annotation

The first module automatically annotates the corpus with linguistic information required at later stages of processing. Reconcile [26] is used to annotate the coreferential links in the English side of the corpus. Reconcile is an off-the-shelf coreference resolution system for English that uses machine learning and was trained on a collection of texts from the Reuters corpus. The system was run as it is and no attempts were made to tune it for our texts. As a result of using the coreference resolver, the noun phrases in the English texts are also annotated.

The Portuguese side of the corpus is annotated with morpho-syntactic information using the PALAVRAS parser [3]. This information includes boundaries of NPs and features such as the head of the NP, number and gender information, and the type of NP, which are used when the Portuguese coreference chains are identified.

3.2 Alignment

The noun phrases identified by the previous module are used by the GIZA++ word aligner [18] to establish mappings between the noun phrases in the two sides of the corpus. This step is necessary because most parallel corpora do not have a word-by-word alignment. Because the word aligner requires that the corpus is aligned at sentence level, we run the TCAlign sentence aligner [4] first.

3.3 Coreference Resolution for Portuguese

The last module of the system is responsible for performing the actual coreference resolution. This process consists of the following three steps: instance generation and projection, feature generation and classification and clustering.

Instance Generation and Projection: The idea of the method is to project the coreferential links from English to Portuguese and use them to train a coreference resolver for Portuguese. Given the errors introduced by the NP extractors and by the word-to-word aligner, it is not possible to directly map English NPs to Portuguese NPs. Instead, for each English anaphor and antecedent pair, the algorithm checks whether their heads have a corresponding word in Portuguese. If so, the pair is projected to Portuguese and used as a positive pair to train the Portuguese coreference resolver. For generating negative pairs (non-anaphoric pairs), the anaphoric expression projected from English is paired with all the Portuguese noun phrases which occur between the projected positive pair. This is the standard in coreference resolution [24], but it generates training data which contain a much larger proportion of negative instances.

Feature Generation: After the pairs are produced for Portuguese, a set of features is extracted for each of the pairs to be used by the learning algorithm. The features were inspired by previous work on English and Portuguese coreference resolution [24,25,22] and contain a mixture of surface-based features (e.g. head match and substring match), semantic information (e.g. number and gender agreement, and type of entity associated by PALAVRAS) and syntactic information (e.g. whether the antecedent or anaphor are the subject of the sentence). A more detailed description of the 11 features used in our research can be found in [10].

Classification and Clustering: The features extracted in the previous step are used to produce training instances for a machine learning algorithm. After experimenting with several algorithms, we decided to use JRip, WEKA's implementation of decision rules. Using the induced rules, each instance is classified as coreferential or non-coreferential. The classified pairs are clustered together using the Closest-First clustering algorithm, in this way producing the coreferential chains.

3.4 Adaptation to Other Languages

The system described in this section was developed for the English-Portuguese language pair, but it can be easily adapted for other languages as long as they have a parallel corpus and the necessary annotation tools. Given the availability of English coreference resolvers, the assumption is that the coreference links will be projected from English, but even this can be changed if a coreference resolver for the source language is available.

In order to develop a coreference resolver for a language other than Portuguese, it is necessary to have an NP extractor for that language, which also provides information about the heads of NPs. If necessary this can be replaced by an NP chunker and a set of heuristics which can approximate the head of the NP. The word alignment algorithm used here can be applied to any language pairs as long as there is a language model for that language pair. The pair projection method proposed here can also be used without modifications, but depending on the language pair and the accuracy of the NP identifiers used, improvements can be brought to the algorithm. The classifier used for Portuguese to decide whether a pair is coreferential or not can be used for other languages as well, but the set of features may need to be changed depending on the characteristics of the language.

4 Evaluation

The system described in the previous section does not depend on a particular parallel corpus. In this section, we explain first how we instantiated the system using the FAPESP parallel corpus. The performance of this instance of the system was evaluated using the Summ-It corpus. The section finishes with an error analysis.

4.1 Instantiation of the System

As explained earlier, the parallel corpus is central to the method developed here. In order to check the performance of the developed system, we used the English-Portuguese parallel corpus extracted from the electronic version of the *Revista Pesquisa FAPESP* Brazilian magazine[3]. The corpus contains 646 texts about domestic and international scientific policy, and about research carried out in Brazil and other countries. The English side contains around 464,000 words, and there are approximately 433,000 words in the Portuguese side.

For the FAPESP corpus, Reconcile generated 94,990 coreference chains in the English part. 82,272 of these chains are singleton (i.e. chains formed by only one expression) which is approximately 86% of the expressions identified in the text. The remaining 14% are chains formed by two or more expressions.

Using the chains extracted by Reconcile, the system generated 21,849 positive pairs (approximately 4.8%) and 436,033 negative pairs (approximately 95.2%)

[3] `http://revistapesquisa.fapesp.br/`

out of 457,882 pairs. The English pairs are projected using the projection algorithm described in section 3. The algorithm successfully projected 3,569 positive pairs (7.6%) and 43,174 negative pairs (92.4%).

The increase in the proportion of positive pairs is explained by the way the pairs are projected. The projection algorithm uses the heads of noun phrases and the sentences where the noun phrases occur. If any of this information is not available (due to problems in syntactic annotation or in the alignment) or if the process of finding the expressions in the aligned corpus fails, the algorithm ignores the instance.

These projected pairs are used to train a supervised machine learning model that is used further on as a classifier in the clustering algorithm. The algorithm used to train the model is the WEKA toolkit [28] implementation of the decision rules [6] algorithm (JRip).

4.2 Evaluation of the System

The system was evaluated on the Summ-It corpus [7], a coreferentially annotated corpus that contains around 17,000 words and 700 coreferential expressions distributed in 50 newswire texts. This corpus was used because it was not employed in the development of the system. The performance of the coreference resolver is scored using the MUC [27] and CEAF [13] measures.

In order to have a better understanding of the performance of the system, a baseline was developed as well. The baseline classifies two expressions as coreferential if they have the same head. The coreferential chains are built using the same Closest-First clustering algorithm used by our system.

The baseline and our system obtained the same scores on the Summ-it corpus: 7.12% MUC f-measure and 14.37% CEAF f-measure. One of the reasons why the MUC score has a lower f-measure is because it penalises missed links and several chains extracted present only part of the expressions they should contain. The next section contains an error analysis which tries to explain the results.

4.3 Error Analysis

Our system relies on several components which address difficult language processing problems and which, even though they represent the state-of-the-art in the field, are still not highly accurate. As a result, each of these components introduces errors which propagate throughout the system, contributing to its low performance. This section focuses on the coreference resolution components in an attempt to understand the low accuracy of the proposed system.

Error Analysis of Output of Reconcile: The authors of Reconcile reported MUC f-measure scores of 68.50% for the MUC-6 corpus and 62.80% for the MUC-7 corpus. In order to assess the accuracy of Reconcile on our data, five texts from the FAPESP corpus with approximately 3,600 words and 846 markables in the English side were annotated with coreferential information. Taking the manual

(sys) ⟨ *the old light microscope, the electron microscope, the electron microscope in Germany, the electron microscope* ⟩

(ref_a) ⟨ *the electron microscope, The electron microscope, The electron microscope, an electron microscope, the electron microscope, an electron microscope, this instrument* ⟩

(ref_b) ⟨ *the light microscope, The light microscope* ⟩

Fig. 2. Chain extracted by Reconcile and its corresponding manual annotation

annotation as reference, Reconcile's output obtained a MUC f-measure of 76.8%. Given the small size of the corpus, we cannot argue that Reconcile's performance on our texts is significantly better than the one obtained on the MUC dataset. However, we believe that it indicates that its performance on our texts is at least in line with that reported by the authors of Reconcile.

Comparing the system annotation and the manual annotation, it is possible to confirm the intuition that many entities in the chains, albeit sharing the same head, belong to different chains. One example of such an error is presented in figure 2. The chain sys is the output produced by Reconcile. The chains ref_a and ref_b are two different chains identified by our annotator. The former is about an electron microscope and the latter is about a light microscope. In the sys chain Reconcile mixed elements from the two chains ref_a and ref_b into one long chain.

The same phenomenon was observed in other chains extracted by the system in this set of 5 texts. It is possible to conclude that longer chains contain more expressions that do not belong to them, generating undesired noise that is projected to the Portuguese side of the corpus.

Given Reconcile's bias towards using head match for classifying entities as coreferential, we analysed all the non-singleton chains identified in the FAPESP corpus. Comparison of all the expressions in the chain in a pairwise fashion revealed that about 53% of the pairs share the same head. Among this 53%, there are a fair number of errors where entities share the same head, but do not refer to the same entity as in the examples above.

Evaluation of the Learnt Rules: The JRip algorithm was run with 10-fold cross-validation and default parameters. The automatically induced classifier correctly classified 45,944 out of 46,743 instance pairs projected (approximately 98%). However, most of the instances fall under only one rule that uses a feature that verifies if the heads of both expressions match. Analysis of the 3,569 coreferent pairs showed that 2,978 (approximately 83%) of them have the same head. This leaves only 591 pairs (17%) that are positive but that do not have the same head. The small amount of positive and non-head matching pairs is not informative enough to help the JRip algorithm employ features other than the head match feature.

Figure 3 shows the only 2 rules induced by the system. The first rule classifies two noun phrases as coreferential if they have the same head and it is applied in the majority of cases. The second rule is applied only in five instances, which explains why our method and the baseline obtain the same results.

```
if (head_match = 1) => class=C
if (number_agrmt = 1) and (ant_appos = 1) and
   (sem_class_agrmt = 1) and (word_overlap = point5) and
   (ana_appos = 0) => class=C
else => class=NC
```

Fig. 3. The rules generated by the JRip algorithm

5 Conclusions and Future Work

This paper presented a system which extracts coreference chains from Portuguese texts without having to resort to Portuguese corpora manually annotated with coreferential information. The system implements a method that automatically obtains data for training a supervised machine learning coreference resolver for Portuguese.

The training data is generated by using an English-Portuguese parallel corpus from which the coreference chains annotated in the English part of the corpus are projected to the Portuguese part of the corpus. The coreference chain extraction system for Portuguese was tested in a corpus annotated with coreference chains in Portuguese. The results of the system on this corpus are comparable to the baseline.

The results of the system described here are strongly influenced by the coreference links identified in the English part of the corpus as the errors generated there are propagated throughout the pipeline. Therefore, the use of a better performing English coreference resolution system might improve the overall performance of the Portuguese resolver. A way to filter out errors introduced by the English coreference resolver is to use gender information from the Portuguese part to identify and remove these errors in a similar manner to what [15] did for pronoun resolution.

The projection algorithm used to transfer pairs has a strong influence on the accuracy of the Portuguese coreference resolver. Different methods for performing the projection might be implemented and tested. As future work, an evaluation of the projected pairs should be carried out in order to evaluate the strong points and the pitfalls of the algorithm employed.

An alternative route for developing the system is not to use a parallel corpus, but instead to automatically translate documents to the target language. This approach could prove useful for languages where there is not enough parallel data, but is likely to introduce additional problems due to the errors introduced by the machine translation step.

Acknowledgements. This work was partially supported by the European Commission, Education & Training, Erasmus Mundus: EMMC 2008-0083, Erasmus Mundus Masters in NLP & HLT programme. The authors would like to thank Sheila Castilho Monteiro de Sousa for her help in the annotation process.

References

1. Aone, C., Bennett, S.W.: Evaluating automated and manual acquisition of anaphora resolution strategies. In: The 33rd Annual Meeting on Association for Computational Linguistics, pp. 122–129 (1995)
2. Bentivogli, L., Pianta, E.: Exploiting parallel texts in the creation of multilingual semantically annotated resources: the MultiSemCor Corpus. Natural Language Engineering 11(03), 247 (2005), `http://www.journals.cambridge.org/abstract_S1351324905003839`
3. Bick, E.: The parsing system PALAVRAS: automatic grammatical analysis of Portuguese in a constraint grammar framework. Phd, Arhus (2000)
4. Caseli, H.D.M.: Alinhamento sentencial de textos paralelos português-inglês. Master thesis, USP (2002), `http://www2.dc.ufscar.br/~helenacaseli/pdf/2002/QualiMestrado.pdf`
5. Chaves, A., Rino, L.: The Mitkov Algorithm for Anaphora Resolution in Portuguese. In: The 8th International Conference on Computational Processing of the Portuguese Language, p. 60 (2008)
6. Cohen, W.: Fast effective rule induction. In: 12th International Workshop Conference on Machine Learning, pp. 115–123. Morgan Kaufmann Publishers, Inc. (1995)
7. Collovini, S., Carbonel, T.I., Fuchs, J.T., Vieira, R.: Summ-it: Um corpus anotado com informacoes discursivas visando à sumarizacao automática. In: TIL - V Workshop em Tecnologia da Informação e da Linguagem Humana, Rio de Janeiro, pp. 1605–1614 (2007)
8. Collovini, S., Vieira, R.: Learning Discourse-new References in Portuguese Texts. In: TIL 2006, pp. 267–276 (2006)
9. Cuevas, R., Paraboni, I.: A Machine Learning Approach to Portuguese Pronoun Resolution. In: The 11th Ibero-American Conference on AI: Advances in Artificial Intelligence, pp. 262–271 (2008)
10. de Souza, J., Orăsan, C.: Coreference resolution for Portuguese using parallel corpora word alignment. In: The International Conference on Knowledge Engineering, Principles and Techniques (KEPT 2011), Cluj-Napoca, Romania (July 2011)
11. Hoste, V., Pauw, G.D.: KNACK-2002: a Richly Annotated Corpus of Dutch Written Text. In: The Fifth International Conference on Language Resources and Evaluation, pp. 1432–1437. ELRA (2006)
12. Konstantinova, N., Orăsan, C.: Issues in topic tracking in wikipedia articles. In: The International Conference on Knowledge Engineering, Principles and Techniques (KEPT 2011), Cluj-Napoca, Romania, July 4-6 (2011)
13. Luo, X.: On coreference resolution performance metrics. In: The Conference on Human Language Technology and Empirical Methods in Natural Language Processing, pp. 25–32 (2005)
14. McCarthy, J.F., Lehnert, W.G.: Using Decision Trees for Coreference Resolution. In: International Joint Conference on Artificial Intelligence, pp. 1050–1055 (1995)

15. Mitkov, R., Barbu, C.: Using bilingual corpora to improve pronoun resolution. Languages in contrast 4(2), 201–212 (2004)
16. Ng, V.: Graph-Cut-Based Anaphoricity Determination for Coreference Resolution. In: NAACL 2009: Human Language Technologies: The 2009 Annual Conference of the North American Chapter of the Association for Computational Linguistics, pp. 575–583. Association for Computational Linguistics, Boulder (2009)
17. Ng, V.: Supervised Noun Phrase Coreference Research: The First Fifteen Years. In: ACL 2010, pp. 1396–1411 (July 2010)
18. Och, F.J., Ney, H.: A Systematic Comparison of Various Statistical Alignment Models. Computational Linguistics 29(1), 19–51 (2003)
19. Padó, S., Lapata, M.: Cross-lingual annotation projection of semantic roles. J. Artificial Intelligence Research. 36, 307–340 (2009)
20. Paraboni, I., Lima, V.L.S.D.: Possessive Pronominal Anaphor Resolution in Portuguese Written Texts - Project Notes. In: 17th International Conference on Computational Linguistics (COLING 1998), pp. 1010–1014. Morgan Kaufmann Publishers, Montreal (1998)
21. Postolache, O., Cristea, D., Orăsan, C.: Transferring Coreference Chains through Word Alignment. In: The 5th International Conference on Language Resources and Evaluation, Genoa, Italy (2006)
22. Recasens, M., Hovy, E.: A deeper look into features for coreference resolution. Anaphora Processing and Applications (i), 29–42 (2009)
23. Recasens, M., Martí, M.A.: AnCora-CO: Coreferentially annotated corpora for Spanish and Catalan. Language Resources and Evaluation 44(4), 341–345 (2009)
24. Soon, W.M., Ng, H.T., Lim, D.C.Y.: A Machine Learning Approach to Coreference Resolution of Noun Phrases. Computational Linguistics 27(4), 521–544 (2001)
25. de Souza, J.G.C., Gonçalves, P.N., Vieira, R.: Learning Coreference Resolution for Portuguese Texts. In: Teixeira, A., de Lima, V.L.S., de Oliveira, L.C., Quaresma, P. (eds.) PROPOR 2008. LNCS (LNAI), vol. 5190, pp. 153–162. Springer, Heidelberg (2008)
26. Stoyanov, V., Cardie, C., Gilbert, N., Buttler, D.: Coreference Resolution with Reconcile. In: The Joint Conference of the 48th Annual Meeting of the Association for Computational Linguistics (ACL 2010). Association for Computational Linguistics (2010)
27. Vilain, M., Burger, J., Aberdeen, J., Connolly, D.: A model-theoretic coreference scoring scheme. In: The 6th Conference on Message Understanding, pp. 45–52 (1995)
28. Witten, I.H., Frank, E.: Data Mining: Practical Machine Learning Tools and Techniques, 2nd edn. The Morgan Kaufmann Series in Data Management Systems. Morgan Kaufmann (2005)
29. Yarowsky, D., Ngai, G.: Inducing multilingual POS taggers and NP bracketers via robust projection across aligned corpora. In: Second Meeting of the North American Chapter of the Association for Computational Linguistics on Language Technologies 2001, pp. 1–8. Association for Computational Linguistics, Pittsburgh (2001)

Abstract Anaphors in Appositive Relative Clauses in Romanian*

Emil Ionescu

Faculty of Letters, University of Bucharest, Romania
emilionescu@unibuc.ro

Abstract. The paper represents a contribution to the study of anaphora linked to linguistic structures denoting events, facts or propositions. These anaphors are called abstract anaphors. Abstract anaphors are studied in sentential structures with appositive relative clauses in Romanian. Three abstract anaphors may occur in such sentences: *care* ('which'), *unde* ('where') and *ceea ce* ('which'). It is shown that *care* ('which') is used to denote events and facts (but not propositions); *unde* ('where') may only be used to denote facts, whereas *ceea ce* ('which') denotes facts propositions and outcomes but not events. The analysis therefore documents the existence of finer-grained realizations of abstract anaphora in natural language. At the same time, the analysis enriches the inventory of lexical items which count as a diagnostic for phrases that denote events, facts or intensional objects.

Keywords: anaphor, event, fact, proposition, Romanian.

1 Introduction

Abstract anaphors examined in this paper establish the link between a variety of appositive relative clause - ARC (a subordinate clause) and a clausal antecedent (the main clause), like in the sentence *John died, which surprised me.* A sample of abstract anaphor in ARCs in Romanian is given below. The anaphor is *ceea ce* ('which'). The main clause (in brackets) is its antecedent:

(1) [Ion a demisionat]$_i$, *ceea ce*$_i$ m-a surprins
[John has resigned]$_i$, which$_i$ has surprised me
'John resigned, which surprised me'[1]

* I am deeply grateful to Ana-Maria Barbu and Gianina Iordăchioaia, who made substantive and valuable suggestions and comments on previous versions of this paper. My gratitude also goes to the three anonymous reviewers of the DAAR Colloquium in Faro, Portugal. Finally, I am indebted to Bogdan Ştefănescu for his assistance in improving the English of the paper. I take exclusive credit for any possible errors in this article.

[1] The first line of translation of the Romanian examples supplies relevant information about anaphoric relations. The second line of translation gives the meaning of the sentence.

I. Hendrickx et al. (Eds.): DAARC 2011, LNAI 7099, pp. 70–81, 2011.

The anaphors discussed in this paper are abstract in that their clausal antecedent may refer to abstract objects, such as events, facts or intensional entities.

Abstract anaphors are a relatively new concern in semantics. Vendler [10] had the intuition of their existence, and Asher [1] mentioned them. Nevertheless, a systematic approach is more recent, and it is due to Delfitto [6][2] and especially Amsili a. o.[3].

In these latter works, abstract anaphors are discourse anaphors: they establish a connection between two independent sentences. Instead, abstract anaphors discussed in this paper are closer to sentence anaphors, because they connect two clauses in a complex sentential structure.

Anaphoric links of this type in Romanian only have been started being addressed from a formal and computational perspective in the past decade (see, for instance, [9,7]). Nevertheless, the study of abstract anaphors in Romanian is just starting.

The main reason in choosing Romanian for the study of ARCs is the diversity in the realization of abstract anaphora: one such anaphor (*care* - 'which') denotes events and facts (but not intensional objects); another one (*unde* - 'where') may only be used to denote facts, whereas the third one (*ceea ce* - 'which') denotes facts and intensional objects but not events. These anaphors thus contrast with the "jolly-joker (discourse) anaphors" *ce, ça, c'* ('that') or *le* ('it') in French, *that* and *it* in English, or *asta* ('that') in Romanian, which may take any abstract object as a value. The present analysis therefore documents the existence of finer-grained (and more constrained) realizations of abstract anaphora in natural language. At the same time, the analysis enriches the inventory of lexical items which count as a diagnostic for phrases that denote events, facts or intensional objects. It thus appears that the cohesion of the constructions under scrutiny here is essentially due to the anaphoric link which is to be presented below.

The approach in this paper constantly resorts to the well-known hierarchy of the degree of abstraction of objects (the world immanence scale), proposed in [1]. Methodologically, the analysis relies on the principle of the identity between the semantic type of the anaphora and the semantic type of the antecedent. To show how this principle works, in the majority of cases under scrutiny here I use the Vendlerian procedure of the paraphrase. This procedure exploits diagnostic nominals for abstract entities, such as *evenimentul* ('the event') for events, *faptul* ('the fact') for facts or *ideea* ('the idea') for propositions.

2 The Data and Some Terminological Specifications

Before passing to the presentation of the data, some terminological specification is needed. This paper deals with anaphors, which, from a logical point of view, acquire their referential force from antecedent expressions, whose functioning is similar to that of constants in logical languages. In other words, the antecedent - a clause - is not a quantifier but an (abstract) definite description, which supplies its reference to the anaphor.

[2] The term abstract anaphor, though, is not used in [3].

As already mentioned, three abstract anaphors may occur in ARCs in Romanian: *care* ('which'), *unde* ('where') and *ceea ce* ('which'). The first two obligatorily appear as complements of the prepositions: *care* is the complement of prepositions *după* ('after'), *la* ('at', 'to', 'relative to') or *drept pentru* ('for'); *unde* is the complement of *de* ('from'). It is only *ceea ce* that is not selected by prepositions; in ARCs, *ceea ce* is either the subject or the (direct) object of the head verb.

Each of these lexical items is able to denote something, due to the preceding adjacent clause. ARCs with *care*:

(2) (a) [Ion a bătut la uşă]$_i$ după care$_i$ a intrat
[John knocked at the door]$_i$ after which$_i$ he came in
'John knocked at the door and then he came in'

(b) [Am intervenit mustrându-l]$_i$ la care$_i$ m-a privit mirat
[I stepped in scolding him]$_i$, at which$_i$ he stared at me in surprise
'I stepped in scolding him, which made him stare at me in surprise'

(c) [Ion a murit]$_i$ drept pentru care$_i$ copiii i-au moştenit averea
[John died]$_i$, fact for which$_i$ his children inherited his fortune
'John died, and consequently his children inherited his fortune'

ARCs with *unde*:

(3) [Pe masă erau cărţi deschise]$_i$ de unde$_i$ se părea că studia
[There were open books on his desk]$_i$, from where$_i$ it seemed to show that he was studying
'There were open books on his desk, which seemed to show that he was studying'

ARCs with *ceea ce*:

(4) [Mexic a bătut Franţa]$_i$ ceea ce$_i$ a fost o surpriză
[Mexico has beated France]$_i$, which$_i$ was a surprise
'Mexico beat France, which was a surprise'

None of these anaphors is exclusively abstract; *care*, for instance, also occurs in restrictive relative clauses, where its antecedent is a NP; *unde* in turn, also occurs in restrictive relative clauses, with an antecedent NP which denotes a place. Finally, *ceea ce* may occur in restrictive relatives (where its antecedent is the quantifier *tot* - 'all') and also in free relatives. Each anaphor discussed here, then, is dual in its most general nature, in that each may be both nominal and clausal.

3 Events and Event Anaphora

According to Asher [1], on the scale of the world immanence (which is a scale of the degrees of abstraction of the objects), events are close to material objects. This means that they are rather concrete. Events may be located in space and time, they may be perceived (eye witnesses are witnesses of events), and also they may be evaluated with respect to observable parameters, such as speed (an event may occur slowly or quickly), or duration.

Events are denoted in Romanian by nominals and clauses. Event-denoting nominals may be the subject argument of diagnostic predicates ('containers'), according to Vendler [10]: *a avea loc* ('to take place'), *a se întâmpla* ('to occur') etc.

Unlike nominals, clauses do not have distinctive features when they denote events. Necessary (but not sufficient) conditions for a clause to denote an event are the polarity form and the action content of its head verb: if the head verb has positive polarity and denotes an action, the clause might denote an event or a fact[3]; if the clause is the subject or the complement of an event container, the clause does denote an event. In ARCs, the pronoun *care* occurs as an event anaphora, if it is the complement of the prepositions *după* ('after') or *la* ('at', 'to', 'towards').

3.1 ARCs of Type *după care* ('after which')

In ARCs, *după* only has temporal meaning. A sentence with ARC containing *după* may be paraphrased by a sentence in which *după* takes a nominal description of an event as its complement. This nominal description comprises the main clause of the paraphrased sentence, as the adjunct of the head noun. Thus, for sentence (5), the paraphrase is (6), below. It may be seen that if in (6) the nominal description of an event is replaced with the nominal description of a fact or proposition, the paraphrase is ill-formed[4]:

(5) [Ion şi-a luat haina din şifonier]$_i$, după care$_i$ a plecat
[John took his coat from the wardrobe]$_i$ after which$_i$ (he) left
'John took his coat from the wardrobe and then he left'

(6) După [evenimentul/*faptul/*ideea [că Ion şi-a luat haina din şifonier]], (a avut loc evenimentul/*faptul/*ideea că) Ion a plecat

'After [the event/*the fact/*the idea [that John took his coat from the wardrobe]] (it took place the event/*the fact/*the idea that) John left'

Intuitively, in (5) the main clause is the antecedent of *care*. This correct intuition, though, has to be proven and it is the paraphrase (6) which supplies the proof. In (6), the main clause from (5) (i. e. *Ion şi-a luat haina din şifonier* - 'John took his coat from the wardrobe') occurs as an embedded clause: *că Ion şi-a luat haina din şifonier* ('that John took his coat from the wardrobe'). This embedded clause in (6) is the adjunct of the distinctive nominal *evenimentul* ('the event') which heads the phrase *evenimentul că Ion şi-a luat haina din şifonier* ('the event that

3 Technically, the requirement of positive polarity means that events are not closed under negation (see [7]).

4 One of the anonymous reviewers of the abstract of this paper notices that (6) is not an exact paraphrase of (5), because in the paraphrased sentence (5) *John's taking the coat* is more salient than *John's leaving*, while in (6) it is the other way round. This is utterly true but it has to be stressed that the purpose of the paraphrases is to reveal the semantic type of the denotatum antecedent (which in most cases remains implicit). From this point of view, the paraphrases do their job well.

John took his coat from the wardrobe'). The fact that the combination between the noun *evenimentul* and the clause *că Ion şi-a luat haina din şifonier* is correct proves that the whole resulting phrase denotes an event. Furthermore, the phrase headed by *evenimentul* is the complement of the preposition *după* ('after'). This shows that the preposition *după* in (6) is an event container (but not a fact, or a proposition container). Since *după* in (6) is identical with *după* in (5), it follows that in (5), the anaphoric complement *care* ('which') of *după* has to denote an event, too. Under the general assumption that anaphoric links hold under the identity of the semantic type of both the anaphor and its antecedent, one may conclude that the main sentence in (5) (i.e. *Ion şi-a luat haina din şifonier* - 'John took his coat from the wardrobe') denotes an event, too.

Additional evidence that both *care* and the main clause denote an event comes from ARCs with negative main clauses. In this case, the anaphoric link does not hold any more:

(7) *[Ion nu şi-a luat haina din şifonier]$_i$ după care$_i$ a plecat
*[John did not take his coat from the wardrobe]$_i$ after which$_i$ (he) left

Here the pronoun *care* denotes an event (because of its head *după*). However, the main clause fails to be the antecedent of *care*. This is because the main clause is negated, and negated clauses cannot denote events.

3.2 ARCs of Type *la care* ('to which')

The meaning expressed by *la* in ARCs is relational. For instance, in a sentence like (8):

(8) [I-am cerut să mă ajute]$_i$, la care$_i$ el m-a refuzat
[I asked him to help me]$_i$, to which$_i$ he refused me
'I asked him to help me, but he refused me'

la has to be interpreted as follows: *regarding my asking to be helped by him*$_i$, *he*$_i$ *refused me*. The paraphrase test does not help to draw the conclusion that both *care* and its antecedent (the main clause) denote an event. This is because the paraphrase of the sentence (8) is itself very bizarre:

(9) *La evenimentul cererii mele de a mă ajuta a avut loc evenimentul refuzului său
*With respect to my asking to be helped by him$_i$ the event of his$_i$ refusal took place

Nevertheless it is still possible to show that the relational meaning of *la* requires *care* to denote the same semantic type as the main clause does, namely an event. If instead of the main clause in positive polarity *I-am cerut să mă ajute* ('I asked him to help me') one uses in (8) its negated counterpart *Nu i-am cerut să mă ajute* ('I did not ask him to help me'), the result is bad; the whole sentence becomes semantically abnormal:

(10) *[Nu i-am cerut să mă ajute]$_i$, la care$_i$ el m-a refuzat
*[I did not ask him to help me]$_i$, to which$_i$ he refused me
'*I did not ask him to help me, but he refused me'

Also, if instead of a verb of action one uses a verb of state in the main clause, the result is at least weird:

(11) ?? [Am fost bolnav]$_i$, la care$_i$ el nu a avut nicio reacţie
?? [I was sick]$_i$ to which$_i$ he had no reaction
'?? I was sick but he had no reaction to that'

In both cases above, the main clause does not denote an event (but a fact or a proposition) and for this reason it cannot serve as an antecedent for *care*. This explains the ill-formedness of the sentences (10)-(11) and leads to the conclusion that well-formed sentences with ARCs of type *la care* owe their well-formedness to the identity of the semantic type of both *care* and the main clause. As the tests of the negated clause and the verbs of state indicate, probably, this semantic type cannot be but an event.

4 Facts and Anaphors of Facts

ARCs with anaphors that denote facts contain the anaphors *care* (as a complement of the compound preposition *drept pentru*), and *unde* (as complement of the preposition *de*). As in the preceding section, I will begin with some basic specifications about facts and their linguistic expression.

Facts occupy an intermediary position on the scale of the world immanence. They are in between events and propositions. Unlike events and similarly to propositions, facts cannot be localized in space or time [10]. For this reason, facts cannot be perceived (one cannot see or hear a fact), nor can they be measured in time. So, they are not sudden, and, also, they do not last.

On the other hand, unlike propositions and close to events, facts have causal force [2]. They are able to cause the emergence of a physical or mental event. A fact therefore may be at the origin of a physical event (the global warming, as a fact, presumably determines the melting of the ice in the polar areas of the earth) and it may yield emotional reactions (the same global warming concerns a lot of people).

As in the case of events, the linguistic expression of facts is also ensured by both nominals and clauses. In Romanian a hallmark of the nominal expression of facts is the noun *faptul* ('the fact'). This noun may have a (clausal or nominal) adjunct, which indicates the content of the fact: *faptul încălzirii globale* ('the fact of the global warming'), *faptul că pământul se încălzeşte* ('the fact that the earth is warming up').

Clauses that denote facts may be main clauses or embedded clauses with the complementizer *că* ('that'). The clausal expression of facts is not constrained. This means that a clause which denotes a fact may be in negative polarity or may express a state.

Clauses in negative polarity, which denote facts show that facts are closed under negation. As for the possibility of a fact to make reference to a state, this simply shows that a state may be presented like a fact (but not like an event). Indeed, one may say *faptul că Ion este bolnav* ('the fact that John is sick') but not **evenimentul că Ion este bolnav* ('*the event that John is sick').

Since clauses that denote facts do not display peculiar features, they can only be identified by means of containers. Containers which show that their clausal arguments denote facts are of two sorts: predicates which take fact-denoting clauses as subject, and predicates which take fact-denoting clauses as complements.

The former class consists of verbs of emotional causality: *a surprinde* ('to surprise'), *a îngrijora* ('to concern'), *a deranja* ('to bother'), like below:

(12) Mă surprinde că Ion a renunţat
'It surprises me that John gave up'

The other class comprises verbs of certain propositional attitude: epistemic verbs, mainly: *a şti, a cunoaşte* ('to know'), *a demonstra* ('to prove', 'to demonstrate'), *a deduce* ('to infer') or factive verbs: *a regreta,* ('to regret'), *a uita* ('to forget'):

(13) Ştiu/Am uitat că Ion a renunţat
'I know/I forgot that John gave up'

Anaphors referring to facts in ARCs are of two types, the *drept pentru care* type and the *de unde* type.

4.1 The *drept pentru care* ('for which') Type

No direct evidence is available, which proves that *care*, as a complement of *drept (pentru)*, denotes a fact. At least, not at first sight. *Care* cannot be the complement of the diagnostic containers mentioned above, because it cannot be but the complement of the preposition *drept (pentru)*. It will be shown that *drept (pentru)* turns out to be itself a diagnostic item for fact-denoting expressions. To this purpose, I will resort once again to the paraphrase test. More specifically, I propose paraphrases for sentences with ARCs of type *drept (pentru) care*, such that the paraphrase makes obvious that the anaphora refers to a fact. For example, the paraphrase which preserves the meaning of the sentence (14) is (15):

(14) [Ion a murit]$_i$, drept (pentru) care$_i$ copiii i-au moştenit averea
[John died]$_i$, fact for which$_i$ his children inherited his fortune
'John died, and consequently his children inherited his fortune'

(15) Pentru faptul/motivul că Ion a murit, copiii i-au moştenit averea
'For the reason that John died, his children inherited his fortune'

As in the case of the event anaphors, in the present case the paraphrase makes the anaphora disappear. What appears instead is the diagnostic nominal *faptul* (in alternation with *motivul* - 'the reason'). This nominal offers a semantic type to the clause *că Ion a murit* ('that John died') which thus explicitly qualifies as denoting a fact.

Notice that in this environment the description *faptul/motivul că Ion a murit* ('the fact/the reason that John died') is the complement of the preposition *pentru* ('for'). Both the meaning of *pentru* (in the paraphrase) and the one of *drept pentru* (in the original sentence) is the same: it is a causal meaning. Additional evidence in this sense is that if one attempts to paraphrase sentence (14) by means of the nominal *evenimentul* ('the event'), the paraphrase is bad:

(16) *Pentru evenimentul că Ion a murit, copiii i-au moştenit averea.
'*For the event that John died, his children inherited his fortune'

The explanation is that the phrase *evenimentul că Ion a murit* ('the event that John died') fails to fulfil the semantic requirement of the preposition. The preposition requires that its complement denote a fact, while the nominal description *evenimentul că Ion a murit* ('the event that John died') actually refers to an event.

So, the conclusion is that the paraphrase *Pentru faptul/motivul că Ion a murit, copiii i-au moştenit averea* ('For the reason that John died, his children inherited his fortune') is the appropriate one for the sentence *[Ion a murit]*$_i$, *drept (pentru) care*$_i$ *copiii i-au moştenit averea* ('John died, and consequently his children inherited his fortune'). The import of this conclusion is twofold. On the one hand, it entitles us to say that for each sentence with ARCs of type *drept (pentru) care*, there must be a paraphrase which shows that in the paraphrased sentence the main clause (that is, the antecedent of the anaphor) denotes a fact. On the other hand, the conclusion allows us to say that *drept (pentru)* is itself a diagnostic container for fact-denoting expressions, as long as its correspondent in the paraphrase takes a fact-denoting phrase as a complement.

4.2 The *de unde* ('from where') Type

Let us now consider the following example:

(17) [Pe masă erau cărţi deschise]$_i$ de unde$_i$ se părea că studia
[There were open books on his desk]$_i$, from where$_i$ it seemed to show that he was studying
'There were open books on his desk, which seemed to show that he was studying'

In ARCs, *unde* exclusively occurs as the complement of the preposition *de* ('from'). I will show that, in this context, preposition *de* is a fact container, too, i.e. its complement must denote a fact.

In ARCs, the meaning of *de* is causal. It is interpreted as *on the basis/ground of x...* This is also supported by the paraphrase test. Any sentence with ARC of type *de unde* is paraphrasable by a sentence in which *de* is replaced with its contextual allomorph, the preposition *din* ('from')[5]. The preposition *din* appears in the main sentence of the paraphrase, where it denotes a fact-denoting nominal (here, *faptul*) as a complement. Since facts have causal force, it is not surprising to find nominals that denote facts as complements of a preposition with causal meaning. Consider then again example (17) and its paraphrase (18):

(18) Din [faptul/*evenimentul/*ideea [că pe masă erau cărţi deschise]], se părea că studia

[5] The use of the preposition forms *de* and *din* in (17) and (18) does not change the meaning in passing from the original sentence to its paraphrase. With respect to these contexts, *de* and *din* are in complementary distribution with no meaning change. This explains the above use of the term 'allomorph'.

'The fact/*the event/*the idea that there were opened books on his desk seemed to show that he was studying'

In (18), the preposition *din* governs a nominal phrase which denotes a fact. This phrase has the main clause of the paraphrased sentence (17) as its adjunct. The complementation of *din* with this nominal phrase shows that *din* accepts a fact-denoting complement but excludes event/proposition-denoting complements. Since *din* in (18) substitutes *de* in the original sentence (17), it follows that in (17) the complement of *de* also denotes a fact. This complement is just *unde*.

5 An Anaphor for Facts, Propositions and Outcomes: *ceea ce* ('which')

Propositions occupy the highest rank in Asher's hierarchy of abstract entities. They are prototypical intensional entities, due to the reputation they come with, in the natural language metaphysics from the philosophy of language. If compared with the other objects in the scale of the world immanence, propositions may be characterized rather negatively. Unlike facts, they do not have causal force. Unlike events they do not manifest in space and time. A conspicuous positive feature, though, is that propositions may be assigned to people ([11]).

Propositions are denoted in Romanian by specialized nominals (e.g. *idea* - 'the idea') and subordinate clauses. A proposition-denoting clause has to be either the subject (as in the case of the predicate *este adevărat* - 'is true') or the complement (as in the case of the predicate *a crede* - 'to believe') of a container of propositions.

In ARCs, *ceea ce* may denote facts, propositions and outcomes but not events. It cannot be selected by a preposition.

5.1 *Ceea ce* as an Anaphor of Facts

The first thing to be noted about sentences with ARC of type *ceea ce* is that the main clause does not seem to be allowed to denote an event. Consider in this sense the following ill-formed example:

(19) *Ion a demisionat, ceea ce s-a petrecut ieri
'*John resigned which happened yesterday'

In this construction, *ceea ce* is the subject argument of the event container *s-a petrecut ieri* ('happened yesterday'), which proves that *ceea ce* denotes an event. Despite that, *ceea ce* cannot be linked to the main clause *Ion a demisionat* ('John resigned'). If it could, the whole complex sentence would become acceptable. So, the ill-formedness of (19) seems to be explained through the missing antecedent for *ceea ce*. This in turn means that the only possible antecedent - the main clause *Ion a demisionat* - does not denote an event. One may now wonder what abstract object the main clause denotes here. The answer is: a fact[6]. This is

[6] Indeed, it is not a paradox that an event may appear in a context as a fact.

firstly proved by a paraphrase (with the descriptor *faptul* - 'the fact'), which accounts for the ill-formedness of (19): this paraphrase, in turn, is ill-formed:

(20) *Faptul că Ion a demisionat s-a petrecut ieri.
'*The fact that John resigned happened yesterday'

This negative argument is strengthened by its positive counterpart: if the event container *s-a petrecut* ('happened') is replaced with a fact container in (19), the whole sentence becomes well-formed:

(21) Ion a demisionat, ceea ce eu uitasem
'John resigned, which I forgot'

So, despite the availability of *ceea ce* to be an argument of containers of events, the main clause in sentences with ARCs of type *ceea ce* is not able to denote events.

5.2 *Ceea ce* as an Anaphor of Propositions

If *ceea ce* is the argument of a container of propositions, it will have an antecedent, provided that the antecedent itself denotes a proposition. This is shown in (22), below:

(22) Toţi credeau [că Ion a demisionat]$_i$, ceea ce$_i$ e adevărat /Toţi au văzut *[că Ion a demisionat]$_i$, ceea ce$_i$ e adevărat
'Everybody believed [that John had resigned]$_i$ / Everybody saw *[that John had resigned]$_i$ which$_i$ is true'

In (22) *ceea ce* is the subject of the container *este adevărat* ('is true'), whereas the clause *că Ion a demisionat* ('that John resigned') is the complement of the container *credeau* ('believed'). Both the subordinate clause and the pronoun denote a proposition. This explains the well-formedness of the sentence as a whole: the subordinate clause is the antecedent of the pronoun. Example (22) shows, at the same time, that if in the main clause the container of propositions *credeau* ('believed') is replaced with a container of facts (*a vedea* - 'to see'), the anaphoric link does not hold anymore. Also, the anaphoric link does not hold if one proposes as the antecedent of *ceea ce* in (22) the main clause. In this case the anaphoric link is not allowed, because the main clause denotes a fact, whereas *ceea ce* still denotes a proposition:

(23) *[Toţi credeau că Ion a demisionat]$_i$, ceea ce$_i$ e adevrat
'*[Everybody believed that John had resigned]$_i$ which$_i$ is true'

5.3 *Ceea ce* as an Anaphor of Outcomes

Outcomes, as species of intensional objects, have been recognised as part of the spectrum of the abstract entities, thanks to the work of Ginzburg and Sag [8]. Ginzburg and Sag informally define an outcome as "a specification of a situation which is futurate relative to some other given situation" ([8]: 79). They consider both propositions and outcomes as instances of the same more general abstract entity, called by them 'austinian'.

Sentences susceptible of denoting outcomes are subjunctive or infinitive clauses in English, and subjunctive clauses in Romanian. Diagnostic containers are verbs *a vrea* ('to want'), *a dori* ('to wish'), *a sfătui* ('to advise'), *a spera* ('to hope'), *a se aştepta* ('to expect'), *a ordona* ('to order'), *a cere* ('to ask') etc., which take subjunctive clauses as their complements.

A simple and convincing example of anaphor of outcomes may be found in (24). In (24), both *ceea ce* and the preceding embedded clause denote an outcome. The anaphoric link holds accordingly:

(24) Toţi sperau [ca Ion să demisioneze]$_i$, ceea ce$_i$ şi eu aşteptam
'Everybody was hoping [that John would resigned]$_i$, which$_i$ I was also expecting

The anaphoric link, though, cannot hold with the whole preceding sentence:

(25) *[Toţi sperau ca Ion să demisioneze]$_i$, ceea ce$_i$ şi eu aşteptam
'*[Everybody was hoping that John would resign]$_i$, which$_i$ I was also expecting

The explanation is that this time *ceea ce* still denotes an outcome, whereas its antecedent denotes a fact. This is proved by the paraphrase below, where the phrase headed by the noun *faptul* ('the fact') becomes the object argument of the outcome container *aşteptam* ('I was expecting'). The result is an ill-formed sentence, because facts are not the kind of entity that could be the object of an expectation:

(26) *Şi eu aşteptam faptul că toţi sperau ca Ion să demisioneze
'*I was also expecting the fact that everybody was hoping that John would resigned'

6 Conclusions and Future Work

Sentences with appositive relatives in Romanian represent a compact area in the investigation of the abstract anaphora, due to the outstanding diversity in their realization and use. No doubt, though, Romanian is not a singular case. One of the promising lines of a future research, then, is the comparative investigation of the other Romance (or Balkan) languages from the point of view of this anaphoric pattern.

Another continuation of the present approach regards its computational applicability. In this respect, the first thing to be done is the disambiguation of the anaphors *care*, *unde* and *ceea ce* which, as mentioned above, may occur either as nominal anaphors or clausal ones (see, for illustration the parallelism in English of pairs, such as *Kim owns a dog, which is regrettable* and *Kim owns a dog, which is a dachshund*). A major challenge for the computational treatment of abstract anaphors is represented by the fact that the algorithm for anaphora resolution cannot exploit the nominal information (gender, number) of the antecedent, because the antecedent is non-nominal (i. e. clausal). It is just in this point that the concept of container might prove its practical import[7].

---

[7] An algorithm for event anaphora resolution has been proposed in [5]. The set of relevant (verbal) containers may be automatically extracted from [4].

Finally, it remains to account for cases (not discussed in this paper), where anaphoric links hold, although the anaphor and its antecedent do not share the same semantic type. Albeit not so frequent, such a pattern can be documented and also requires an explanation.

References

1. Asher, N.: Reference to Abstract Objects in Discourse. Kluwer (1993)
2. Asher, N.: Events, Facts Propositions and Evolutive Anaphora. In: Higginbotham, J., Pianesi, F., Varzi, A. (eds.) Speaking of Events, pp. 123–151. Oxford University Press, New York (2000)
3. Amsili, P., Denis, P., Roussarie, L.: Anaphores abstraites en français: reprèsentation formelle. Traitement Automatique des Langues 46(1), 15–39 (2005)
4. Barbu, A.M.: Conjugarea verbelor româneşti (The Conjugation of Romanian Verbs), Editura Coresi, Bucureşti (2007)
5. Bittar, A.: Un algorithme pour la rèsolution d'anaphores événementielles. Mémoire de master recherche, Université Denis Diderot, Paris 7 (2006)
6. Delfitto, D.: On Facts in the Syntax and Semantics of Italian. In: Geerts, T., van Ginneken, I., Jacobs, H. (eds.) Romance Languages and Liguistic Theory, pp. 15–35. John Benjamins, Amsterdam (2005)
7. Dinu, A.: Quantifying over Eventualities in Continuation Semantics. University of Bucharest (2011) (manuscript)
8. Ginzburg, J., Sag, I.A.: Interrogative Investigations. The Form, Meaning and Use of English Interrogatives. CSLI Publications, Stanford (2000)
9. Pavel, G., Postolache, O., Pistol, I., Cristea, D.: Rezoluţia anaforei pentru limba romnă (Anaphora Resolution for Romanian). In: Forăscu, C. Tufiş, D., Cristea, D. (eds.): Resurse Lingvisticc Şi Instrumente Pentru Prelucrarea Limbii Romne (Linguistic Resources and Tools for Processing Romanian). Editura Universităţii Al. Ioan Cuza, Iaşi (2006)
10. Vendler, Z.: Linguistics in Philosophy. Cornell University Press, Ithaca (1967)
11. Vendler, Z.: Causal Relations. In: Davidson, D., Harman, G. (eds.) The Logic of Grammar, pp. 255–261. Dickenson Publishing Company Encino and Belmont, CA (1975)

The Choice between Verbal Anaphors in Discourse

Philip Miller

Université Paris Diderot, Sorbonne Paris Cité
CLILLAC-ARP, EA 3967, 75004 Paris, France
philip.miller@univ-paris-diderot.fr

Abstract. This paper investigates the conditions of choice in discourse between various verbal anaphors in English, namely Post-Auxiliary Ellipsis with auxiliary *do*; *do so*; and *do it/this/that*. On the basis of an extensive corpus survey, the following factors are shown to be relevant: (i) register, (ii) the presence or absence of an accessible polar alternative, (iii) whether the sentence containing the anaphor refers to the same state of affairs as that which contains the antecedent, (iv) the presence of a non contrastive adjunct, (v) the identity of the subject of the anaphor and its antecedent, (vi) the saliency of the antecedent.

Keywords: Anaphora, Verb Phrase Ellipsis, *do so*, *do it*, *do this*, *do that*, discourse, accessibility, saliency, register, verbal anaphors, verbal antecedent accessibility.

1 Introduction

Various VP anaphor constructions in English (viz. Post-Auxiliary Ellipsis (=PAE, usually referred to by the misnomer VP-ellipsis), *do so*, and *do it/this/that*) have been extensively studied both from a theoretical (e.g. Hankamer and Sag, Hardt, Kehler, Culicover, Houser [5,6,9,3,7]) and from a discourse-oriented perspective (e.g. Bos and Spenader[1]). However very little research has been carried out on factors affecting the choice between such anaphors in naturally occurring discourse. The present paper presents a preliminary investigation of the choice between these constructions in American English (AmE) on the basis of an extensive corpus analysis (based on the COCA[1] and the Brown corpus). Discussion of PAE is limited to cases involving auxiliary *do*, excluding other auxiliaries.

2 Register

A first result is that register is a crucial factor. Table 1 shows the frequency of each type across 4 registers based on a random sample of 100 occurrences of

[1] Corpus of Contemporary American English (COCA): 425 million words, 1990-present. Available online at http://www.americancorpus.org. All examples cited here are from the COCA unless otherwise stated.

I. Hendrickx et al. (Eds.): DAARC 2011, LNAI 7099, pp. 82–95, 2011.

finite forms of the relevant verbal anaphors from each register except for Spoken, for which the sample had 150 occurrences[2] . It appears that *do so* is much more frequent in Academic and Newspaper than in Spoken or Fiction whereas PAE with finite auxiliary *do* is more frequent in the latter than in Academic and Newspaper. As will be shown below, these register effects are largely explainable as resulting from an interaction between the discourse properties of each of these constructions and the use of language typical of the different registers. Table 1 also provides a baseline for the relative frequency of the different constructions across the COCA as a whole and in each register.

Table 1. Frequency of finite verbal anaphors

COCA	Spoken	Fiction	Newspaper	Academic	Total
PAE with finite aux *do*	120 occ. (80%)	88	64	55	327 (72.7%)
do so	3 (2%)	2	16	27	48 (10.7%)
do it	12 (8%)	1	13	8	34 (7.6%)
do this	9 (6%)	2	2	7	20 (4.4%)
do that	6 (4%)	7	5	3	21 (4.7%)
do it + do this + do that	27 (18%)	10	20	18	75 (16.7%)
	150	100	100	100	450

3 Semantic Constraints on Possible Antecedents

It has been claimed in the literature (Lakoff and Ross, Culicover and Jackendoff [11,3], Huddleston and Pullum [8] (who qualify their claim by 'in general')) that *do so* cannot have stative antecedents. The present study confirms the contrary claims of Michiels [12] and Houser [7]. This is especially frequent when *do* is nonfinite (i.e. when auxiliary *do*, which has no non finite uses in AmE, is not in competition) but finite occurrences, as in (1a), are also far more widely attested than Houser's data suggest. Similarly, it has been claimed by Culicover and Jackendoff [3] that *do it/this/that* must have action antecedents. In fact, non agentive causes and certain patient/theme subjects (1b,c) are possible though not frequent. However, contrary to *do so*, no occurrences with stative antecedents were found.

(1) a. If I represent a wholly different Christianity, I do so only because I have found a way to help us recognize as Christians what extraordinary things we say when we worship God. [#I do it only because. . . ; #If I am representing]

b. Although straight narrative can advance a plot faster and less circuitously, dialogue often does it more interestingly.

c. I just— you know, we're all going to die. I mean, everybody does it eventually.

---

[2] Only cases where alternation with *do so, do it/this/that* is possible were counted, so that e.g. question tags and various comparative and relative structures are excluded (see section 4).

4 Syntactic Constraints

As is well known, certain syntactic structures only allow PAE. These include (2a) tag questions, (2b) certain comparative structures, (2c) certain relative clause structures, (2d) the *so/neither* AUX NP construction.

(2) a. He didn't actually know Laura Silsby at all, did he? [*did he do it/this/that/so]
b. She is unjustified in behaving as she does. [*as she does it/this/that/so]
c. A man has to be confident to wear the pastels that Poulter does in public. [*that Poulter does it/this/that/so]
d. That chocolate mousse looks excellent but so does the strawberry tart. [*so does it/this/that/so the strawberry tart]

A detailed discussion of these constraints is beyond the scope of this paper. It should be noted however that they were excluded from all statistics on the frequency of PAE as contrasted with other verbal anaphors since there is no alternation possible for reasons independent of discourse.

It is also worth recalling that the syntactic status of *do* is completely different in PAE and in *do so/it/this/that*. As is well known, in the former it is an auxiliary and inverts with the subject and is directly compatible with *not*; in the latter it is the main verb, requiring *do* support with negation and SAI. It has been claimed that the main verb status of *do* explains the putative restriction against stative (and more generally non-agentive) antecedents mentioned in section 3 but this argument is weakened by the exceptions discussed.

5 Factors Affecting the Choice of Post-Auxiliary Ellipsis

As noted by Kertz [10], there are two main uses of PAE. In the first, (3a), the subject-predicate relation is presupposed and focus is on the polarity; in the second, as in (3b), the open proposition denoted by the predicate is presupposed and the focus is on the subject. In the sample examined (122 occurrences) 101 (82.8%) cases were of the polarity-focus type and 21 (17.2%) were of the subject-focus type. We will examine these in turn.

(3) a. A—Well, that doesn't make it your property. B—Technically, it does. [polarity-focus]
b. The boys cheered. I did too. [subject-focus, conforming subjects]

Contexts involving contrasts in polarity and, more generally, the choice between two branches of a salient polar alternative $p \vee \neg p$ strongly favor PAE. Among these one can distinguish various recurrent configurations. A yes/no question raises a $p \vee \neg p$ alternative and the answer (by the addressee, as in (4a), or the same speaker (4b)) chooses one branch. Simply asserting a proposition puts it on the table, so to speak, making the $p \vee \neg p$ alternative available and allowing for contradiction or confirmation as in (4c,d,e).

(4) a. A—Senator Brown, does this bill end too-big-to-fail? B—Yeah, it does. [#Yeah, it does it/this/that/so]
b. It is too soon to know whether he will use it that way. Let us hope that he does. [#that he does it/this/that/so].
c. A—He shops in women's. B—No, he doesn't. [#No, he doesn't do it/this/that/so]
d. A—[...] her friend grew up in Florida. And in the Northeast, and at the end of the book [she] returns to Vietnam. B—She does. I mean, the story is really touching. [#She does it/that/so]
e. He dances really well with me. He really does. [#He really does it /this/that/so]

Table 2 shows comparative frequency of the various verbal anaphors in contexts of type (4c) and (4e) in the COCA. It appears clearly, in comparison with the overall frequencies given in table 1, that PAE is very significantly preferred in these contexts.

Table 2.

Total occurrences	no (,) [pp*] did n't|not .	no (,) [pp*] did n't|not do it|this|that .	no (,) [pp*] did n't| not do so .
551	536 = 97.3%	14 = 2.5%	1 = 0.2%
	[pp*] really [do] .|,	[pp*] really [do] it|this|that .|,	[pp*] really [do] so .|,
1485	1440 = 97%	45 = 3%	0 =0%
	sure [do] .|,	sure [do] it|this|that .|,	sure [do] so .|,
668	663=99.3%	5=0.7%	0

On the other hand, if the answer to a yes/no question does not limit itself to choosing one branch of the alternative, PAE is dispreferred. Consider example (5a) where the situation 'you argue with him' is presupposed, the question bearing on the degree of arguing. The addressee chooses to answer the question repeating the main verb[3]. In the variant in (5b) the answer with PAE is infelicitous because it provides information on the degree, rather than just a yes/no choice, as is the case in the felicitous (5c). The variant with *do it* in (5d) is felicitous, contrasting with (5b).

(5) a. A—Do you argue with him a lot? B—Oh, we argue constantly.
b. A—Do you argue a lot? B— #Oh, we do constantly.
c. A—Do you argue a lot? B— Oh, we do.
d. A—Do you argue a lot? B— Oh, we do it constantly.

[3] This is encouraged because the argument structure of *argue* changes from transitive in the question to symmetric predicate in the answer. This change makes PAE slightly dispreferred even if *a lot* is removed and the focus of the question is on polarity (*Do you argue with him? #Oh, we do.*). In order to avoid this independent problem, *with him* has been removed in the question (5b,c,d) so that *argue* is used as a symmetric predicate throughout.

Similarly, examples such as (6a,b) exhibit an accessible alternative in the previous context (in (6a) the epistemic verb *think* implicitly brings up the other possibility; in (6b) *whether* brings up the alternative) and the PAE construction provides a choice.

(6) a. A—I think she's going to get a job out of this. B—I hope she does. [alternative = she's going to or she's not going to; #I hope she does it/this/that/so]

b. The question remains, however, whether Moscow will let go of the carrot and, even if it does, whether it would ever support more than a slap on Tehran's wrist. [alternative = Moscow will let go of the carrot or not; #even if it does it/this/that/ so]

Because they implicitly bring up an alternative, conditional clauses, as in (6b), are a frequent context for PAE of this type.

We now turn to the case of subject-focus PAE as in (7). In such cases there is a contrastive nucleus on the subject (e.g. *Congress* in (7a)) as opposed to the cases in (5) and (6) where the stress is on the auxiliary.

(7) a. Presidents don't write policy and spend money, the Congress does. [#does so]

b. She didn't say anything, and I didn't either. [#didn't do it/this/that /so either]

Table (7) provides comparative frequency in the COCA for the different verbal anaphors in the *either* and *too* contexts (conforming-subjects) exhibited in (7b) and (3b). The difference in frequency (as compared with table 1) between PAE and *do it/this/that* in the *too* context is smaller than in the *either* context because the *too* construction is in fact used with *do it/this/that* when the intended antecedent is not sufficiently salient (see section 6 below). However, though acceptable, the *too* construction does appear to be less frequent than would be expected.

Table 3.

<table>
<tr><td>Total occurrences</td><td>[do] n't either .</td><td>[do] n't do it|this|that either.</td><td>[do] n't do so either .</td></tr>
<tr><td>204</td><td>197 = 96.6%</td><td>7 = 3.4%</td><td>0</td></tr>
<tr><td></td><td>[pp*] [do] (,) too .</td><td>[pp*] [do] it|this|that (,) too .</td><td>[pp*] [do] so (,) too .</td></tr>
<tr><td>623</td><td>537 = 86.2%</td><td>78 = 12.5%</td><td>8 =1.3%</td></tr>
</table>

Many of these characteristic uses of PAE are typical of spoken language (e.g. contradiction, confirmation, answering yes/no questions, ...). This explains the higher frequency of PAE in the spoken register, as shown in table 1, as opposed to the academic and newspaper registers. As for the fiction register, the high proportion of PAE is apparently due to its frequent appearance in direct speech, imitating the spoken register.

Another important property of PAE is that the antecedent must be salient in the context. Table 4 provides data from our sample on the distance between verbal anaphors and their antecedents (only finite uses of *do* are considered).

Strikingly, it appears that PAE occupies the middle ground in its requirement for saliency of the antecedent, between *do so*, which requires a highly salient antecedent and *do it*, which allows activated antecedents. The requirement for saliency of the antecedent in PAE would appear to be a logical consequence of the fact that auxiliary *do* in PAE exercises no restrictions on its antecedent (except that it not contain another auxiliary), so that it provides almost no semantic

Table 4. Distance between anaphor and antecedent

Antecedent in:	Same sentence	Previous sentence, no turn	Previous sentence with turn
do it	8 (16%)	19 (38%)	3 (6%)
do in PAE	29 (23%)	41 (32.5%)	42 (33.3%)
polarity focus	13 (12.9%)	37 (35.2%)	41 (39%)
subject focus	16 (76.2%)	4 (19%)	1 (4.8%)
do so	49 (75.4%)	15 (23.1%)	1 (1.5%)

Table 5. (Table 4 continued)

Antecedent in:	2 sentences before	3 or more sentences before	Antecedent trigger is very different or unavailable	Total sample
do it	8 (16%)	0 (0%)	12 (24%)	50 (100%)
do in PAE	6 (4.8%)	4 (3.2%)	4 (3.2%)	126 (100%)
polarity focus	6 (5.7%)	4 (3.8%)	4 (3.8%)	105 (100%)
subject focus	0 (0%)	0 (0%)	0 (0%)	21 (100%)
do so	0 (0%)	0 (0%)	0 (0%)	65 (100%)

information allowing one to identify its antecedent. In this, it appears at first glance to be similar to *it*, see Gundel et al. [4]. In fact, as table 4 shows, it is necessary to distinguish polarity-focus and subject-focus PAE for an obvious reason. In polarity focus cases, the subject of *do* appears as a pronoun coreferent with the subject of the antecedent. Thus, a potential antecedent with an incompatible subject is automatically excluded. Consider the following invented example:

(8) A—I wonder whether he$_i$ smokes. It$_j$ worries me. B—No, he$_i$ doesn't. /No, it$_j$ doesn't.

Though there are two candidate VPs in the previous context, B's two possible replies are unambiguous because of the choice of the subject pronoun. In subject-focus cases, on the other hand, no clue of this type is generally available[4] and there is a higher requirement of saliency. It should be noted however that naturally occurring examples of type (8) (in its *no he doesn't* variant) are in fact hard to find. Only in 7.2% of the cases of PAE examined is the antecedent 2 or 3 sentences back. And, in these cases, the saliency constraint is generally not in fact violated. For instance, in (9a), the two intervening sentences between the antecedent and the PAE are a clarification request by the second speaker and the first speaker's clarification. In (9b), the distance leads the speaker to use the wrong auxiliary and she appears to repair her violation of the saliency constraint by adding the full version of what she intended.

(9) a. A—Does your character make those sounds? B—What are the sounds? A—Oh. B—Yeah. Yeah. He does.
  b. It's very upsetting. But, you know, what am I going to do? I have to deal with it. I don't know. But it does. It stresses me out a lot.

In Miller and Pullum [13] we argue that the observation by Hankamer and Sag [5] that PAE usually does not allow exophoric antecedents is a consequence of the fact that the appropriate types of referents (situations and open propositions) are usually not salient enough in the context and that the exceptions to this involve special cases where they are.

Another important factor affecting the choice of PAE is the presence of an adjunct after the elliptical auxiliary. Though this is not ungrammatical, it is rare. Out of 249 cases of PAE examined, only 4 exhibited this pattern, i.e. 1.6%. We will return to these cases below (cf. (19)) when we discuss the extremely frequent presence of adjuncts with *do so*.

6 Factors Affecting the Choice of *do it/this/that*

Do it, *do this* and *do that* have been mentioned together up to now because they form a coherent group as opposed to PAE on the one hand and to *do so* on the other. Beyond the semantic restrictions on possible antecedents mentioned in section 3, the most important difference between these forms and PAE and *do so* is that they do not require the same degree of saliency for their antecedent. The data suggest that an activated referent (in the sense of Gundel et al. [4]) is sufficient for use of *do it*, *do this* and *do that*. It appears furthermore that *do that* allows for exophorically recoverable non activated referents. We will concentrate on *do it* and make some further remarks on *do this* and *do that*.

As shown in Table 4 above, out of a random sample of 50 examples (25 of spoken and 25 of academic), there are 12 where the antecedent-trigger (in the sense of Cornish [2]), i.e. the segment of previous discourse from which an appropriate antecedent is inferred) is very different from the necessary antecedent, e.g. (10a). Among these 12 there are 5 where it is in fact impossible to even guess what

[4] Factors of plausibility given general world knowledge may allow disambiguation in some cases of course.

the intended antecedent is from the 5 previous lines of context provided by the COCA (these are all from the spoken register and it is likely that part of the difficulty in interpretation comes from lack of access to the exophoric context). Among the 38 remaining, there are 9 where the antecedent-trigger is not a verb (it is usually a noun), e.g. (10b). 30 examples out of 50 have an adjunct, 23 have the same subject as their antecedent, 17 have a different subject and 10 are unclear in this respect.

(10) a. The roads were less congested in early morning, but it was still a relief to leave the garish tourist excrescences near the lake and navigate the narrow switchbacks up and back into time. I parked the car near the base of the hill and hoofed it, like generations of pilgrims before me. The steep climb is the whole idea: to work for one's salvation, not stroll down a garden path. Being oblivious, or American, I did it wrong.

b. The Diabetes Prevention Program: how the participants did it.

By contrast it is very difficult (though not impossible) to find attested examples of PAE with non verbal antecedents and, in written text, it is very difficult to find cases where the antecedent of PAE is unclear with 5 lines of previous context.

Though an activated referent is sufficient for *do it*, it is also the most usually used form in cases where the referent is highly salient but the usual conditions on PAE are not met. For instance, in (11a, b), there is no accessible alternative and the anaphor is followed by a manner adjunct, making PAE infelicitous. In (11c,d), despite the absence of a manner adjunct, the variant with PAE is infelicitous because there is no accessible alternative in the context. Note in particular that the implicit subject of the infinitival VP in (11c) antecedent is generic, so that a contrast in polarity or in subjects is impossible. The difference in acceptability of PAE between the COCA example (11d) and the constructed variant (11e) is also interesting. The deontic modal *should* makes the question of whether or not the obligation will be fulfilled by the subject accessible in the context. Dynamic *could*, on the other hand simply states a fact without triggering an alternative. (11e) is also interesting in that *did it* remains felicitous, despite the saliency of the antecedent, the presence of an alternative, and the absence of an adjunct. (11f) is a COCA example of this type (*want* triggers the alternative), where *do it* appears, but PAE would have been equally felicitous.

(11) a. Using 19th century technology they not only accomplished it but did it so well that it was later incorporated into the London subway system and remains in use in the 21st century. [#but did so well that...]

b. Although straight narrative can advance a plot faster and less circuitously, dialogue often does it more interestingly. [#often does more interestingly]

c. It was just a question of how to crack the code, and he did it. [#and he did]
d. I didn't know I couldn't do this... so I just did it! [#so I just did!]
e. I thought I should do this, so I did/so I did it!
f. If Kipp wants to set fire to the town garage, he does it. [OK: he does]

It has been impossible at present to find a difference between the two variants of (11e) and (11f), which suggests that in cases like these the gricean quantity effect described by Gundel et al. [4] (e.g. for the choice between *it* and *that*) does not hold for the choice between PAE and *do it*, i.e. use of *do it* in (11e) and (11f) does not lead the addressee to search for a less accessible antecedent. This contrasts with the examples given above in (6) and (7) where the variants with *do it* seem to suggest, in contextually implausible ways, that some different antecedent is intended, which leads to infelicity. It may be the case that the difference between these cases has to do with the degree of accessibility of the alternative. When it is explicit and thus very salient, as in the examples in (6) and (7), *do it* is infelicitous, but when the alternative is inferable, *do it* becomes felicitous. Further study is required to verify this hypothesis. As for the contrast between *do it* and *do this* and *do that*, a detailed study is beyond the scope of this paper. However, it is clear that the gricean quantity effects described by Gundel et al. [4] *do* apply in these cases. Use of *do that* or *do this* in contexts where *do it* is sufficient to recover the intended antecedent leads the addressee to attempt to recover a less accessible antecedent with infelicitous results. Similarly, it is quite usual for the first reference to an antecedent to be made using *do this* or *do that* and subsequent references with *do it*, as in (11d). This is exactly similar to what Gundel et al. [4] find for pronominal *this*, *that* and *it*. Inverting the order of *do it* and *do this* in (11d) leads to infelicity as well as repeating *do this* or *do that*. To conclude, consider the following constructed example which suggests that familiar status is sufficient for the antecedent of *do that*.

(12) [addressee is making an annoying noise tapping his pencil against the table while speaker is trying to concentrate; no mention of this noise has occurred in the discourse context]. Stop doing that! /#Stop doing it.

Presumably, in this context, the annoying activity is familiar but not activated in the sense of Gundel et al. [4], since it would be possible to say simply: *That's annoying* (of course, *it* and *this* are impossible, as predicted by Gundel et al.).

7 Factors Affecting the Choice of *do so*

As briefly mentioned in section 3, there is a large difference in the properties of *do so* depending on whether it is finite or non finite. In the latter case, it is not in competition with PAE (there are no uses of non-finite auxiliary *do* in AmE) and its uses are much less restricted. This section will center on finite *do so* though a few remarks on non finite cases will be made at the end. A first factor which conditions the choice of finite *do so* is that the antecedent must be highly salient and syntactically very close to its antecedent. As shown in Table 4 above, the great majority of examples examined have *do so* and its antecedent in the same sentence and the rest have it in the previous sentence. Furthermore, there is almost never a turn between the antecedent and *do so* (only one example of this type was found in the sample). It is very likely that this property explains the classical observation of Hankamer and Sag 1976 that *do so* has no exophoric uses. The second central property of *do so* is the identity of the state of affairs denoted by the antecedent and by *do so*. This property explains two other typical properties of *do so*, the first of which has not, to my knowledge, ever been noted in the literature, namely that (i) the subject of *do so* is almost always the same as that of the antecedent (the state of affairs denoted would otherwise be different); (ii) there is typically a non contrastive adjunct specifying some additional property of the state of affairs (otherwise the *do so* sentence would simply be redundantly repeating the previous sentence). Consider first the identity of subjects between *do so* and its antecedent, The sample of 65 occurrences studied contains only one case (less than 2%) of subjects with clearly disjoint references given in (13a). In 4 other cases, there is a relation of either partial overlap, inclusion, or metonymy (13b).

(13) a. Decades earlier, his father did not avenge his mother's murder by a Shia. Jamil does so now, triggering eye-for-eye bloodshed.

b. [Saddam Hussein is topic of previous discussion] Iraq does not possess nuclear weapons. The best intelligence that anybody can find, certainly that I can find, is that it will be at least a year before he does so and maybe five years.

Turning to the presence of non contrastive adjuncts, 54 out of 65 cases (83%) have a non contrastive adjunct. Thus (14a,b) are typical examples. The type illustrated in (14c) is far less frequent: *do so* allows a second reference to the same state of affairs, but does so in order to temporally locate another event, rather than in order to allow specification of an additional property of the initial state of affairs.

(14) a. [He$_i$ recently retired as vice president of technology standards at Sony Electronics]$_j$. [He$_i$ did so]$_j$ because the Stooges need him again. [additional property of singular event]

b. Motorino is having a moment. That seems fair. [It$_i$ serves the city's best pizza.]$_j$ [It$_i$ does so]$_j$ consistently, at both locations,... [additional property of habitual event]

c. An old man from the same village corroborates his story. As he does so, there is a reminder of just how close we are to the war,

Adjuncts of all varieties are attested. Manner and means adjuncts are the most frequent, but one also finds location, time, conditional, concessive, causal, consequence, etc. Let us examine more closely the precise nature of the identity of state of affairs requirement. Consider the COCA example (15a) and the constructed variants (15b,c,d):

(15) a. and Mom hugged me and told me she hated hitting me and did it for my own good and I told her I knew that and then she [...]
b. and Mom hugged me and told me she hated hitting me and did so for my own good and I told her I knew that and then she [...]
c. My Mom hits me almost every day. She does so for my own good. [habitual>habitual]
d. My Mom hits me almost every day. #She did so yesterday. [habitual>specific]
e. My Mom hit me yesterday. She did so for my own good. [specific>specific]
f. My Mom hit me yesterday. #She does so for my own good. [specific>habitual]

Out of context, (15a) has two possible interpretations: either *did it* is habitual/generic, like its antecedent, or it refers to a specific event of hitting. The latter interpretation appears to disappear in the constructed variant (15b) with *do so*. The constructed data in (15c, d, e, f) suggest that if *do so* has an habitual/generic antecedent, then it must itself have an habitual/generic reading and that if it has an antecedent referring to a specific event, it must itself refer to a specific event. Data from the sample suggest that this constraint is very generally respected. No such constraint exists with *do it* and (15d) and (15e) become perfectly felicitous if *do so* is replaced by *do it*. The following is an attested example of the latter type, where substitution of *do it* by *do so* is infelicitous, despite the presence of adjuncts, and where the events denoted by the sentences with *do it* are tokens of the event-type denoted by the antecedent.

(16) After all, the old saying that every country is three meals away from revolution turned out to be sadly incorrect in the twentieth century; it is possible for leaders to survive even when millions die. Stalin did it in the 1930s, Mao did it in the 1960s, and Kim Jong Il has done it more than once in the last two decades.

There is a pattern of data which lends further support to this hypothesis, namely that *do so* is much less frequent than would be expected in combination with *again*, namely the pattern "[do] so again" occurs 189 times in the COCA, whereas "[do] it again" occurs 2949 times. Table 1 indicates that the overall frequency of *do it* is approximately 71% of that of *do so*, so that *do so again* occurs 11 times less frequently than it should if all other things were equal. The example in (17) is one of the infrequent cases which violate the identity of state of affairs constraint.

(17) Smithson's writings spread his ideas the moment they were published, and after they were collected in book form in 1979, they did so again.

It may be that in this case *do it* was avoided because of its bias towards an actional antecedent (it is really the document and not the author which is the cause in this example and a metonymic reading should be avoided) and PAE is not available as there is no accessible alternative.

Further properties of *do so* include the identity of speech acts performed by *do so* and its antecedent (typically an assertion, there are only 5 occurrences of *do so* with subject auxiliary inversion in the whole COCA) and absence of contrasting polarity. There is also a dispreference for *do so* followed by intensifier *so*, so that an example like (18) becomes infelicitous if *did so* replaces *did it*, despite the fact that all other conditions for the presence of *do so* are satisfied (as evidenced by the fact that removing intensifier *so* before *effectively* makes *do so* perfectly felicitous).

(18) The first radical known to man who rebelled against the establishment and did it so effectively that he at least won his own kingdom. [#did so so effectively; OK: and did so effectively.]

As pointed out, the presence of a non contrastive adjunct is typical for *do so* (83% of cases). It is worth comparing with the other constructions on this point. With *do it*, as mentioned, 60% of the cases have an adjunct. And with PAE only 1.6% of cases do. (19) is an example of the latter type:

(19) Brother Laurence has rarely grasped for words. He does now. [#He does so now]

In (19) there is a clear polar alternative between the usual situation and the present situation. Specifically, the adjunct does not characterize the situation referred to by the antecedent, as is the case in all the examples of *do so* with adjuncts cited above, but rather contrasts the specific situation referred to by *do* with the habitual situation referred to by the antecedent.

As pointed out in section 2, *do so* is much more frequent in formal written registers. It can be assumed that this is in large part due to the analytic type of discourse typical in these registers, where it is normal to come back on events and analyze their causes, consequences, manners, etc. It does appear, however, that use of *do so* has become available as a marker of formality in spoken discourse. A close examination of the spoken data from the COCA shows that non prototypical uses of *do so* are more frequent than in academic discourse and that some speakers seem to use *do so* on occasion simply as a marker of higher register.

To conclude this section, let us turn briefly to non finite uses of *do so*. Houser [7] establishes that stative antecedents are more frequent with non finite uses of *do so* than with finite uses and that native speakers tend to accept stative antecedents more easily with non finite uses of *do so* than finite uses. He links this to the impossibility of non finite auxiliary *do* in AmE. Building on this idea, it can be shown that more generally the discourse constraints on finite uses of *do so* just discussed are much less constraining in the non finite cases. It is significant in this respect that, for instance, *to do so* is 4 times more frequent in the COCA than one would expect given the frequency of finite *do so* and the average proportion of non finite to finite uses of verbs. (*Do it/this/that* also exhibit unexpectedly high frequencies in their non finite forms, though to a lesser extent than *do so*). This suggests that in non finite uses, *do so* (and to a lesser extent *do it/this/that*) appear in contexts where VPE would have been preferred if, all other things being equal, the example had been finite.

8 Conclusion

This paper has provided results of a preliminary investigation into the factors governing the choice between PAE, *do so*, and *do it/this/that* in discourse, concentrating on discourse-pragmatic factors. The statistical results and the hypotheses presented need to be confirmed by testing them on a larger data-base. This work is in progress. It has been suggested that the following are all relevant factors in the choice: (i) register, (ii) the presence or absence of an accessible polar alternative, (iii) the question of whether the sentence containing the anaphor refers to the same state of affairs as that which contains its antecedent, (iv) the presence of a non contrastive adjunct, (v) the identity of the subject of the anaphor and its antecedent, (vi) the saliency of the antecedent. One point that needs to be stated with more precision is the exact criteria for determining whether an alternative is salient or inferable in a given discourse context. Similarly, the analysis of the relevance of saliency of the antecedent is challenging. It appears that the categories proposed by Gundel et al. [4] ('in focus', 'activated', 'familiar') are at least partly useful in explaining the facts linked to the accessibility of the antecedent. However it has also been shown that in some cases, no gricean effects of the type expected under the givenness hierarchy hypotheses appear. These cases will have to be further investigated and, more generally, it will be necessary to reflect further on the precise way in which the categories proposed by Gundel et al. can be applied to abstract entities such as open propositions and states of affairs.

References

1. Bos, J., Spenader, J.: An annotated corpus for the analysis of VP ellipsis. Language Resources and Evaluation (2011)
2. Cornish, F.: Anaphora, discourse, and understanding: evidence from English and French. Oxford University Press (1999)
3. Culicover, P.W., Jackendoff, R.: Simpler Syntax. Oxford University Press, Oxford (2005)
4. Gundel, J.K., Hedberg, N., Zacharski, R.: Cognitive status and the form of referring expressions in discourse. Language 69(2), 274–307 (1993)
5. Hankamer, J., Sag, I.: Deep and surface anaphora. Linguistic Inquiry 7, 391–428 (1976)
6. Hardt, D.: Verb phrase ellipsis: Form, meaning, processing. Unpublished PhD dissertation, University of Pennsylvania, IRCS report 93-23 (1993)

7. Houser, M.J.: The Syntax and Semantics of *do so* Anaphora. Unpublished PhD dissertation, University of California at Berkeley (2010)
8. Huddleston, R., Pullum, G.K.: The Cambridge Grammar of the English Language. Cambridge University Press (2002)
9. Kehler, A.: Coherence, Reference, and the Theory of Grammar. CSLI Publications (2002)
10. Kertz, L.: Ellipsis Reconsidered. Unpublished PhD Dissertation, University of California at San Diego (2010)
11. Lakoff, G., Ross, J.R.: Why you can't do so into the sink. In: McCawley, J.D. (ed.) Syntax and Semantics. Notes from the Linguistic Underground, vol. 7. Academic Press (1976)
12. Michiels, A.: A note on the relation between agent and stativity. Neophilologus Groningen 62(2), 172–177 (1978)
13. Miller, P., Pullum, G.K.: Exophoric verb phrase ellipsis (In preparation)

Abstract Anaphors in German and English

Stefanie Dipper[1], Christine Rieger[2],
Melanie Seiss[2], and Heike Zinsmeister[2]

[1] Ruhr-University Bochum, 44780 Bochum, Germany
dipper@linguistics.rub.de
[2] University of Konstanz, 78457 Konstanz, Germany
{christine.enzinger,melanie.seiss,heike.zinsmeister}@uni-konstanz.de

Abstract. Abstract anaphors refer to abstract referents such as facts or events. Automatic resolution of this kind of anaphora still poses a problem for language processing systems. The present paper presents a corpus-based comparative study on German and English abstract anaphors and their antecedents to gain further insights into the linguistic properties of different anaphor types and their distributions. To this end, parallel texts from the Europarl corpus have been annotated with functional and morpho-syntactic information. We outline the annotation process and show how we start out with a small set of well-defined markables in German. We successively expand this set in a cross-linguistic bootstrapping approach by collecting translation equivalents from English and using them to track down further forms of German anaphors, and, in the next turn, in English, etc.

Keywords: Abstract anaphora, corpus annotation, contrastive linguistics.

1 Introduction

Abstract anaphora denote anaphoric relations between some anaphoric expression and an antecedent that refers to an abstract object like an event or a fact.[1] The antecedents are normally expressed by verbal or clausal constructions, and sometimes also by their corresponding nominalizations. In the classical example by Byron [4], the pronoun *it* (underlined in (1a)) refers to an *event*: the migration of penguins to Fiji. In the alternative sequence, (1b), the demonstrative pronoun *that* refers to the *fact* that penguins migrate to Fiji in the fall.

(1) a. Each Fall, penguins migrate to Fiji. <u>It</u> happens just before the eggs hatch.
b. Each Fall, penguins migrate to Fiji. <u>That</u>'s why I'm going there next month.

[1] We would like to thank the reviewers for helpful comments. Heike Zinsmeister's research was financed by Europäischer Sozialfonds in Baden-Württemberg.

I. Hendrickx et al. (Eds.): DAARC 2011, LNAI 7099, pp. 96–107, 2011.

Abstract anaphora are analyzed as discourse deixis within a mental discourse model [22,24]. According to this approach, discourse units correspond to underspecified abstract referents which can be coerced into different types of referents when they are referred to in the text [2]. Abstract anaphora contribute to the coherence of a text in that they make previously mentioned events (or facts etc.) available for further modification in subsequent sentences. Compared to other tasks in Natural Language Processing such as tagging or parsing, automatic resolution of concrete anaphora is still a difficult challenge for language processing systems. Consequently, automatic resolution of abstract anaphora is an even harder task.

We pursue a corpus-based approach to investigate the properties that characterize different instantiations of abstract anaphora. In the long run, we envisage to derive features from the corpus annotation that will serve us to tackle the automatic resolution of abstract anaphors. In this paper we investigate what kind of anaphoric elements are employed to refer to abstract objects. The range of possible realizations includes pronouns, lexical NPs (e.g. *this issue, this situation*, etc.) and adverbials (e.g. *likewise*). We take a cross-linguistic, bootstrapping approach and present a comparative corpus study on the realization of abstract anaphora in a parallel corpus of English and German. We present results on the following question: to what extent do English and German use the same kind of strategies to refer to abstract objects.

The paper is organized as follows. In Sec. 2, we present related work. Sec. 3 provides a description of our approach: the corpus, methodological considerations, and the annotation procedure. Sec. 4 presents the results from our comparative study in detail while Sec. 5 discusses the results more generally. Sec. 6 concludes with an outline of future research.

2 Related Work

In comparison to work on nominal anaphora, considerably less research has focused on abstract anaphora. A recent overview of projects annotating abstract anaphora is provided by [8]. Studies based on English (monolingual) corpora, e.g., include [23,16,5,10,13,18,17]. Languages other than English have been studied by [12,15] (Czech), [1] (Basque), and [9] (German).

Contrastive analyses based on multilingual *comparable* corpora have been made, e.g., by [19] for Spanish and Catalan, which investigates all kinds of pronouns and full NPs. The data shows that in Catalan, demonstrative pronouns are used slightly more frequently than personal pronouns to refer to abstract entities (thus reflecting tendencies that can be found also in English). In contrast, Catalan uses personal pronouns twice as much as demonstratives.

In a diachronic study of English data from the 17th–20th centuries, [3] finds that the use of the personal pronoun *it* as an abstract anaphor has decreased over time, and the demonstrative pronoun *that* came into use instead; throughout the entire period, *this* is rarely used as an abstract anaphor.

Annotation of *parallel* texts has been performed, e.g., by [21], who extract a French-Portuguese subcorpus from the parallel MLCC corpus. The MLCC corpus contains written questions asked by members of the European Parliament and the corresponding answers from the European Commission. [21] investigate the use of demonstrative NPs. Although French has a higher number of demonstratives, the overall results are highly similar, and French and Portuguese seem to share relevant syntactic and semantic properties.

[14] annotates pronominal abstract anaphora in Andersen's fairy tales in Danish (the original language), and their English and Italian translations. The data shows that whereas English mostly uses demonstrative pronouns to refer to abstract entities, there is no such preference in Danish and Italian, which also use personal pronouns quite often. In original Italian data, abstract anaphors occur less frequently than in the translations.

Our project deals with the annotation of the full range of abstract anaphora (including full NPs anaphors and anaphoric adverbs) in a parallel corpus in German and English. In this paper, we present the first two annotation rounds of a bi-directional bootstrapping approach which concentrates mainly on pronominal anaphors.

3 Our Study

3.1 The Corpus

For our study, we extracted about 100 German and English turns (contributions by German and English speakers) along with their sentence-aligned translations from the Europarl Corpus (Release v3, 1996–2006, [11]). The Europarl corpus consists of transcripts of European Parliament debates. Individual contributions ('turns') in the debates were delivered (and transcribed) in one of the official EU languages. Professional translators provided official EU translations.

The original contributions were spoken but might have been based on written scripts. Speakers had the option to edit the transcripts before publication. Hence, the register of the turns is of a mixed character, between spoken and a more standardized written language.

Preprocessing of the data included the addition of missing tags to indicate the speaker's original language. More importantly, it included tokenizing, POS tagging and chunking based on the TreeTagger [20].

We created two parallel subcorpora: (i) "DE-EN" based on German original turns and their aligned English translations; (ii) "EN-DE" based on English originals and German translations. DE-EN contains 94 German turns, with an average of 19.5 sentences per turn. The turns contain contributions by 61 German and Austrian speakers. The turns were randomly sampled from those turns of the German Europarl corpus that contain at least one markable, i.e. one of pronominal *dies, das, es* 'this, that, it' (see below). For the annotation task, all 871 markables in the turns were highlighted; among them, 223 were identified as abstract anaphors by the annotators (Ø 2.37 abstract anaphors per turn). 203 of them could be aligned with English equivalents.[2]

EN-DE is about the same size as DE-EN. It contains 95 English turns with an average length of 21.0 sentences. 296 abstract anaphora were identified on the basis of 1,224 markables and aligned with their German translations (Ø 3.12 anaphors per turn).[3]

The results presented in Sec. 4 are based on the set of aligned anaphora pairs of both translation directions.

3.2 Methodological Considerations

One way to learn about the distribution of abstract anaphora would be to go through a text and check sentence by sentence whether it contains a reference to an abstract referent. We do not pursue this approach. Instead, we start out with a well-defined set of markables in the original language and collect all variants of translations on the side of the "target" language (the translation of the original language).

In the first round of annotation, we chose original texts from German, because in German —in contrast to English— one pronoun is unambiguously used as an abstract anaphor: the uninflected singular demonstrative pronoun *dies* ('this'). In addition to this, we defined as markables the (ambiguous) demonstrative pronoun *das* ('that') and the (ambiguous) third person neuter pronoun *es* ('it'). The target language was English.

For the second round of annotation, we considered the reversed translation direction: English original texts and their German translations. We extended our set of markables and included the adverbs *as, so* and *likewise*, because these adverbs frequently served as translations of German anaphors in the first round. We will apply this method of bootstrapping back and forth to extend the set of markables iteratively. For instance, in the third round, German pronominal adverbs (e.g. *davon* 'thereof') and the adverb *wie* ('as') will be added to the set of markables. In contrast to the first approach described above, this bootstrapping approach allows for a fast and efficient way of extracting anaphors in both languages.

3.3 Annotation Procedure

For cross-lingual annotation of German and English texts, two MMAX2 annotation windows were used, which were put side by side on the screen.[4]

[2] The alignment is not complete since it is based on the automatic sentence alignment provided by Europarl, release v3, which does not contain alignments for all turns. If a translation is not literal, the turn structures of the parallel texts are not necessarily isomorphic.

[3] The slightly higher density of abstract anaphors in English is due to the fact that we extracted turns containing at least two markables and started out with the extended set of markables available after the first annotation round, see Sec. 3.2.

[4] MMAX2: `http://mmax2.sourceforge.net/`

The annotators were first asked to annotate the German text. For each anaphor, they had to specify its type (demonstrative or personal pronoun), function (subject, object, other) and position (pre-field, matrix, embedded, other).

Next the annotators checked whether some item could be identified in the corresponding English align unit which served a similar function as the German anaphor. If such an item was found on the English side, it was marked and, similarly to the annotation of German, its type, function, and position were specified. For the annotation of English, the feature 'type' could be specified as: pronoun, NP, *likewise, so, as* or other); the features 'function' and 'position' have the same values as in German, except for the position *pre-field* ('Vorfeld'), which is replaced by a *topic* position in English. The English anaphoric item was linked to the German anaphor via the token-ID of the German anaphor.[5] Obviously, in the first round of annotation, only anaphors of a very restricted, predefined set were annotated, and only anaphors that were present in the German texts were considered at all. To complete the picture, we therefore looked at original English texts, too, and started out from English anaphors (as defined above) and searched for corresponding items in the German translations. This way, we came across new forms of abstract anaphors in German, which can be used in the bootstrapping approach, to search, again, for new forms in English.

4 Results

We start this section by testing two hypotheses: that English in general avoids the use of pronominal abstract anaphors, and that English prefers demonstrative pronouns to personal pronouns in abstract anaphora. We then compare the grammatical functions and positions of abstract anaphors in German and English.

4.1 Avoidance of Pronominal Abstract Anaphors in English

We used our annotations to test the hypothesis that English avoids the use of *pronominal* abstract anaphors. The results from the German-to-English ('DE-EN') and English-to-German ('EN-DE') annotations do not to support this hypothesis. Table 1 shows that in both directions, the majority of pronouns (65% and 70%) are translated to a pronoun in the target language, while a small part is translated to full NPs and the rest to some other expression (e.g. anaphoric adverbials).[6] The differences between the two translation directions are not statistically significant.

[5] To ensure reliable annotations, annotation guidelines were provided, a detailed one for monolingual annotation, which includes tests for antecedents etc. [7], and more general guidelines, describing the process of bilingual annotation in two MMAX2 windows [6]. Due to space limitations, we cannot go into the details of the guidelines here.

[6] EN-DE: 39 pronominal adverbs are counted among the German pronouns.

Table 1. Translations of pronouns

	Pronoun-to-pronoun	Pronoun-to-other	Sum
DE-EN	65% (132)	35% (19 NPs, 52 other)	100% (203)
EN-DE	70% (173)	29% (18 NPs, 55 other)	100% (246)

The data shows that both languages use pronominal abstract anaphors to a similar extent, but the uses overlap in around 70% of the cases only. One possible explanation could be that the contexts of the abstract anaphors are at the root of the discrepancies: while the contexts are semantically more or less equivalent (because one is the translation of the other), they can differ at the syntactic level, with the effect of disallowing a source pronoun in the target language.

We observe the following main differences in the translations of pronominal abstract anaphors from German to English and vice versa.

- there is no corresponding material in the translation, e.g. a different argument frame is employed, see Ex. (2)[7]
- use of full NPs rather than pronouns (*all these things, the whole thing, this approach, these measures, this situation, this thread ...*), see Ex. (3)
- use of adverbials or conjunctions (*likewise, so, as*), see Ex. (4)

(2) a. *DE$_o$*: Wenn dies nicht geschieht, verlieren wir das Vertrauen der Bürger.
EN$_t$: If we do not, the public will lose confidence in us.
DE-LIT: ... If this does not happen, the public will lose confidence in us.
b. *EN$_o$*: There are absolute assurances of that and provisions made for it in the White Paper.
DE$_t$: Hierfür sind absolute Sicherungsmaßnahmen vorgesehen, und das Weißbuch enthält die notwendigen Vorkehrungen.
DE-LIT: ... the White Paper lists the necessary provisions.

(3) a. *DE$_o$*: Das konnte durch die glänzende Vorsitzführung von Frau Cederschiöld, aber auch durch die sehr substanzielle Hilfe der Kommission abgewendet werden, und deswegen können wir diesem Kompromissergebnis zustimmen.
EN$_t$: Thanks to Mrs Cederschiöld's inspired leadership, but also due to the very substantial support from the Commission, this threat has been averted, so we can now vote in favour of this compromise result.
DE-LIT: ... this could be averted
b. *EN$_o$*: I do not necessarily support this.
DE$_t$: Diesem Standpunkt schließe ich mich nicht notwendigerweise an.
DE-LIT: This position I do not necessarily follow.

[7] In the examples, the a.-examples stem from the DE-EN corpus, the b.-examples from the EN-DE corpus. The lines displayed first contain the original version, additionally marked by the subscript "o". The second lines, with subscript "t", show the corresponding translation from the Europarl corpus. The "DE-LIT" lines provide a literal translation of (parts of) the German lines.

(4) a. *DE*$_o$: ... — auch das wurde bereits gesagt — ...
EN$_t$: As has also been said already, ...
DE-LIT: — this too has been said already —
b. *EN*$_o$: Whatever European Union policies flow from this conference at The Hague will have to come to this Parliament for debate, amendment and agreement, that is the European policies.
DE$_t$: So sieht es das europäische Regelwerk vor.
DE-LIT: So it is regulated by the European regulations.

4.2 Preference of Demonstrative Pronouns in English

Following [16,14], we hypothesized that English prefers demonstrative pronouns to personal pronouns in abstract anaphora in comparison to other languages.

Fig. 1 shows the translation equivalents of pronoun types from both translation directions. The EN-DE bar plot indeed confirms that English prefers demonstrative pronouns (> 80%).[8] The DE-EN bar plot, however, shows that German shows a similar preference. Such strong preferences did not show up for the languages studied by [14,19] (Danish, Italian, Spanish, Catalan). In both directions, only about 2/3 of the demonstratives (DE-EN: 60%, EN-DE: 65%) are translated as such, and considerably less of the personal pronouns.

It is assumed that the personal pronoun *it* in English can only refer to events and states, but not, e.g., to situations or facts, see, e.g., [10]. This constraint does not seem to apply to German anaphors, which could explain part of the variance observed above. To validate such a hypothesis, we would need to annotate the semantic types of the abstract objects that are referred to by the anaphors.

Ex. (5a) shows a relevant type mismatch: German *es* 'it' refers to the *fact* that the states have not transposed the directive. The English translation uses the demonstrative *this* instead. A converse example is Ex. (5b): English *it* is translated by a German demonstrative.[9]

(5) a. *DE*$_o$: Frau Kommissarin, Sie haben jede Unterstützung dieses Parlaments, die Staaten, die diese Richtlinie nicht ordentlich umgesetzt haben, vor den EuGH zu bringen, es öffentlich zu machen und so den Druck dafür zu erzeugen, dass diese Richtlinie endlich umgesetzt wird.
EN$_t$: If, Commissioner, you want to bring before the ECJ those states that have not properly transposed this directive, in order to bring this out into the open and thus to bring pressure to bear in order to get this directive transposed at last, then this House is behind you all the way.
DE-LIT: ... to bring it out into the open ...
b. *EN*$_o$: The fact that an agreement was reached on very difficult issues should not be underestimated. It was a huge task.
DE$_t$: Die Tatsache, dass zu sehr schwierigen Fragen Übereinstimmung erzielt wurde, sollte nicht unterschätzt werden. Das war eine gigantische Aufgabe.
DE-LIT: ... This was a huge task.

[8] EN-DE: German pronominal adverbs are not considered here since their pronominal part is ambiguous between personal and demonstrative.

[9] It is not entirely clear to us to which kind of abstract object the anaphors refer to in Ex. (5).

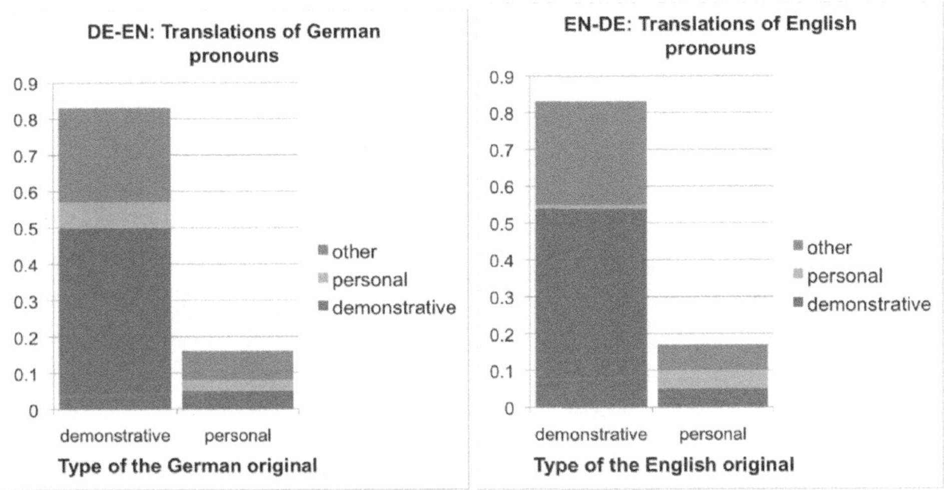

Fig. 1. Translation equivalents of the pronominal types (percentages). The columns encode the types of the original texts, the colors the types of the translated texts.

Comparing the uses of personal and demonstrative pronouns in English and German is hindered by the fact that the German neuter pronoun *es* 'it' is usually not used after prepositions and, instead, pronominal adverbs, such as *davon* 'thereof' or *daraus* 'out of it', are used—this holds for both concrete and abstract *es*-anaphors, see Ex. (6). Pronominal adverbs do not allow us to distinguish between personal or demonstrative use. Conversely, English seems to prefer personal to demonstrative pronouns after prepositions: *out of it/*that* [16].

(6) EN_o: The role of this Parliament is to ensure that the rules are complied with. That is what we should concentrate on.
DE_t: Die Aufgabe des Parlaments besteht darin, dafür zu sorgen, daß die Regeln eingehalten werden. Und genau darauf sollten wir uns konzentrieren.
DE-LIT: ... And exactly thereon we should concentrate.

4.3 Function

In both languages, abstract anaphors (of the types that we have annotated up to now) most often occur in the subject position ($\geq$ 60%), see Fig. 2. The majority of subjects remain subjects (about 2/3), whereas only half of the objects are translated as such, in both directions. The overall picture of both translation directions is highly similar.

4.4 Position

In the annotation, we distinguished between three different positions: the prefield/topic position, a position within the matrix clause, and a position within

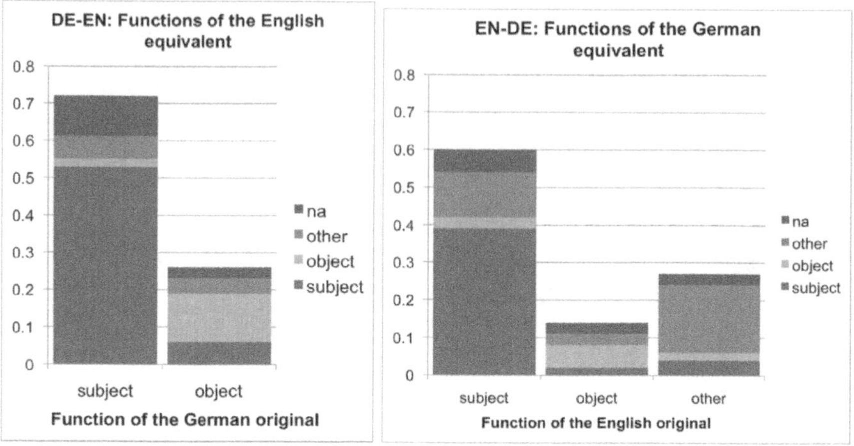

Fig. 2. Translation equivalents of functions (percentages)

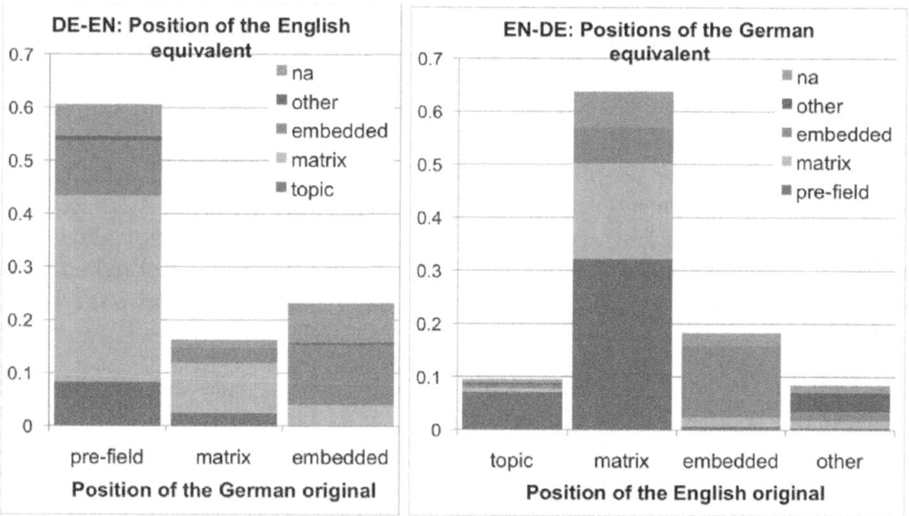

Fig. 3. Translation equivalents of positions (percentages)

the embedded clause. In Ex. (7), the original German anaphor is in an unmarked, post-verbal position. In contrast, its English counterpart has been realized in the marked topic position.

(7) DE_o: Man glaubte in verschiedenen europäischen Staaten, man müsste rasch handeln, man müsste die Amerikaner unterstützen. Ich verstehe <u>das</u> auch. Nur jetzt müssen wir wieder zur Rechtsstaatlichkeit zurückfinden ...
EN_t: It was believed in various European states that rapid action was called for and that we had to support the Americans, and <u>that</u> I can understand. Now, though, we have to get back to the rule of law ...
DE-LIT: ... and I understand <u>that</u> well. ...

According to Fig. 3, most abstract anaphors do not occur in embedded position. The figure further shows that the German pre-field position has other properties than the English topic position: The majority of German pre-field anaphors are translated as an ordinary matrix constituent in English. Conversely, English topicalized anaphors are usually translated to German pre-field anaphors. Columns 2 and 3 indicate that a minority of anaphors switch their position from a matrix clause into an embedded one, or vice versa.

5 Discussion

We performed a bidirectional comparison of the expression of abstract anaphora to interpret observed divergences between English and German.

The major finding of our study is that English and German pattern very much alike in contrast to findings on different language pairs. Despite the observed similarities, there are language-specific preferences that manifest themselves in cross-linguistic divergences. It is still open to future research whether these differences point to features that could be employed in automatic anaphora resolution. A larger annotated corpus is needed to answer this question in a conclusive way. Models of preferences and divergences in the expression of abstract anaphora are also important for applications such as machine translation.

Another explanation for the observed divergences would be that they are due to idiomatic preferences of the speaker on the one hand and the translator on the other hand and would not be related to different types of anaphors. In a study by [11], it has been investigated to what extent translators differ when they are asked to translate one and the same text. Mismatches that occur between such multiple translations concern syntactic variation, clause subordination vs. anaphorically linked sentences, different argument realization, etc. The same types of mismatches have also been found in comparing original texts and their translations [10]. We think that the Europarl corpus is a suitable database to overcome these objections as it consists of contributions of many speakers and translations by a variety of translators, which is, unfortunately, not documented in the metadata of the corpus.

6 Future Steps

An open question is whether (some of) the cross-linguistic differences can be attributed to differences on the semantic level. In future work, we would like to address the two following hypotheses: (i) English demonstratives conflate different functions of German anaphors, (ii) (Some) differences between both languages could be related to the abstract types of the anaphor and antecedent.

In addition to exploring new features, a larger database will allow us to investigate correlations between already described features such as function, position, and pronoun type. Multivariate analyses could point to hidden preferences and divergences. We expect this deeper approach allows us to explore whether the observed differences can be mapped onto language-specific structures or principles.

Another question not yet investigated is to what extent the use of lexical NP anaphors (e.g., *this situation*) can be exploited to derive features for annotation in a semi-automatic and less subjective way than manual annotation of pronominal anaphors. A further investigation will be on whether the alignments of the parallel corpus can be employed for this endeavor in making use of lexical NP translations to determine the abstract type of a pronominal anaphor in the original text.

References

1. Aduriz, I., Ceberio, K., Díaz, I.D.: Pronominal anaphora in Basque: annotation of a real corpus. In: DAARC 2009, pp. 99–104 (2009)
2. Asher, N.: Reference to Abstract Objects in Discourse. Kluwer Academic Publishers, Boston (1993)
3. Azuma, H.: A diachronic view of pronominal reference in English. In: Second Workshop on Anaphora Resolution, WAR II (2008)
4. Byron, D.K.: Resolving pronominal reference to abstract entities. In: ACL 2002, pp. 80–87 (2002)
5. Byron, D.K.: Annotation of pronouns and their antecedents: A comparison of two domains. Technical Report, University of Rochester (2003)
6. Dipper, S., Müller, M., Rieger, C., Seiss, M., Zinsmeister, H.: Discourse-deictic anaphora — comparison EN–GE, Annotation Guidelines (2011)
7. Dipper, S., Zinsmeister, H.: Discourse-deictic anaphora, Annotation Guidelines (2009)
8. Dipper, S., Zinsmeister, H.: Towards a standard for annotating abstract anaphora. In: LREC 2010 Workshop on Language Resources and Language Technology Standards, Valletta, Malta, pp. 54–59 (2010)
9. Dipper, S., Zinsmeister, H.: Annotating abstract anaphora. Language Resources and Evaluation, Online First (2011)
10. Hedberg, N., Gundel, J.K., Zacharski, R.: Directly and indirectly anaphoric demonstrative and personal pronouns in newspaper articles. In: DAARC 2007, pp. 31–36 (2007)
11. Koehn, P.: Europarl: A parallel corpus for statistical machine translation. In: MT Summit 2005 (2005)
12. Kučová, L., Hajičová, E.: Coreferential Relations in the Prague Dependency Treebank. In: DAARC 2004, pp. 97–102 (2004)
13. Müller, C.: Resolving *it*, *this*, and *that* in unrestricted multi-party dialog. In: ACL 2007, pp. 816–823 (2007)
14. Navarretta, C.: A contrastive analysis of the use of abstract anaphora. In: DAARC 2007, pp. 103–109 (2007)
15. Nedoluzhko, A., Mírovský, J., Ocelák, R., Pergler, J.: Extended coreferential relations and bridging anaphora in the Prague Dependency Treebank. In: DAARC 2009 (2009)
16. Passonneau, R.J.: Getting at discourse referents. In: Proceedings of ACL 1989 (1989)
17. Poesio, M., Artstein, R.: Anaphoric annotation in the ARRAU corpus. In: LREC (2008)
18. Pradhan, S., Ramshaw, L., Weischedel, R., MacBride, J., Micciulla, L.: Unrestricted coreference: Identifying entities and events in OntoNotes. In: IEEE-ICSC (2007)

19. Recasens, M.: Discourse deixis and coreference: Evidence from AnCora. In: Second Workshop on Anaphora Resolution (WAR II), pp. 73–82.
20. Schmid, H.: Probabilistic part-of-speech tagging using decision tree. In: International Conference on New Methods in Language Processing (1994)
21. Vieira, R., Salmon-Alt, S., Gasperin, C.: Coreference and anaphoric relations of demonstrative noun phrases in a multilingual corpus. In: DAARC 2002 (2002)
22. Webber, B.L.: A Formal Approach to Discourse. Garland (1979)
23. Webber, B.: Discourse deixis: Reference to discourse segments. In: ACL 1988, pp. 113–122 (1988)
24. Webber, B.L.: Structure and ostention in the interpretation of discourse deixis. Language and Cognitive Processes 6, 107–135 (1991)

Nominal Associative Anaphors – A Text-Based Analysis at the Semantics-Pragmatics Interface

Nicolas Kimm[1] and Christian Horn[2]

[1] Department of Computational Linguistics
[2] Department of General Linguistics, Institute for Language and Information, Heinrich-Heine University Düsseldorf, Universitätsstraße 1, 40225 Düsseldorf, Germany
{kimm,chorn}@phil.hhu.de

Abstract. This pilot study investigates the proportion of nominal associative anaphors (NAAs) in German texts. The research is motivated by a study that shows a high proportion of nonpossessive uses among two-place predicates (cf. [16]). Such cases could be explained by NAAs, in that their anchor may provide the required possessor argument. The question is for how many of the nonpossessive uses NAAs account for. Methodologically, we present a preliminary manual for the annotation of NAAs and apply it to a text collection of two text sorts. The results show that a large proportion of nonpossessive uses are NAAs. On closer examination not only do we find that the NAA occurrences reflect the distinction between one- and two-place predicates, but also that the distribution of NAAs exhibits differences with respect to their concept types (functional, relational, sortal, individual) proposed in the theory of concept types and determination (cf. [21]).

Keywords: Associative anaphors, concept types, CTD, text analysis, corpus linguistics.

1 Nominal Associative Anaphors

In this study, we analyze associative anaphors (AA) with nominal anchors. We call these nominal associative anaphors (NAA)[1] and define them by the following five conditions:

(i) The referent of the anaphoric NP is determined by associating it with a referent previously introduced in the discourse (this referent is often called "anchor").
(ii) The anchor is given by an NP.
(iii) The reference to the anchor is successful.
(iv) The anaphoric NP may be used with definite or indefinite determination.
(v) Both the anaphoric NP and the anchor do not co-refer.

[1] Our definition NAA is in line with [1,20,22,30]. We consider indefinite NPs as potential AAs since their reference might also be determined by an association with a referent previously introduced in the discourse (see also [27,28,20]).

I. Hendrickx et al. (Eds.): DAARC 2011, LNAI 7099, pp. 108–118, 2011.

Consider the following example from German.

(1) *Peter ging an* <u>*einem Haus*</u> *vorbei.* ***Das Dach*** *sah alt aus.*
'Peter passed <u>a house</u>. The roof looked old.'

The reference of the definite NP *das Dach* 'the roof' in (1) is determined by drawing on the anchor provided by the NP *einem Haus* 'a house'. Hence, the reference is successful and both NPs do not co-refer. In sum, all conditions for an NAA are fulfilled.

Nouns like *Dach* 'roof' constitute two-place predicates and are termed relational, as opposed to one-place noun predicates (e.g., 'tree')[2]. [16,15,17,24] show that two-place noun predicates occur more often with possessive constructions than one-place noun predicates.

The paper is structured as follows: In the next section, we summarize the theory of concept types and determination (CTD) and give an overview of theoretical approaches to AAs. Section 3 presents a preliminary manual for the annotation of NAAs and co-referential NPs. This forms the basis for our empirical study on German texts in section 4. Subsequently, the results are discussed and summarized.

2 Theoretical Background for the Analysis

2.1 The Theory of Concept Types and Determination

The theory of concept types and determination (CTD) is developed in ([21]). The principle claims of CTD relevant here are the following:

(i) Nouns differ with respect to their inherent referential properties; these properties are relationality [±R] and uniqueness [±U] The distinction between [+R] and [-R] reflects the traditional distinction between one- and two-place predicates. Two-place predicates require their possessor argument saturated for reference. For [+U] nouns, the number of potential referents is restricted to one. From the potential values of the two properties four basic noun types are derived: sortal concepts (SC; *tree*, *stone*) are [-R][-U], relational concepts (RC; *sister*, *branch*) [+R][-U], individual concepts (IC; *earth*, *God*) [-R][+U], and functional concepts (FC; *mother*, *head*) [+R][+U]. The distinction is claimed to hold cross-linguistically.

(ii) Different modes of determination (e.g., the definite article in singular, the indefinite article, demonstratives, possessive or nonpossessive uses) exhibit semantic predispositions for certain noun types; they are considered "natural" for their respective noun types. Uses of noun types with their natural determination are considered congruent, others as incongruent. Incongruent uses are seen as triggering type shifts of the respective noun type.

Typological investigations on the basis of unrelated languages ([10,21,25]) support the distinction. [16] present results of an empirical analysis of concept

[2] For the distinction between relational and non-relational nouns see [2,21,26,31].

types[3] in German texts. In their paper, they distinguish between the level of linguistic (in)congruency and the level of pragmatic (in)congruency. They only investigate the former which includes all kinds of linguistic determination. Pragmatic (in)congruency on the other hand is based on contextual clues and mutual knowledge. Both kinds together make up "overall" (in)congruency. NAAs contribute to pragmatic (in)congruency and are addressed in this paper. [16] group the modes of determination in German into operative determination classes[4]; among others the following two relevant here: DET_{+R} is used for modes of determination congruent with [+R] concepts (RC, FC), i.e., possessive uses expressed by possessive pronouns, genitive markers in left-adjacent or right-adjacent constructions, prepositions that express possessive relations, and predicative possession with verbs. DET_{-R} is used for modes of determination congruent with [-R] concepts (IC, SC), that is, nonpossessive uses. The results of the study for the [±R] distinction are summarized in table 1 (taken from [16]).

Table 1. [+R] concepts and [-R] concepts with $DET_{\pm R}$

	DET_{+R}	DET_{-R}	TOTAL
[+R] concepts	71 30.1%	165 69.9%	236 100.0%
[-R] concepts	17 4.9%	331 95.1%	348 100.0%

The results show that although [+R] concepts occur more often with DET_{+R} than [-R] concepts, they still occur with roughly two third DET_{-R}; that is, the linguistic congruency is rather low for [+R] concepts. The authors argue that this may be explained by economic communicative effort drawing on [12] maxim of quantity and mutual knowledge (cf. [6]). Accordingly, AAs could perfectly account for a proportion of these results (cf. [21]:300) and thus contribute to a higher overall congruency. This is tested for NAAs in this paper.

In the following we give a brief overview of approaches to associative anaphors.

2.2 Approaches to Associative Anaphors

AAs[5] are investigated in the literature with different foci. They are often analyzed with respect to the given-new distinction, i.e., the assumptions made by the speaker about the hearer's knowledge (see for example [5,28]). In other approaches, AAs are classified based on the semantic relation that holds between the anaphor and its respective anchor (cf. [11,18]; [9]). AAs also play a crucial role in theories of definiteness since in contrast to earlier assumptions they do

[3] In accordance with [16], we use 'concept' for the meaning variant of a noun.

[4] [21] classifies the modes of determination of English.

[5] The technical term varies from bridging (cf. [5]), indirect anaphor (cf. [4]), associative anaphor (cf. [13]; [20]), inferrables (cf. [1]) and contiguity anaphor (cf. [11]).

not constitute exceptional cases (cf. [8]). [14] analyzes definiteness in her theory of File Change Semantics. She points out the necessity of accommodation in order to "remedy the infelicity" (1982: 372) that the referent of the AA has not been directly referred to in the discourse up to that point. Within his theory of identifiability, Hawkins([13]: 123) considers AAs as a "textual appeal to general knowledge". [30] analyzes AAs with respect to cognitive aspects. She distinguishes between different types of activation of the ([3]:16) call on [29] qualia theory to explain AAs. They argue that the knowledge needed to determine the reference of the AA is said to be retrieved from the implicit lexical information and is used to coerce the missing (direct) antecedent.

In accordance with his (2011) assumptions of CTD, [20] argues that the head noun of a definite AA is interpreted as [+U][+R] irrespective of its lexical concept type. Lexically [+U][+R] concepts remain unchanged. If the concept is lexically [-U] (SC, RC), it undergoes a type shift triggered by the definite article. [-R] concepts are shifted accordingly. Since the concept is thus interpreted [+R], a possessor argument is needed to determine the reference of the AA. Given that the possessor argument is not explicitly realized in case of AAs, it is to be retrieved from the context.

In this paper, we do not consider such type shifts or other semantic operations. Our focus is on the analysis of the quantitative relation between the lexical concept types of nouns and their occurrences as NAAs, and we provide the results of an empirical pilot study of two text sorts. In the following we present preliminary guidelines for the annotation of NAAs.

3 Preliminary Guidelines for the Annotation of NAAs

This section outlines the guidelines[6] for the annotation of NAAs and co-referential NPs. We take the two as mutually exclusive in that two NPs cannot be co-referential and associatively anaphoric at the same time (condition (v)). To keep both cases apart is not only theoretically plausible but also allows us to identify sets of co-referential expressions. As illustrated in the examples below, two co-referential NPs may (2) or may not (3) be identical on the linguistic surface.

(2) *Peter ging an <u>einem Haus</u> vorbei.* ***Das Haus*** *sah alt aus.*
'Peter passed <u>a house</u>. **The house** looked old.'

(3) *Peter ging an* <u>einem Haus</u> *vorbei.* ***Die Hütte*** *sah alt aus.*
'Peter passed <u>a house</u>. **The shack** looked old.'

[6] On the one hand, the guidelines should be restrictive enough to provide consistency of annotation. On the other hand, however, they should be flexible enough to account for an annotator's individual interpretation.

Part A: The Definition of Markables

In accordance with our definition of NAAs, we define a markable[7] as a simple or a complex NP. Simple NPs consist only of a noun and a determiner[8]. Complex NPs are all other NPs; they might for instance include other NPs, pre- or postmodification of a different kind or genitive constructions. Each NP that is part of a complex NP also constitutes a possible markable, depending on the annotator's individual interpretation. Consider the following example.

(4) *Peter ging an* [*einem Haus*]$_{\text{NP}}$ *vorbei.* [[**Das Dach**]$_{\text{NP}}$ **mit** [**seinen roten Ziegeln**]$_{\text{NP}}$]$_{\text{NP}}$ *sah alt aus.*

'Peter passed [**a house**]$_{\text{NP}}$. [[**The roof**]$_{\text{NP}}$ **with** [**its red tiles**]$_{\text{NP}}$]$_{\text{NP}}$ looked old.'

The annotator chooses the markable for further annotation. In (4), annotator A might choose *Das Dach* 'The roof' whereas annotator B might include the adjunct and thus use *Das Dach mit seinen roten Ziegeln* 'The roof with its red tiles' as a markable.

Part B: The Annotation of NAAs and Co-referential NPs

Each markable defined in part A is analyzed whether it is co-referent with another markable or whether it is an NAA. Steps 1-5 are conducted for each markable defined.

Step 1: Identification of a Co-referential NP

The first step comprises the identification of the markable as co-referential since we expect this is easier to detect than NAAs. The annotator is to identify whether the NP in question exhibits identical reference with another NP. If the markable is marked as co-referential, the annotator proceeds with step 2, otherwise with step 3.

Step 2: Annotation of the Co-referential NP

The annotator assigns the markable co-referential and links it with one (of the) co-referential NPs. Afterwards, the annotator proceeds with the next markable in step 1.

Step 3: Identification of NAAs

In step 3, the annotator analyzes whether the referent of the markable in question requires an additional possessor argument for reference from the context. To do this, the annotator searches for a plausible possessor argument in the linguistic environment that helps to determine the referent. If this possessor argument is given by an NP, the markable is assigned NAA. As an example, the NP "*das Dach* [*mit seinen roten Ziegeln*]" 'the roof [with its red tiles]' in (4) triggers the

[7] We borrowed the term 'markable' from the annotation tool MMAX2 we used (cf. [23]).

[8] These comprise (in-)definite articles, possessive pronouns among others.

search for an appropriate possessor argument (cf. [13]), i.e., for an entity that may have a roof. In our example, the NP *einem Haus* 'a house' delivers the required possessor argument of the NAA. NAAs may form transitive chains of reference as for instance in part-of relations (e.g., *finger* < *hand* < *arm* < *body*).

If the annotator identifies the markable as an NAA, he proceeds with step 4; if not, he proceeds with step 5.

Step 4: Annotation of the Anchor of the NAA
In this step, the anchor of the NAA identified in step 3 is annotated. Afterwards, the annotator is to proceed with the next markable in step 1.

Step 5: Annotation of "Other" Cases
If an NP is neither classified as co-referential nor as an NAA, it is assigned "other" and the annotator proceeds with the next markable in step 1.[9]

4 The Case Study

4.1 Setting of the Study

The study presented here is based on the German text collection from [16]. The nouns in the texts are already annotated for their concept types and their grammatical uses. The text collection comprises both fictional (42.78%) and newspaper (57.22%) written texts from various websites with an overall size of 4405 tokens and 1059 noun tokens. The proportions of concept types are given by the following table taken from Horn et al [16].

Table 2. Distribution of concept types among the text sorts

Concept type	Fiction	%	Newspaper	%	Total	%
FC	72	27.1%	80	25.2%	152	26.0%
RC	43	16.2%	41	12.9%	84	14.4%
IC	18	6.8%	91	28.6%	109	18.7%
SC	133	50.0%	106	33.0%	239	40.9%
Total	266		318		584	

In line with their study, we only counted the first occurrence of a concept to ensure an equal distribution of the concepts. Hence, we analyze 584 concepts. The annotation of the NAAs is carried out by two native speakers of German following the manual. They are given only the running text without any annotations. The annotation procedure is conducted using the tool MMAX2 (cf. [23]). We expect that FCs and RCs occur more often as NAAs than ICs and SCs since this reflects their inherent relationality. In the next section, we present the results of our study.

[9] At the current stage, we only distinguish between co-reference and NAAs and subsume other types of AAs as well as extraphoric references in this category.

4.2 Analysis of the Data

We separately capture whether (i) an NP is annotated as NAA and (ii) which NP is marked as the respective anchor. For our analysis, we take into account each NP identified as an NAA by both annotators irrespectively of its assigned anchor. Annotator A in total identifies 285 NAAs (134 for the fictional texts and 151 for the newspaper texts). Annotator B in total identifies 258 NAAs (149 for the fictional texts and 109 for the newspaper texts). The number of NAAs in the intersection of the annotators is 144 for the entire text collection (75 for the fictional texts and 69 for the newspaper texts). The consideration of (i) allows us to investigate whether the high amount of linguistically incongruent DET_{-R} uses among [+R] concepts (69.9%, cf. table 1) can be explained by their occurrences in NAAs, i.e., part of the pragmatic congruency.

Table 3 illustrates the annotation of NAAs for each concept type for the entire text collection. The second and the third column give the DET_{+R} and DET_{-R} uses for each concept type, i.e., the proportions of possessive and nonpossessive uses for the concept types. Within CTD, DET_{+R} is seen as predisposed for FCs and RCs whereas DET_{-R} is considered linguistically congruent with ICs and SCs. The fourth column shows the respective use as an NAA, which is pragmatically congruent for FCs and RCs and pragmatically incongruent for ICs and SCs. The last two columns illustrate the respective proportion of (in-)congruent uses for each concept type.

Table 3. Concept types and NAAs in the entire text collection

Concept type	DET_{+R}	DET_{-R}	NAA (of DET_{+R} uses)	Overall congruency	Overall incongruency
FC	51 **33.6%**	101 66.4%	47 46.5%	98 **64.5%**	54 35.5%
RC	20 **23.8%**	64 76.2%	29 45.3%	49 **58.3%**	35 41.7%
IC	1 0.9%	108 **99.1%**	13 12.0%	95 **87.2%**	14 12.8%
SC	16 6.7%	223 **93.3%**	55 24.6%	168 **70.3%**	71 29.7%

The results for FCs and RCs show that the proportion of NAAs constitutes almost half of the DET_{-R} uses. As an effect, the proportion of congruent uses among FCs (33.6%) is doubled and amounts to 64.5%. For RCs, we observe similar effects; the proportion of congruent uses among RCs rises from 23.8% to 58.3%.

Whereas the occurrence as an NAA is seen as pragmatically congruent for FCs and RCs, it is expected to be pragmatically incongruent for ICs and SCs. The data show 12.0% NAA uses for ICs with DET_{-R}. This leads to a decrease of congruent uses by roughly 10%. The proportion for SCs is 24.6% and in combination with the 6.7% DET_{+R} uses, this amounts to 29.7% incongruent uses.

As expected, FCs and RCs show considerably higher proportions of NAAs than ICs and SCs in the entire text collection. Table 4 summarizes the overall congruency (including NAAs) for [+R] and [-R] concepts.

Table 4. (In-)Congruency for [±R] concepts

Concepts	Linguistic congruency	Linguistic incon-gruency	Overall congru-ency	Overall incongruency	Total
[+R]	71	165	147	89	236
	30.1%	69.9%	**62.3%**	37.7%	100.0%
[-R]	331	17	263	85	348
	95.1%	4.9%	**75.6%**	24.4%	100.0%

For [+R] concepts, the proportion of linguistically congruent uses is roughly one third. This proportion of overall congruent uses is considerably increased by taking into account NAAs. On the other hand, the proportion of congruent uses for [-R] decreases from 95.1% to 75.6%.

We now sum up the results for NAAs among nonpossessive uses:

1. Although we only consider first occurrences, we find a large proportion of NAAs (29%). One might expect even higher proportions for subsequent mentions.
2. Among associative anaphors, we only considered those with nominal anchors. One might expect even higher proportions for all kinds of AAs.
3. The proportions of NAAs are considerably higher for two-place predicates than for one-place predicates.
4. The proportions of NAAs for FCs and RCs are equally distributed with roughly 45%.
5. The proportion of NAAs for SCs is twice the proportion for ICs.

4.3 Interpretation of the Results

The high proportions of uses with NAAs for [+R] concepts support the distinction between the [±R] concept types. Whereas the consideration of linguistically congruent uses only shows roughly 30%, the integration of NAAs increases their overall congruent proportions to almost two-thirds. At the same time, the proportions for SCs and ICs remain relatively low which is in line with their semantic predispositions. In other words, the semantic predispositions of the concept types are not only reflected on the linguistic surface but also at the pragmatic level. The results show that both factors equally contribute to overall congruency.

4.4 Critical Discussion of the Study

Which factors limit the generalizability of our pilot study? First, although we developed a systematic manual for the annotation of NAAs, it is still preliminary. The markables defined differed between the annotators to a large extent.

We dealt with this problem by only taking into account the intersection of the annotations. As a consequence, we aim at a refinement of part A in the manual to increase the proportion of this intersection. We consider this refinement a prerequisite for the measurement of inter-annotator-agreement. Second, the annotation was conducted by two annotators; additional annotators will provide more generalizable results. Third, a larger size of the text collection and a greater choice of text sorts would be desirable for future studies.

5 Conclusion

The paper investigates whether nominal associative anaphors contribute to the high proportion of nonpossessive uses of two-place concepts. The results show that in fact NAAs account for a large proportion of such uses. With respect to the concept type distinction, the proportion of NAAs shows the following distribution: FCs, RCs > SCs > ICs; corresponding to [+R] > [-R], respectively. The proportion of NAAs for FCs and RCs is considerably higher than for SCs, and the proportion for the latter is considerably higher than for ICs. The overall congruency of concept types clearly benefits from the consideration of NAAs. On the other hand, NAAs provide further evidence for the distinction of one- and two-place predicates.

Acknowledgements. The research for this paper was supported by the German Science Foundation (DFG), grant FOR 600, Research Unit "Functional Concepts and Frames", project A5 "Automatic classification of concept types" (http://www.phil-fak.uni-duesseldorf.de/fff/). We would like to thank the project leaders Sebastian Löbner and James Kilbury, and we express our gratitude for helpful discussions and comments to Doris Gerland, Anja Latrouite and especially to our fellow annotators Elisabeth Morgner and Jessica Nieder.

References

1. Ariel, M.: Accessing NP Antecedents. Routledge, London (1990)
2. Behagel, O.: Deutsche Syntax. Eine geschichtliche Darstellung. Bd. I: Die Wortklassen und Wortformen. A. Nomen. Pronomen. Carl Winter's Universitaetsbuchhandlung, Heidelberg (1923)
3. Bos, J., Buitelaar, P., Mineur, A.: Bridging as Coercive Accommodation. In: Klein, E., Manandhar, S., Nutt, W., Siekman, J. (eds.) Working Notes of CLNLP 1995, pp. 1–16. South Queensferry, Scotland (1995)
4. Chafe, W.: Givenness, Contrastiveness, Definiteness, Subjects, Topics, and Point of View. In: Li, C.N. (ed.) Subject and Topic, pp. 25–55. Academic Press, New York (1976)
5. Clark, H.H.: Bridging. In: Schank, R.C., Nash-Webber, B.L. (eds.) Theoretical Issues in Natural Language Processing, pp. 169–174. ACM Press, New York (1975)
6. Clark, H.H., Marshall, C.R.: Definite reference and mutual knowledge. In: Joshi, A.K., Webber, B., Sag, I. (eds.) Elements of Discourse Understanding, pp. 10–63. Cambridge University Press, Cambridge (1981)

7. Erkü, F., Gundel, J.K.: The pragmatics of indirect anaphors. In: Verschueren, J., Bertuccelli-Papi, M. (eds.) The Pragmatic Perspective: Selected Papers from the 1985 International Pragmatics Conference, pp. 533–545. John Benjamins, Amsterdam (1987)
8. Fraurud, K.: Definiteness and the processing of NP's in natural discourse. J. Semantics 7, 395–433 (1990)
9. Gardent, C., Manuelian, H., Kow, E.: Which bridges for bridging definite descriptions? In: 4th International Workshop on Linguistically Interpreted Corpora, Budapest, Hungary (2003)
10. Gerland, D., Horn, C.: Referential properties of nouns across languages. In: Kang, Y.-S., Yoon, J.-Y., Hong, J., Wu, J.-S., Rhee, S., Kim, K.-A., Choi, D.-H., Kim, K.-H., Kang, H.-K. (eds.) Universal Grammar and Individual Languages, SICoL 2010. University of Korea, Seoul (2010)
11. Greber, E.: Zur Neubestimmung von Kontiguitätsanaphern. Sprachwissenschaft 18, 361–405 (1993)
12. Grice, P.: Logic and Conversation. In: Cole, P., Morgan, J.L. (eds.) Syntax and Semantics, vol. 3, pp. 41–58 (1975)
13. Hawkins, J.: Definiteness and Indefiniteness. Croom Helm, London (1978)
14. Heim, I.: The semantics of definite and indefinite noun phrases. Dissertation. Schriftenreihe des Sonderforschungsbereichs 99, Linguistik, Nr. 73. Universität Konstanz, Konstanz (1982)
15. Horn, C., Kimm, N.: Conceptual noun types in a German fictional text. In: Gamerschlag, T., Gerland, D., Osswald, R., Petersen, W. (eds.) Concept Types and Frames, Applications in Language, Cognition, and Philosophy. Springer, Heidelberg (to appear)
16. Horn, C., Kimm, N., Gerland, D.: Empirical Evidence for Concept Types in German Texts. J. Semantics (submitted)
17. Jensen, P.A., Vikner, C.: The English prenominal genitive and lexical semantics. In: Kim, J.-Y., Lander, Y.A., Partee, B.H. (eds.) Possessives and Beyond: Semantics and Syntax, pp. 3–27. GLSA Publications, Amherst (2004)
18. Kleiber, G.: Associative Anaphora and Part-Whole Relationship: The Condition of Alienation and the Principle of Ontological Congruence. J. Pragmatics 31(3), 339–362 (1999)
19. Löbner, S.: Definites. J. Semantics 4, 279–326 (1985)
20. Löbner, S.: Definite Associative Anaphora. In: Botley, S. (ed.) Approaches to Discourse Anaphora, DAARC 1996, Lancaster (1998)
21. Löbner, S.: Conceptual Types and Determination. J. Semantics 28(3), 279–333 (2011)
22. Mitkov, R., Evans, R., Orasan, C., Barbu, C., Jones, L., Sotirova, V.: Coreference and anaphora: developing annotating tools, annotated resources and annotation strategies. In: DAARC 2000, Lancaster, UK, pp. 49–58 (2000)
23. Müller, C., Strube, M.: Multi-Level Annotation of Linguistic Data with MMAX2. In: Braun, S., Kohn, K., Mukherjee, J. (eds.) Corpus Technology and Language Pedagogy. New Resources, New Tools, New Methods. English Corpus Linguistics, vol. 3, pp. 197–214. Peter Lang, Frankfurt (2006)
24. Nissim, M.: Lexical Information and Choice of Determiners. In: Kim, J.-Y., Lander, Y.A., Partee, B.H. (eds.) Possessives and Beyond: Semantics and Syntax, pp. 133–152. GLSA Publications, Amherst (2004)
25. Ortmann, A., Handschuh, C.: Semantic factors of valence-changing processes with nouns: possession in the Mayan languages. In: DGfS-Meeting. Handout, Mainz (2004)

26. Partee, B.: Uniformity vs. versatility: the genitive, a case study. Appendix to Theo Janssen (1997): Compositionality. In: van Benthem, J., ter Meulen, A. (eds.) The Handbook of Logic and Language. Elsevier (1983/1997)
27. Poesio, M.: Associative descriptions and salience: a preliminary investigation. In: ACL Workshop on Anaphora, pp. 31–38. Budapest (2003)
28. Prince, E.: Toward a taxonomy of given-new information. In: Cole, P. (ed.) Radical Pragmatics, pp. 223–256. Academic Press, New York (1981)
29. Pustejovsky, J.: The Generative Lexicon. Computational Linguistics 17(4) (1991)
30. Schwarz, M.: Indirekte Anaphern in Texten. Studien zur domänengebundenen Referenz und Kohärenz im Deutschen. Niemeyer, Tübingen (2000)
31. Vikner, S., Jensen, P.A.: A semantic analysis of the English genitive. Interaction of Lexical and Formal Semantics. Studia Linguistica 56, 191–226 (2002)

Perspective in the Processing of the Chinese Reflexive *ziji*: ERP Evidence

Petra B. Schumacher, Walter Bisang, and Linlin Sun

Department of English and Linguistics,Johannes Gutenberg University Mainz, Jakob-Welder-Weg 18,55099 Mainz, Germany
{petra.schumacher,wbisang}@uni-mainz.de, linsun@students.uni-mainz.de

Abstract. We investigated the comprehension of the Chinese reflexive *ziji*, which is typically subject to long-distance binding. However, this preference can be overridden by verb semantics (some verbs require local binding) as well as by subtle feature combinations of intervening noun phrases (NPs) (e.g., $1^{st}/2^{nd}$ person pronouns block dependencies with more distant 3rd person antecedents). The processing of *ziji* was examined in sentences containing two verb types (local/self-oriented, distant/other-oriented) and three different intervening NPs (1st, 2nd, 3rd person). The event-related potential data revealed an early interaction of verb and intervener: other-oriented verbs showed more processing effort for 1st and 2nd person interveners (blocking), while self-oriented verbs showed a disadvantage for 2nd person (associated with directive speech acts). We argue that two distinct animacy hierarchies are the source for these early verb-specific patterns. The blocking effect showed an additional later effect independent of verb semantics.

Keywords: Reflexivity, Chinese, long-distance binding, blocking effect, animacy hierarchy, perspective, language comprehension, event-related brain potentials.

1 Introduction

Much research has focused on the resolution of the Mandarin Chinese reflexive *ziji*. This anaphoric element has first and foremost received extensive attention because it disrespects the classical binding account (i.e. binding of a reflexive with a local antecedent – cf.[3] et seq.), and thus led to analyses in terms of long-distance binding (e.g., [21]) and to analyses beyond syntax, which integrate aspects of semantics, pragmatics and discourse (cf. among others the Prominence Computing Algorithm [13], the pragmatics-based approach [11], and the logophoricity- and discourse-based approach [12]). In our approach, we will start from long-distance binding and the preference for the highest subject. As we will show, this preference can be overruled by verb-inherent properties, since the semantics of some verbs require a local antecedent, while others require a distant antecedent. In addition, a closer look at the interpretation of *ziji* reveals that it is subject to subtle restrictions, one of which has become known as the blocking

I. Hendrickx et al. (Eds.): DAARC 2011, LNAI 7099, pp. 119–131, 2011.

effect. In the present research, we wanted to investigate the referential resolution of *ziji* by recording event-related brain potentials (ERPs), and we examined the role of restrictions enforced by verb-inherent properties and the blocking effect.

This paper is structured as follows. In the next subsections, we first discuss the three aspects of *ziji* that we seek to disentangle in the present research: i) the preference for long-distance binding, ii) the blocking effect, with a focus on person features, iii) verb-specific constraints on binding. In section 2, we briefly review the literature on ERPs and reflexivity, and then present an ERP study on the processing of Chinese *ziji* in section 3. Section 4 closes with the general discussion of the data and their implications for linguistic theory.

1.1 Long-Distance Binding of *ziji*

In contrast to classical binding conditions, which state that a reflexive must be bound in its local domain (e.g., [3]), the monomorphemic Chinese reflexive *ziji* can undergo long-distance binding in many instances. In particular, it shows a strong orientation to refer to the subject or speaker of an utterance (for an overview see [12]). For example in (1), *ziji* can refer not only to the local antecedent *Lisi*, but also – and preferably – to the distant *Zhangsan*.

(1) Zhangsan$_i$ renwei Lisi$_j$ hen ziji$_{i/j}$.
Zhangsan think Lisi hate SELF
'Zhangsan thinks that Lisi hates himself/him.'

One account of this phenomenon has proposed that the perspective conveyed by an utterance is of central concern and that *ziji* is speaker-oriented ([12], based on [16], [23]), yielding a reformulation of (1) in direct discourse as in (1'):

(1') Zhangsan renwei: "Lisi hen wo"
Zhangsan think: Lisi hate I
'Zhangsan thinks: "Lisi hates me."'

1.2 Blocking Effect

Long-distance binding, however, can be blocked by intervening noun phrases (NPs) carrying phi-features distinct from those of the potential long-distance antecedent. For instance, if *Lisi* is replaced by the 1st person singular pronoun *wo*, the distant antecedent is no longer available (2). 1st and 2nd person NPs thus block long-distance binding with a 3rd person antecedent; likewise, a local plural NP blocks distant singular antecedent (but interestingly not the other way round) (cf. [12]).

(2) Zhangsan$_i$ renwei wo$_j$ hen ziji$_{*i/j}$.
Zhangsan think I hate SELF
'Zhangsan thinks that I hate myself.'

Within the perspective-based account [12], the blocking effect is attributed to conflicting perspectives of an internal speaker *(Zhangsan)* and an external speaker (*I*). The latter wins, reflecting the blocking effect.

(2') Zhangsan renwei: "wo hen wo"
Zhangsan think: I hate I
'Zhangsan thinks: "I hate me." '

1.3 Verb-Inherent Restriction

In addition, long-distance binding may be overruled (or enforced) by verb-specific properties, which require local (or distant) binding. Some verbs express actions that are typically performed on somebody else (so-called extroverted or other-oriented verbs – such as *hug, approach* (3)); others express actions that are performed on the agent him/herself (so-called introverted or self-oriented verbs – such as *self-examine* (4); cf. e.g., [9, 15, 23]). The former conform to long-distance binding principles (3); the latter, however, overrule *ziji's* preference for long-distance binding on the basis of verb-inherent semantic requirements (4).

(3) Zhangsan$_i$ rang Lisi$_j$ kaojin ziji$_{i/*j}$.
Zhangsan CAUSATIVE Lisi approach SELF
'Zhangsan asked Lisi to approach him.'

(4) Wangwu$_i$ rang Zhaoliu$_j$ fanxing ziji$_{*i/j}$.
Wangwu CAUSATIVE Zhaoliu (self-)examine SELF
'Wangwu asked Zhaoliu to (self-)examine himself.'

2 ERPs and Reflexivity

By now, the electrophysiology of language has generated a wealth of data on language processing, and in the following, we mainly focus on findings related to reflexivity. Reflexivity has first and foremost been used to assess morphosyntactic mismatches, where a feature mismatch between antecedent and anaphor has evoked a positive deflection starting around 600 ms after the onset of the reflexive (P600) [19]; for a recent overview of agreement related ERP effects see [18]. The contrast between locally and long-distance bound reflexives has been addressed in a few studies [1, 10, 17][1]. For English, agreement mismatches in sentences involving a locally bound reflexive ("The pilot's mechanics browbeat themselves/*himself.") and a non-locally bound reflexive ("The pilot's mechanics browbeat Paxton and themselves/himself.") registered a P600 for the mismatch in the local binding condition, as well as an early positivity for non-local binding [10]. A direct comparison between locally bound reflexives ("Three participants said that James had painted himself.") and non-locally bound reflexives ("Three participants said that James had painted both himself and Erin.") revealed an anterior negativity (300–450 ms) for non-local dependencies relative to local relations [1]. The different ERP signatures evoked by the reflexive may be associated

[1] For the review of the English investigations [1, 10], we use the term "non-local" binding relations to refer to reflexive-antecedent relations between two non-co-arguments (called "logophors" in both studies), because the long-distance dependency in Chinese may be qualitatively different from the non-coargument relations in English.

with distinct underlying mechanisms, i.e. the detection of mismatches and the establishment of referential dependencies. Utilizing verb semantics as an indicator of the binding domain in Chinese, the processing of *ziji* was investigated in three constellations - local binding (triggered by self-oriented verbs), long-distance binding (other-oriented verbs) and ambiguous binding (verbs allowing local and long-distance readings) [17] – and long-distance reference evoked a more pronounced positivity between 300-400 ms (here referred to as EarlyPos) and a subsequent P600.

Overall these data suggest that local and long-distance binding relations exert distinct computational demands. P600 has been associated with morphosyntactic violations, but also with discourse updating (e.g., when new referents are introduced [1, 22]). While referential processing has further shown to involve an earlier processing stage of linking with discourse representation, reflected by a negative potential between 300-500 ms after the onset of the anaphor (for an overview see [22]), more enhanced discourse linking costs for long-distance reflexives were only observed for English [1]. The other studies reported an earlier positivity [10, 17], which may have to do with task-specific restrictions associated with acceptability and referent identification tasks (vs. comprehension task in [1]) that may be directly linked to the detection of integration difficulties (cf. [18] for functionally dissociable mechanisms during agreement processing).

3 ERP Experiment

The present study sought to investigate the processing of *ziji* when its interpretation is constrained by verb-specific properties and the blocking effect. While previous research has already shown effects of verb semantics [17], we are interested in the interaction of verbal features and perspective. In particular, if the interpretation of *ziji* is primarily guided by perspective, the conflict evoked by competing perspectives (blocking effect) should engender processing demands. In addition, perspective may interact with verb-specific properties.

3.1 Methods and Materials

Participants. Twenty-three right-handed and monolingually raised native speakers of Mandarin Chinese (12 women; mean age: 24.1) participated in this study. All participants had normal or corrected-to-normal visual acuity and no history of neurological disorder by their own report. They were paid for their participation.

Materials. Thirty sets of critical sentences were constructed for other- and self-directed verbs each (illustrated in (5) and (6) below). Each set included three different NP instantiations, i.e. 1st (*wo)*, 2nd (*ni)*, 3rd person (name, e.g., *Lisi*). This amounted to 180 critical sentences, which were interspersed with 180 distractor sentences – representing different sentence structures and sentences with reflexives in other positions. Critical and filler items were presented in a pseudo-randomized order.

(5) other-directed verb (EV1/EV2/EV3): name+*rang*+*wo*/*ni*/name+EV+*ziji*
Zhangsan rang wo / ni / Lisi kaojin ziji
Zhangsan CAUSATIVE I / you / Lisi approach SELF
'Zhangsan asked me/you/Lisi to approach him.'

(6) self-directed verb (IV1/IV2/IV3): name + *rang* + *wo*/*ni*/name + IV + *ziji*
Wangwu rang wo / ni / Zhaoliu fanxing ziji
Wangwu CAUSATIVE I / you / Zhaoliu (self-)examine SELF
'Wangwu asked me/you/ Zhaoliu to examine myself/yourself/himself.'

Verbs were classified in a series of pretests. The first pretest was a forced-choice sentence completion, in which participants were presented with sentence fragments consisting of a proper name and a verb (*Zhangsan kaojin*_____, 'Zhangsan come close to _____.') and were asked to indicate whether this sentence could be completed with either *ziji* or a proper name like *Lisi*. 22 native speakers of Chinese filled out this questionnaire containing 100 sentence fragments. The results identified 60 verbs as other-directed and 40 as self-directed (i.e. requiring a proper name or a reflexive respectively). To determine how these verbs behaved with respect to local or long-distance binding (see e.g. the classification of [14]), a second pretest was designed containing sentences as in (5) and (6) with the structure "proper name *rang* ['causative verb'] proper name verb *ziji*". 28 participants were asked to perform two tasks. In the first part, they were asked to read a questionnaire consisting of 136 randomized sentences and indicate as quickly as possible to whom *ziji* referred. Out of the 60 other-directed verbs identified in the previous pretest, 49 were confirmed to be extroverted (by 95% of the participants). Among the 40 self-directed verbs, 32 were confirmed to be introverted (by 85% of the participants). Verbs that were clearly classified in this task were then selected as stimuli for the ERP study. In the second part of this pretest, we also wanted to assess the blocking effect arising from an intervening 1st person pronoun for other-directed verbs. Participants read 20 sentences each with either a proper name or 1st person pronoun preceding the other-directed verb as in (5) and were presented with an interpretation of *ziji* (e.g., "In this sentence, *ziji* tends to refer to 'me'."). Then they were asked to judge whether this interpretation was highly acceptable, relatively acceptable or unacceptable[2]. The data showed a long-distance preference in both cases, with a stronger preference in the proper name condition (82% of participants). This provided a first indication for verb semantics outranking blocking effects.

Procedure. Participants sat comfortably in front of a computer monitor and their task was to read the sentences for comprehension and respond to a referent identification task after each trial. This task assessed how participants interpreted *ziji* (i.e. they saw one of the referents on the screen – e.g. *Lisi* – and had to indicate whether this was the antecedent of *ziji* by pressing a 'yes' or 'no' button on a gamepad). Stimuli were presented visually in the center of the computer screen in yellow letters against a blue background. Each trial started

[2] Ten clearly unacceptable trials were also included in the questionnaire.

with the presentation of a fixation asterisk for 500 ms, before the sentence was presented in segments (as indicated by '+' in the schematic illustration of the examples above) for 550 ms, followed by an inter-stimulus interval of 150 ms. After the presentation of the last word of a sentence, the screen went blank for 1200 ms, followed by the referent identification task, which stayed on the screen until participants responded or for a maximum of 4000 ms.

Each experimental session was preceded by a brief practice session to familiarize the participants with the experimental modalities and the task requirements. The subsequent experimental session consisted of 360 pseudo-randomized sentences, distributed across eight blocks. The pauses between the blocks were individually determined by the participants.

The electroencephalogram (EEG) was recorded from 25 Ag/AgCl scalp electrodes mounted in an elastic cap, which conformed to the standard 10-20 system for electrode placement. The ground was placed at AFz, and the recordings were digitized at a rate of 250 Hz, referenced to the left mastoid online and rereferenced offline to linked mastoids. Horizontal and vertical eye movements were monitored by means of two sets of additional electrode pairs, placed at the outer cantus of each eye and above and below the participant's left eye, to control for ocular artifacts. Electrode impedances were kept below 4 KΩ.

Data Analysis. Repeated-measures analyses of variance (ANOVAs) of the behavioral data for the referent identification task were computed for mean accuracy rates and reaction times per condition. Incorrectly answered trials and time-outs (>4000 ms response time) were excluded from the reaction time analysis. Analyses included the factors Verb type (EV/IV) and NP2 type ($1^{st}/2^{nd}/3^{rd}$ person).

Grand-average ERPs were computed relative to the onset of *ziji* with the factors Verb type (EV/IV) and NP2 type ($1^{st}/2^{nd}/3^{rd}$ person). Prior to grand averaging, average ERPs were calculate per condition and participant. To exclude slow drifts that could lead to stimulus-independent differences, data were filtered offline with a bandpass filter (0.3–20 Hz). Automatic ($\pm 40\mu$V threshold for ocular electrodes) and manual artifact rejections were carried out. Trials that registered an incorrect or timed-out response in the behavioral task or that contained ocular or other artifacts were excluded from averaging. This amounted to the rejection of 3.45% of the critical trials. Statistical analyses are based on the mean amplitude value per condition in temporal windows determined by visual inspection. ANOVAs were performed with the factors Verb type and NP2 type, and the topographical factor Region-of-interest (ROI) with lateral and midline electrodes considered in separate analyses. The lateral ROI analysis included 4 levels: left anterior (F3/F7/FC1/FC5), right anterior (F4/F8/FC2/FC6), left posterior (CP1/CP5/P3/P7), right posterior (CP2/CP6/P4/P8).The midline ROI analysis included 3 levels: anterior (Fz/FCz), central (Cz/CPz), posterior (Pz/POz). The analysis was carried out in a hierarchical manner. The data were corrected using the Huynh-Feldt procedure in order to control for potential type I errors due to violations of sphericity. Statistical analyses are based on the mean amplitude value per condition in predetermined time-windows.

3.2 Results

Accuracy was coded according to verb semantics, i.e. the correct referent for other-directed verbs was the distant NP1 and for self-directed verbs the local NP2. The mean accuracy rates indicate that participants performed at ceiling level (see Table 1), and the analysis of the accuracy rates registered no reliable differences. The ANOVA for the reaction time measures revealed a main effect of Verb type ($F(1,22) = 7.40$, $p<.02$), which was reflected by longer reaction times to constructions with other-directed verbs (EV) over self-directed verbs (IV).

Table 1. Mean accuracy rates and mean reaction times for the behavioral task. Standard deviations are in parentheses.

Condition	Accuracy (in %)	Reaction time (in ms)
EV1	95.07 (0.07)	1535 (488)
EV2	96.37 (0.05)	1475 (524)
EV3	98.26 (0.03)	1509 (516)
IV1	97.53 (0.03)	1435 (487)
IV2	97.97 (0.04)	1449 (492)
IV3	97.10 (0.04)	1492 (487)

The ERP data revealed two positive deflections, the first one (EarlyPos) demonstrating an interaction of Verb type and NP2 and the second (P600) showing a main effect of NP2. Statistical analyses were performed in time windows between 320-420 ms and 800-1000 ms. Since the oscillations of the early positivity may well influence the region for the negativity with an onset latency around 400 ms, we refrained from computing a separate analysis for this time window.

Analyses in the 320-420 ms window registered main effects of Verb (lateral: $F(1,22) = 5.56$, $p<.03$; midline: $F(1,22) = 6.34$, $p<.02$) and NP2 (lateral: $F(2,44) = 5.14$, $p<.02$; midline: $F(2,44) = 6.39$, $p<.005$) and an interaction of Verb x NP2 (lateral: $F(2,44) = 5.67$, $p<.007$; midline: $F(2,44) = 5.75$, $p<.007$). Resolution of this interaction by Verb revealed significant effects of NP2 for both verb types (EV: lateral: $F(2,44) = 7.03$, $p<.003$; midline: $F(2,44) = 6.69$, $p<.003$; IV: lateral: $F(2,44) = 3.89$, $p<.05$; midline: $F(2,44) = 5.48$, $p<.008$). Subsequent pairwise comparisons registered a reliable effect for the conflict between verb type and the blocking effect for other-oriented verbs (EV), reflected in more pronounced early positive deflections for EV1 over EV3 and marginally EV2 over EV3, and no difference between EV1 and EV2 (see Table 2 for statistical details). For the self-directed verbs, the analysis registered an effect for IV2 over IV1 and IV2 over IV3, and no significant effect between IV1 and IV3 ($F<1$). These effects are illustrated in Figure 1.

The pattern observed in the 320-420 ms time window represents an interesting finding, since it shows early influences of both factors examined in the present study, and more crucially, it demonstrates that the perspective influences the processing of self- and other-directed events in discrete ways. Other-directed

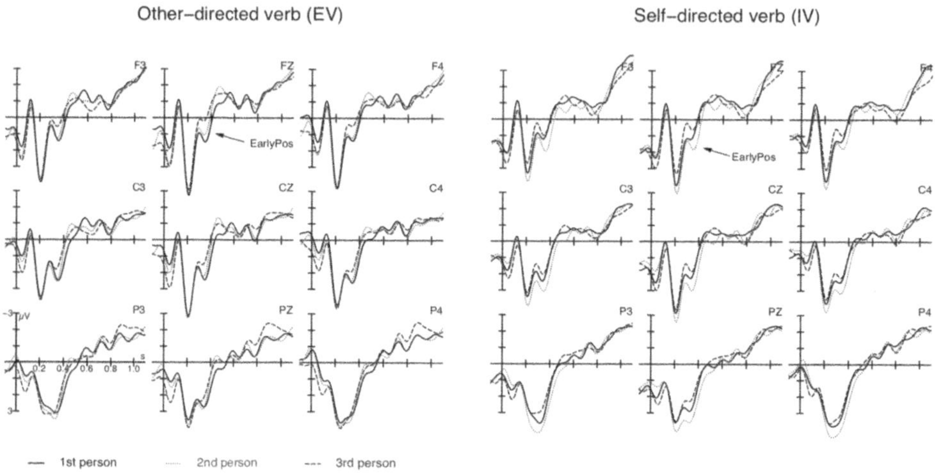

Fig. 1. Grand-average ERPs from 9 selected electrodes relative to the onset of *ziji* (at the vertical bar). The left panel shows the pattern for other-directed verbs (EV) and the right panel shows the ERPs for self-directed verbs (IV) for second NPs representing first (solid), second (dotted) or third person (dashed line). Negative voltage is plotted upward. The horizontal bar shows the time axis from 100 ms before *ziji* until 1100 ms after. EarlyPos shows distinct patterns of noun type intervention as a function of verb type.

Table 2. Pairwise comparisons for the ERP data in the 320-420 ms time window

Comparison	Lateral Regions			Midline Regions		
	df	F	p	df	F	p
EV1 - EV2	1,22	<1.7	-	1, 22	<3	-
EV1 - EV3	1,22	5.42	.02	1,22	9.25	.006
EV2 - EV3	1,22	<2.4	-	1, 22	3.19	.08
IV1 - IV2	1, 22	8.50	.008	1, 22	7.14	.01
IV1 - IV3	1,22	<1	-	1, 22	<1	-
IV2 - IV3	1,22	14.04	.001	1, 22	14.12	.001

verbs (EV) – which ideally refer to an external argument relative to the local predicate – engendered costs from blocking of 1st and 2nd person, indicating that blocking constraints (or rather constraints on perspective) conflict with verb-semantic constraints. 1st person interference further showed more reliable effects than 2nd person interference. In contrast, self-directed verbs (IV) – which challenge the long-distance orientation of *ziji* – showed enhanced processing costs only for an intervening 2nd person, suggesting that the speaker (1st person) has a more privileged role than the addressee.

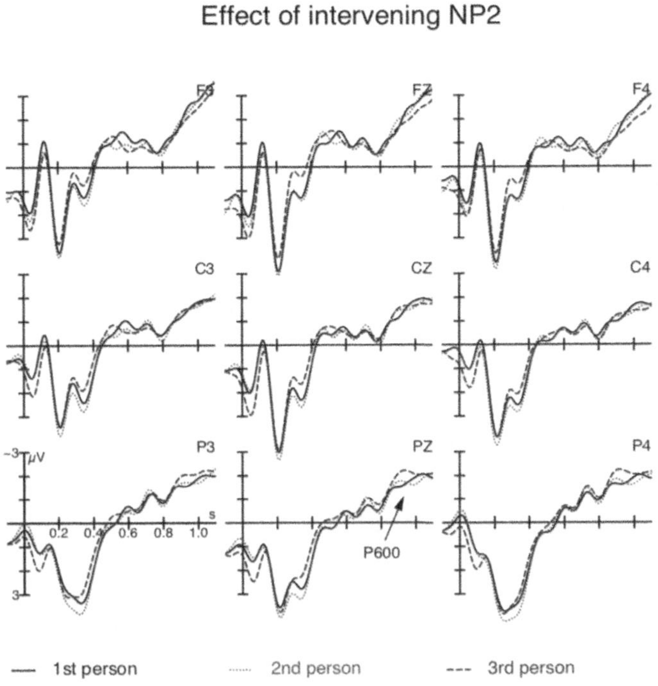

Fig. 2. Grand-average ERPs at 9 selected electrodes for intervening NPs representing first (solid), second (dotted) or third person (dashed line). The Figure reveals a late positivity effect for first and second person pronouns over posterior electrode sites. Negative voltage is plotted up; time ranges from -100 ms till 1100 ms relative to the onset of *ziji*.

The analysis between 800-1000 ms revealed a highly significant interaction of NP2 x ROI over lateral regions of interest ($F(6{,}132) = 5.11$, $p<.001$) as well as over midline regions ($F(4{,}88) = 7.84$, $p<.001$). Resolution of these interactions yielded effects over the posterior midline region ($F(2{,}44) = 3.42$, $p<.04$). Pairwise comparisons in this region showed reliable effects between $1^{st}/2^{nd}$ person and 3rd person, reflected by a more enhanced positivity (P600) for the blocking effect inducing NPs (1st vs. 3rd: $F(1{,}22) = 5.36$, $p<.03$; 2nd vs. 3rd: $F(1{,}22) = 6.05$, $p<.03$; 1st vs. 2nd: $F<1$). Figure 2 demonstrates this effect of phi-feature specification of NP2 averaged over both verb types. It should be noted that while the statistical analyses only registered a verb-type independent effect, a closer look at the figures suggests that this positivity for first and second person pronouns appears to be mainly driven by the other-directed verbs (cf. Figure 1).

Overall, the pattern suggests that blocking effects are reassessed at a relatively late point in time, and that the conflict between *ziji's* long-distance orientation and the intervening NPs exerts additional demands independent from verb-specific information.

4 General Discussion

The ERP data provide support for the influence of both verb-semantics and the blocking effect during online comprehension of *ziji*, and a close look at the data patterns reveals even more fine-grained effects associated with animacy hierarchies and speech acts. The data demonstrate that blocking by certain NP types affects two discrete processing stages and influences language comprehension as early as around 300 ms after the onset of *ziji*. During the early processing stage, NP-specific information further interacts with verb-specific information. Importantly, there is also an asymmetry between 1st and 2nd person as a function of verb semantics – a finding that has not received attention in the literature so far and which we discuss here with respect to distinct animacy hierarchies [4–6, 8, 24].

First, an early positivity registered verb-specific gradations. For other-directed verbs, the EarlyPos was most pronounced for 1st and 2nd person pronoun interference, suggesting that blocking via person features encumbers reference resolution that by virtue of the verbal properties has to bind with a non-local antecedent. It thus reflects a conflict between verb semantic requirements and the blocking effect. From the more general perspective of the animacy hierarchy [24] (see also Dixon [5]:85), it reflects the extended animacy hierarchy represented by 1, 2>3, as proposed by Croft ([4]:130,161),according to which speech-act participants (1st and 2nd person) tend to show different grammatical properties than 3rd persons (pronouns and nouns).

By contrast, for self-directed verbs – which should not be affected by blocking, since they require binding with the local antecedent anyway – the EarlyPos was most pronounced for 2nd person pronouns over the other two conditions. This corresponds more directly to another realization of the animacy hierarchy, proposed by Greenberg, i.e. 2 >3 >1 ([8]:44-45), which operates in the context of imperatives and hortatives ([4]:161). A look at the illocutionary-force status of IV2 vs. IV1 and IV3 reveals that sentences with a 2nd person antecedent express a directive speech act ("Zhangsan asked you to make a self-examination"), while sentences with a 1st or 3rd person antecedent yield an assertive speech act ("Zhangsan asked me/Lisi to make a self-examination."). The directive speech act of the 2nd person fits with the imperative function, which is responsible for the 2 >3 >1 hierarchy. The fact that 2nd person is higher than 1st and 3rd person with self-directed verbs can be accounted for under the assumption that the imperative-based version of the animacy hierarchy is stronger than the extended hierarchy. Even though such a ranking of the different versions of the animacy hierarchy has not been discussed in linguistic typology so far, the high dominance of imperatives and directives over other grammatical contexts is highly plausible if one keeps in mind that the imperative is the ultimate stronghold of nominative syntax. As pointed out by Dixon [6], there is no language, not even Dyirbal, in which imperatives show ergative syntax. The motivation for this type of ergative split has to do with the pragmatic prominence of the actor role in imperatives.

Crucially, the effect of differences in illocutionary-force types only shows up in the case of self-directed verbs. This is due to the fact that the illocutionary force of the embedded verb only matters if binding of *ziji* takes place within the scope of the embedded verb. Since the scope of the governing category includes the matrix verb in the case of other-oriented verbs and since the matrix verb is invariably in an assertive context, this type of construction follows the extended animacy hierarchy.

Why should these specific processing patterns of person features engender an early positivity? First, a few studies have demonstrated that the processing of person features takes precedence of number and gender features, supporting the early influence of NP2 (e.g., [2]). However, since the person features associated with NP2 in the present study interacted with verb type, a general explanation on the basis of processing person agreement cannot account for the ERP patterns. An early positivity (in conjunction with a subsequent P600) has also been observed in the analysis of garden-path sentences, where it has been proposed that it reflects the detection of integration difficulties [7] (see also [17]). In this vein, the current early positivities may be indicative of processing conflicts arising either from mere blocking (in the EV-case) or pragmatic demands arising from speech act demands and their association with different realizations of the animacy hierarchy (in the IV-case). Positivities have further been associated with constraint competition, and the early onset of the current positivity may thus reflect the predominance of semantic and pragmatic constraints in the processing of Chinese.

Second, the later positivity was only modulated by NP2 type, revealing a more pronounced positivity for 1st and 2nd person over 3rd person NP2. The visual inspection suggests that this effect is largely driven be the other-directed constructions. Accordingly, the positivity reflects considerations of well-formedness, since EV1 and EV2 engender a conflict between the verb-semantic need to select a distant antecedent and the person blocking effect. It thus converges with P600-findings from agreement mismatches in morphosyntax [19], but also semantics (i.e. gender stereotypes [20]). Clearly, the current effect occurs rather late, which may further be indicative of evaluatory processes associated with the referent identification task. Along these lines, the behavioral data also suggest that reflexive interpretation in constructions with other-directed verbs is more demanding, since the reaction times to the referent identification task were reliably longer. In the case of self-directed verbs, the effect of illocutionary force was resolved within the scope of the embedded verb itself, while the blocking effect with other-directed verbs operated over the scope of the matrix clause as a whole.

In sum, the current data reveal that verb semantics, perspective, speech act and animacy exert demands on the processing of *ziji* very early on – as reflected by the Early Positivity – supporting accounts that claim that semantic and pragmatic information play a prominent role in the resolution of the Chinese reflexive. In the case of other-directed verbs, the long-distance interpretation motivated by verbal semantics clashes with perspective, that is, the blocking effect triggered by $1^{st}/2^{nd}$ person. Perspective wins and induces a split, which harmonizes with the extended animacy hierarchy (1, 2 >3) as it applies in assertive speech acts (declarative illocutionary force). In the case of self-directed verbs, which favor local binding, perspective is irrelevant. What matters are differences concerning speech act/illocutionary force. Since NP2 in the 2nd person leads to an imperative interpretation, the animacy hierarchy associated with that speech act is selected (2 >3 >1).

Overall, the findings indicate that semantic and pragmatic cues must be incorporated into models of anaphora resolution and that speaker- and hearer-directed information may exert distinct computational demands (as suggested by the current speech act account). The idea that speech acts influence the processing of reflexives in Chinese further substantiates the claim that a principle trait of Chinese language processing is its pragmatic orientation.

References

1. Burkhardt, P.: The Syntax-Discourse Interface: Representing and Interpreting Dependency. John Benjamins, Amsterdam (2005)
2. Carminati, M.N.: Processing Reflexes of the Feature Hierarchy (Person >Number >Gender) and Implications for Linguistic Theory. Lingua 115, 259–285 (2005)
3. Chomsky, N.: Lectures on Government and Binding. Foris, Dordrecht (1981)
4. Croft, W.: Typology and Universals. Cambridge University Press, Cambridge (2003)
5. Dixon, R.M.W.: Ergativity. Language 55, 59–138 (1979)
6. Dixon, R.M.W.: Ergativity. Cambridge University Press, Cambridge (1994)
7. Friederici, A.D., Mecklinger, A., Spencer, K.M., Steinhauer, K., Donchin, E.: Syntactic Parsing Preferences and Their on-Line Revisions: A Spatio-Temporal Analysis of Event-Related Brain Potentials. Cognitive Brain Research 11, 305–323 (2001)
8. Greenberg, J.H.: Language Universals, With Special Reference to Feature Hierarchies. Mouton, The Hague (1966)
9. Haiman, J.: Natural Syntax. Cambridge University Press, Cambridge (1985)
10. Harris, T., Wexler, K., Holcomb, P.J.: An Electrophysiological Investigation of Binding and Coreference. Brain and Language 75, 313–346 (2000)
11. Huang, Y.: The Syntax and Pragmatics of Anaphora. Cambridge University Press, Cambridge (1994)
12. Huang, C.T.J., Liu, C.S.L.: Logophoricity, Attitudes, and Ziji At the Interface. In: Cole, P., Hermon, G., Huang, C.T.J. (eds.) Long-Distance Reflexives, pp. 141–196. Academic Press, San Diego (2001)
13. Hu, J., Pan, H.: NP Prominence and the Chinese Reflexive *Ziji*. Modern Linguistics 4, 46–60 (2002)
14. Jin, Z.-H.: Verb Restraint Function to Ziji Long-Distance Binding. Chinese Language Learning 4, 9–12 (2003)
15. König, E., Vezzosi, L.: The Role of Predicate Meaning in the Development of Reflexivity. In: Bisang, W., Himmelmann, N., Wiemer, B. (eds.) What Makes Grammaticalization?: A Look From Its Fringes and Its Components, pp. 213–244. Mouton de Gruyter, Berlin (2004)
16. Kuno, S.: Functional Sentence Perspective: A Case Study From Japanese and English. Linguistic Inquiry 3, 269–320 (1972)

17. Li, X.Q., Zhou, X.L.: Who is Ziji? ERP Responses to the Chinese Reflexive Pronoun During Sentence Comprehension. Brain Research 1331, 96–104 (2010)
18. Molinaro, N., Barber, H.A., Carreiras, M.: Grammatical Agreement Processing in Reading: ERP Findings and Future Directions. Cortex 47, 908–930 (2011)
19. Osterhout, L., Mobley, L.A.: Event-Related Brain Potentials Elicited By Failure to Agree. Journal of Memory and Language 34, 739–773 (1995)
20. Osterhout, L., Bersick, M., McLaughlin, J.: Brain Potentials Reflect Violations of Gender Stereotypes. Memory and Cognition 25, 273–285 (1997)
21. Reuland, E.: Anaphors, Logophors and Binding. In: Cole, P., Hermon, G., Huang, C.T.J. (eds.) Long-Distance Reflexives, pp. 343–370. Academic Press, San Diego (2001)
22. Schumacher, P.B.: Definiteness Marking Shows Late Effects During Discourse Processing: Evidence From ERPs. In: Lalitha Devi, S., Branco, A., Mitkov, R. (eds.) DAARC 2009. LNCS (LNAI), vol. 5847, pp. 91–106. Springer, Heidelberg (2009)
23. Sells, P.: Aspects of Logophoricity. Linguistic Inquiry 18, 445–479 (1987)
24. Silverstein, M.: Hierarchy of Features and Ergativity. In: Dixon, R.M.W. (ed.) Grammatical Categories in Australian Languages, pp. 112–171. Australian National Institute of Aboriginal Studies, Canberra (1976)

Effects of Reference Form on Frequency of Mentionand Rate of Pronominalization

Sofiana Iulia Chiriacescu

Institute of Linguistics, University of Stuttgart
Keplerstr. 17, 70174 Stuttgart, Germany
Sofiana.Chiriacescu@ling.uni-stuttgart.de

Abstract. Comprehension studies find that a referent, which is expected to be picked up more often in the subsequent discourse, is also more prone to be realized by means of a more reduced type of referring expression (typically a pronoun), compared to a referent that is less expected to be re-mentioned ([1,2]). This paper evaluates this assumption and shows that it does not always hold. Specifically, I take a closer look at the effects of choice of indefinite referential form in English and German on likelihood of subsequent mention and likelihood of subsequent pronominalization. The results of two experimental studies suggest that these two factors, which pertain to the upcoming discourse, should be separated, as they point into different directions. While the type of referring expression used to introduce a referent impacts its frequency of subsequent mention, the rate of pronominalization seems to be dependent on other characteristics of the referent.

Keywords: German, English, reference, pronominalization, topic, psycholinguistics.

1 Introduction

One of the fundamental questions underlying theories of language production and comprehension concerns referent tracking, including what referents are preferred to be picked up in the subsequent discourse and what types of referring expressions are used for this purpose. Psycholinguistic studies concerned with some of these aspects showed that different factors play a role in determining the referent that will be more readily and more often talked about in the subsequent discourse ([8,2,4]). Syntactic or semantic prominence, parallel constructions, or particular coherence relations can be enumerated as examples of such factors that impact the likelihood of subsequent mention. The high expectancy of subsequent mention of a referent correlates with the tendency of that referent to be realized by means of a more reduced type of referring expression (typically a pronoun). The association between likelihood of subsequent mention and rate of pronominalization have been considered epiphenomena of a referent's high accessibility or activation level ([2,1]).

This paper presents and discusses two studies that investigate the effects of choice of indefinite referential form in English and German on likelihood of

I. Hendrickx et al. (Eds.): DAARC 2011, LNAI 7099, pp. 132–143, 2011.

subsequent mention and likelihood of subsequent pronominalization. The two constructions that are of special interest for the present investigation are given in (1) for English, and (2) for German, respectively.

(1) He put on **this 31 cent** stamp on the envelope, and realized only later that it was worth a fortune because it was unperforated. ([13]: 88)

(2) In unserer Stadt gibt's **so'nen Mann**, er ist nicht irgendeiner, nein, er ist unser neuer Bürgermeister, er sieht wie ein Vogelstrauß, [...][1].
'In our city there is **so-a man**, he is not anyone, no, he is our new mayor, he looks like an ostrich [...].'

The general picture about English is that it developed the indefinite determiner *this* for referents that are (going to be) more accessible, activated or topical in the subsequent discourse ([14,13]). This is mirrored by the high referential continuity of such referents. German has not only one, but two indefinite demonstratives that correspond to English *this*, namely the indefinite *dieser* and *so'n* ([15]). In this paper, I focus on indefinite *so'n*, which is formed from the demonstrative for properties *so* and the reduced form of the simple indefinite article *'n*. I test whether German *so'n*, as in (2), has similar discourse effects to English indefinite *this*. If the assumption about the higher accessibility of these referents is true, and in light of previous findings (see [7], among others), then passages should more often continue talking about referents preceded by *this* or *so'n* as compared to a simple indefinite noun phrase, and perhaps such re-mentions should be pronominalized more often as well.

The results of the sentence-completion studies presented in this paper only partially confirm this assumption. Participants prefer to continue talking about referents, whenever these referents are preceded by English *this* or German *so'n*. However, the prediction about a higher rate of pronominalization for the marked referents is not met, as referents headed by *this* and *so'n* tend to be picked up by lexically more elaborated types of noun phrases. This latter finding underlines the necessity to dissociate between likelihood of pronominalization and referential persistence (confirmation of more recent studies conducted by [11,6,10]). Overall, the findings of this paper cast new light on the notions of accessibility, activation or prominence operationalized in terms of referential persistence and likelihood of pronominalization as equally weighted factors. The structure of this paper is as follows. In Section 2 I sketch out the main observations made with respect to the discourse behaviour of indefinite noun phrases headed by *this* in English and *so'n* in German. Section 3 presents and discusses two sentence-completion experiments that investigate the discourse effects of indefinite noun phrases preceded by indefinite *this* in English and *so'n* in German. The findings made in this paper and directions for further research are discussed in the last section.

[1] `http://www.mzee.com/forum/archive/index.php/t-100000620.html` [viewed: May 2010]

2 English Indefinite *this* and German *so'n*

Depending on the context of use, the English determiner *this* can be either definite or indefinite ([14,13], among others). This paper focuses on the latter use of *this*, which occurs in colloquial, mainly conversational English. In (3), only the first two instances of *this* (i.e. *this guy, this story*) are indefinite, whereas the third *this* in *Look at this book* is an instantiation of the stressed, deictic, definite use of *this*.

(3) Well, I met **this guy** last night that is a year older than me at a pool party in San Francisco (Well I live in LA but I was visiting family) and he told me **this** story about dolphins. Look at this book he gave me [...].[2] (emphasis mine)

An analysis of English indefinite *this* is interesting for several reasons. First, as opposed to the proximal demonstrative *this*, indefinite *this* does not bear main stress and serves to introduce hearer-new and discourse-new referents in the discourse. Second, indefinite noun phrases headed by *this* tend to have referential readings (i.e. take wide scope with respect to different operators, are epistemically specific, etc.). And third, besides being semantically specific, indefinites headed by *this* serve as a signal to the hearer that more information about the referent in question will follow ([14,16,7]), thus, being (discourse-) pragmatically specific as well[3].

The discourse effects of indefinite *this* as opposed to those of the simple indefinite article a(n) have been tested in few studies. [16], for example, extended an experimental investigation initially conducted by [14]. They recorded eight- and nine-year-old children telling one another stories and found out that children chose to use *this* for referents that they would continue talking about and a(n) for referents that they would rather not pick up in the following discourse. More exactly, the average was 5.32 times for concepts introduced by *this* and 0.68 times when concepts were introduced by (an).

In a more ample investigation, [7] explained the use of *this* over a(n) in terms of different degrees of accessibility of a referent on the hearer's side. They assume that accessible referents are: (i) mentioned more often in the subsequent discourse (this metric corresponds to [8] textual method referential persistence), are (ii) mentioned earlier in the subsequent discourse, and are (iii) taken up with more attenuated types of referring expressions (i.e. pronouns) in the subsequent discourse. Less accessible referents are predicted to show low values for all three factors. In an auditory sentence-continuation task participants were asked to continue narratives within 30 seconds after hearing the last sentence of each target narrative. The last sentence of each target consisted of a noun phrase which

[2] `http://www.ihav.net/vb/introductions/i-met-him-last-night-358268.html` [viewed: March 2009]

[3] This paper deals only with the discourse effects of *this*-referents, but see [4,5] and [15] for a more ample presentation of the characteristics of *so'n*.

was either headed by indefinite *this* or by the simple indefinite article a(n). Their findings confirm their predictions, as referents headed by *this*, as opposed to referents headed by the simple indefinite article are mentioned more often (i.e. 4.05 times for *this*-indefinites vs. 2.76 times for *a-indefinites)* in the immediately following sentence after being introduced in the discourse. Moreover, indefinites headed by *this*, as opposed to the *a-indefinites*, were show to need less lexical material (e.g. zero anaphors and pronouns) to be picked up for the first time in the subsequent discourse. Based on these results, [7] consider that entities introduced by indefinite *this*, as opposed to a(n), are "more accessible (i.e. more focussed, foregrounded or topical) from listeners' mental representations" and therefore more easily retrievable from memory.

More recent studies showed that other languages developed similar means to introduce referents that play a preferential role in the subsequent discourse ([9,12]). The use of the German determiner *so'n* in 'out-of-the-blue' contexts (i.e. in contexts in which the noun phrase preceded by *so'n* lacks an antecedent or an accompanying pointing gesture) comes close to that of English indefinite *this*. First, similar to English indefinite *this*, indefinite noun phrases headed by *so'n* are used to introduce new referents in the discourse and show a preference for referential readings. Second, *so'n* indefinites are more prone to be picked up in the following discourse compared to noun phrases headed by the simple indefinite article [4,5,15].

In the following section, I test the discourse effects of indefinite noun phrases headed by *so'n* in German and compare the results of this study with a parallel experiment, which tested the impact of English indefinite *this* on the subsequent discourse along the same lines. The current investigations differ from previous experimental studies (e.g. [14], or [7]), as the referents headed by the two indefinite markers are characterized by the semantic feature [+human] (vs. [7]) and appear in direct object position. I coded for two factors: (i) whether referents introduced by means of indefinite *so'n* in German are more frequently re-mentioned in the subsequent discourse compared to their simple indefinite counterparts, and (ii) whether the preferred type of anaphoric expression used to pick up these referents for the first time in a matrix clause is less elaborate than the type of anaphoric expression used to re-mention the referents associated with simple indefinite noun phrases. In light of previous findings on the accessibility of referents in general and on the discourse effects of English indefinite *this* in particular, the predictions with respect to the two factors can be formulated as follows:

(4) *Prediction* 1 (*referential persistence*)
Referents headed by indefinite *this* in English and *so'n* in German will show a higher frequency of subsequent re-mention compared to their simple indefinite counterparts.

(5) *Prediction* 2 (*first anaphoric expression*)
Referents headed by indefinite *this* in English and *so'n* in German will show a higher likelihood of pronominalization compared to their simple indefinite counterparts.

3 The Sentence-Completion Experiments

To evaluate the discourse effects of indefinite noun phrases preceded by indefinite *this* in English and *so'n* in German, two similar experiments were constructed. I will refer to the experiment testing the English data as Exp1 and to the experiment testing the German data as Exp2. I coded for two parameters of the referents in question, namely: (i) referential persistence (i.e. the frequency of mention of a referent in the subsequent discourse) and (ii) the type of co-referential expression used to refer back for the first time to the referent introduced by the target referent[4]. The referents associated with both types of indefinite noun phrases are predicted to be more referentially continuous in the subsequent discourse and to require less lexical material when being picked up for the first time in the subsequent discourse. Furthermore, if the presence of German *so'n* has comparable discourse effects to those of the English indefinite determiner *this*, then the results of the two experiments are expected to be similar.

3.1 Method, Procedure and Data Analysis

The methodology used was an open-ended sentence continuation task with three test items (see [7], or [6] for a detailed description of similar tasks). As both English *this* and German *so'n* are more frequently used in direct object position, all target referents were constructed in this syntactic position. Moreover, the given mini-discourses were kept in a colloquial tone, because both English indefinite *this* and German *so'n* occur in conversational language. Participants (n=20 for Exp1 and n=20 for Exp2) read 3 mini-discourses and were instructed to add 5 logical and natural-sounding sentence continuations to each of them. I manipulated the morphological realization of the target referents, which resulted in two conditions for each experiment, i.e. one in which the direct object realized as an indefinite unmodified noun phrase is headed by *this*, in Exp1, and by *so'n* in Exp2, (see the left columns of Tables 1 and 2), and one in which the same direct object is headed by the simple indefinite article (*an*) in English and *ein(e)* in German (see the right columns of Tables 1 and 2). This was a between-subjects manipulation, which means that a participant either completed a version of the study where all three targets contained simple indefinites, or a version where all three targets contained *this*-indefinites in Exp1 or *so'n*-indefinites in Exp2, respectively.

The fact that each test item consisted of two or three sentences made it difficult to control and eventually code every aspect of the mini-discourses, but it

[4] Independently of these two factors, in [5] I also investigated the topic shift potential of referents headed by *this* in English and *so'n* in German (i.e. the potential of referents mentioned in non-subject positions to become subjects in a subsequent matrix clause). I will not discuss the findings of this metric in this paper, but note that under controlled situations, referents realized as direct objects and which were preceded by indefinite *this* and *so'n* make better candidates to shift the topic of the current discourse (i.e. to become subjects), compared to similar referents preceded by the simple indefinite article.

Table 1. Sample experimental item from Experiment 1 on English

this-condition	*a(n)-condition*
Yesterday evening was so warm that James$_1$ decided to hang out with friends at the local coffee shop. On his$_1$ way downtown, he$_1$ saw **this kid$_2$** coming down the street.	Yesterday evening was so warm that James$_1$ decided to hang out with friends at the local coffee shop. On his$_1$ way downtown, he$_1$ saw **a kid$_2$** coming down the street.

Table 2. Sample experimental item from Experiment 2 on German

so'n-condition	*ein(e)*-condition
Draußen war es warm. Peter$_1$ hiel es zu Hause einfach nicht mehr aus und ging in die Stadt. Auf dem Weg dorthin sah er$_1$ **so'nen Jungen$_2$** einen Laden betreten. 'It was warm outside. Peter$_1$ didn't endure staying home any longer and went downtown. On the way there he$_1$ saw **so'nen boy$_2$** entering a store.'	Draußen war es warm. Peter$_1$ hielt es zu Hause einfach nicht mehr aus und ging in die Stadt. Auf dem Weg dorthin sah er$_1$ **einen Jungen$_2$** einen Laden betreten. 'It was warm outside. Peter$_1$ didn't endure staying home any longer and went downtown. On the way there he$_1$ saw **a boy$_2$** entering a store.'

provided the greater advantage of creating a natural discourse and of combining comprehension and production processes. For each continuation story provided by a participant, I coded the first five main clauses (and any associated subordinate clause). The grammatical subject of the first and second sentence (e.g. *Peter* in the test item in Table 2) received subscript 1. Subscript 2 was used for the indefinite noun phrase whose form was manipulated in the critical sentence (e.g. *so'nen Jungen* ('so'nen boy') in Table 2).

The ***referential persistence*** of each referent introduced in the mini-discourse was explored. Each occurrence of the same referent in every continuation sentence was added up to a sum representing the referential persistence of that referent (i.e. cumulative value). Comparing the values for referential persistence of all referents, we gain insights into the exact stage in the discourse at which the critical referent has a greater cumulative persistence value than the initial subject referent.

The second aspect coded was the ***type of referring expression*** used to pick up the target referent for the first time in the upcoming discourse. For each continuation, I investigated whether participants used a zero anaphor, a pronoun, a definite unmodified noun phrase, or a definite modified noun phrase as the first co-referential expression in a matrix clause. I did not consider following anaphoric expressions referring to the same target referent after its first mention in the subsequent discourse.

3.2 Results

Participants provided 20 responses for each of the two experiments (Exp1 and Exp2). Overall, the results underline the preferential discourse status of indefinite noun phrases headed by English *this* and German *so'n* compared to that of indefinite noun phrases headed by the simple indefinite article. In the following, I discuss the findings from both experiments in more detail.

Referential Persistence. Several observations can be made with respect to the findings of the referential persistence of the referents in Exp1 and Exp2. Figure 1 summarizes the mean values for referential persistence of the referents of test items 1-3 (TI1-TI3) in Exp1 on English. Prediction 1 in (4) was confirmed for the English data, as referents associated with *this*-indefinites were more frequently picked up in the subsequent discourse compared to the referents of the a(*n*)-indefinites.

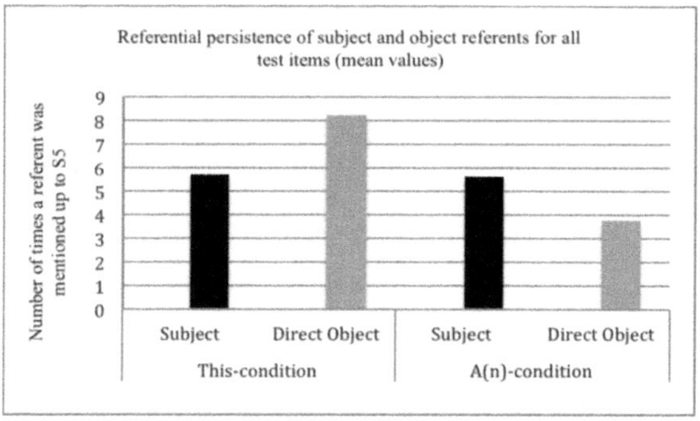

Fig. 1. Referential persistence of all referents introduced in the initial mini-discourses in all test items up to S5 (average per continuation stories) in Experiment 1

Similar to the findings of Exp1, the referents associated with indefinite noun phrases preceded by German *so'n* behave differently with respect to their referential persistence compared to simple indefinite noun phrases. Specifically, for the *so'n*-condition, we notice a high likelihood for the direct object referents to be picked up frequently in the following discourse. In contrast, in the *ein(e)*-condition, direct object referents are mentioned less often in the subsequent discourse. The results reported so far confirm the Prediction 1 in (4), as the marked referents display a higher rate of subsequent mention compared to the referents preceded by the simple indefinite article.

The First Anaphoric Expression. The second factor investigated was the type of referring expression used to refer back to the target items for the first time in the continuation sentences provided by the participants. Tables 3 and 4 display the absolute and mean values of this characteristic for the target referents in Exp1 (*this* vs. a(*n*) referents) and Tables 5 and 6 display the same

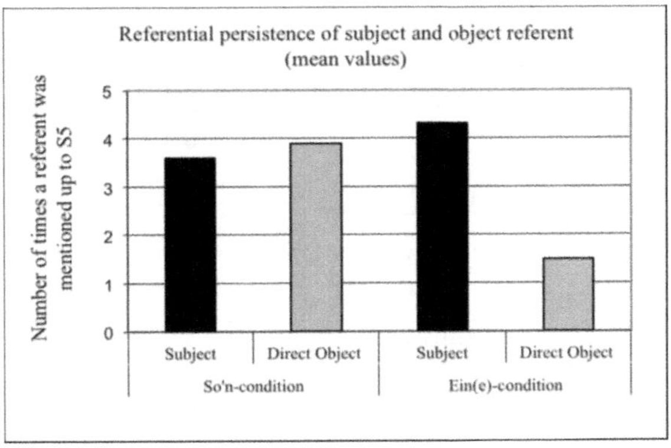

Fig. 2. Referential persistence of all referents introduced in the initial mini-discourses in all test items up to S5 (average per continuation stories) in Experiment 2.

values for the target referents in Exp2 (*so'n* vs. *ein(e)*). Recall that ten different participants provided continuations for each of the three target items per condition, resulting in 30 continuations for the this-condition, another 30 for the a(*n*)-condition, 30 continuations for the *so'n*-condition and 30 continuations for the *ein(e)*-condition. The tables show that for the *this-condition*, two participants (i.e. 7.7% in Table 3) chose not to mention the direct object referent again in a matrix clause, whereas for the *so'n* condition, only one target referent was left unmentioned (i.e. 3.3% in Table 5). In the simple indefinite conditions more referents were left unmentioned in a matrix clause up to S5 (i.e. 16.7% in the a(*n*)-condition in Table 4 and 26.7% in the *ein(e)*-condition in Table 6).

Table 3. Type of referring expression used for the first re-mention of the referent in the *this*-condition

This-referents for all test items (mean and absolute values)					
Continuation Sentence	Pronoun	Name	Def. unmod. NP	Def. modified NP	Sum
S1	10% (3)	(0)	40% (12)	(0)	50% (15)
S2	13.3% (4)	(0)	6.7% (2)	(0)	20% (6)
S3	3.3% (1)	3.3% (1)	6.7% (2)	3.3% (1)	16.7% (5)
S4	3.3% (1)	(0)	(0)	(0)	3.3% (1)
S5	(0)	(0)	(0)	3.3%(1)	3.3% (1)
Sum	30% (9)	3.3% (1)	53.3% (16)	6.7% (2)	93.3 % (28)

More importantly, the data presented in Tables 3 through 6 show that the two types of indefinite noun phrases (headed by *this* or *so'n* vs. by the simple indefinite article a(*n*) or *ein(e)*) seem not to impact the type of referring expression chosen to pick up their associated referents in the subsequent discourse. In other words, both attenuated and less attenuated types of referring expression were used for the referents associated with both indefinite *this* and indefinite *so'n* and simple indefinites. Thus, Prediction 2 in (5) is not met, as the preferred type of

Table 4. Type of referring expression used for the first re-mention of the referent in the a(n)-condition

A(n)-*referents* for all test items (mean and absolute values)					
Continuation Sentence	Pronoun	Name	Def. unmo-d. NP	Def. modified NP	Sum
S1	10% (3)	(0)	26.7% (8)	6.7% (2)	43.3% (13)
S2	6.7% (2)	(0)	6.7% (2)	6.7% (2)	20% (6)
S3	3.3% (1)	3.3% (1)	3.3% (1)	(0)	10% (3)
S4	(0)	(0)	(0)	6.7% (2)	6.7% (2)
S5	(0)	(0)	(0)	3.3% (1)	3.3% (1)
Sum	20% (6)	3.3% (1)	36.7% (11)	23.3% (7)	83.3% (25)

Table 5. Type of referring expression used for the first re-mention of the referent in the *so'n*-condition

So'n-referents for all test items (mean and absolute values)					
Continuation Sentence	Pronoun	Name	Def.unmo-d.NP	Indef. NP	Sum
S1	20% (6)	(0)	60% (18)	3.3 % (1)	83% (25)
S2	(0)	(0)	(0)	(0)	(0)
S3	(0)	(0)	6.7% (2)	(0)	6.7% (2)
S4	(0)	(0)	(0)	(0)	(0)
S5	(0)	3.3% (1)	3.3% (1)	(0)	6.7% (2)
Sum	20% (6)	3.3% (1)	70% (21)	3.3% (1)	96.7 % (29)

referring expression used to pick up the direct object referents, independently of their morphological marking, are definite (unmodified) noun phrases.

At first glance, it seems that the findings presented in Tables 3 to 6 contradict Gernsbacher & Shroyer's ([7], 539) results, which showed that participants used more pronouns to pick up the referents associated with *this*-referents compared to referents introduced by indefinite a(n). One of the reasons for the different results in the two studies is due to the different ways in which the mean values for the first anaphoric item were calculated. In [7] study, the likelihood of pronominalization of the referents preceded by *this* was calculated relative to the likelihood of pronominalization of referents preceded by the simple indefinite article. In contrast, in the studies conducted in this paper, I investigated the type of referring expression used more frequently to pick up the *this*-referents independently of the pick-up preferences for the a(n)-referents.

If we recalculate the mean values in [7] study so that the type of referring expression used for the *this*-referent is independent of that of its simple indefinite counterpart, then the results come close to those reported in this paper, as Table 7 shows. More concretely, the tendency observed in both studies is the same: the type of referring expression used to introduce the direct object referents (i.e. *this*-indefinite vs. a(n)-indefinite) does not influence the type of referring expression used to re-mention that referent.

Table 6. Type of referring expression used for the first re-mention of the referent in the *ein(e)*-condition

Ein(e)-referents for all test items (mean and absolute values)					
Continuation Sentence	Pronoun	Name	Def. unmod. NP	Def. modified NP	Sum
S1	13.3% (4)	3.3% (1)	16.7% (5)	13.3 % (4)	46.7% (14)
S2	(0)	(0)	(0)	(0)	(0)
S3	3.3% (1)	(0)	3.3% (1)	6.7% (2)	13.3% (4)
S4	(0)	(0)	3.3% (1)	6.7% (2)	10% (3)
S5	(0)	(0)	(0)	3.3% (1)	3.3% (1)
Sum	16.7% (5)	3.3% (1)	23.3% (7)	30% (9)	73.3 % (22)

Table 7. Mean and absolute values for the type of referring expressions used to take up the referents of indefinite *this* and a(*n*) in [7] study

	This-indefinites	A(n)-indefinites
Pronoun	69% (214)	67% (161)
Definite NP	31% (95)	33% (81)
Sum	(309)	(242)

Despite the similar results observed, it is still interesting to ask why participants chose to refer back to both types of target referents by means of a pronoun in [7], and not by means of a definite (unmodified) noun phrase, as in my investigation? What is the crucial factor that reversed the preference of anaphoric continuation in the two studies? I argue that the animacy of the introduced referents might play the crucial role in yielding different continuation patterns with respect to the anaphoric type of referring expression used. Note that the target items introduced in direct object position in [7] study were semantically inanimate (e.g. a(*n*)/*this* egg, a(*n*)/*this* vase, etc.) and the initial subject referents given in the same sentence were semantically human (usually proper names referring to persons). In the story-continuation experiments presented in this paper, *both* subject and target referents were semantically human. Different studies [3] showed that the presence of multiple referents in a discourse reduces the use of less specified types of referring expressions to refer back to one of them. Even though the participants in the experiment reported here could have opted for more reduced types of referring expressions, as there was no competition between the referents in terms of gender (except for TI1 in Table (1)), they nevertheless chose more specified types of referring expressions (i.e. definite noun phrases). However, the findings of the study conducted here compared to [7] results, show that not only the mere presence of several referents is responsible for reducing the use of shorter anaphoric types of referring expressions, but their competition in terms or animacy[5] as well. As the two referents mentioned

[5] In a language like Romanian, which does not differentiate between [+human] and [-human] personal pronouns as English does, we would expect lower pronoun rates for multiple referents within one sentence, irrespectively of their animacy.

in Gernsbacher & Shroyer's study differ in animacy, shorter types of anaphoric referring expressions were preferred to pick up the direct object referents. In the study conducted in this paper, however, due to ambiguity-avoidance strategies, low pornominalization rates can be observed for both referents found in direct object position. All in all, the results of the present study confirm the Prediction in (4), but not the Prediction in (5).

4 Conclusion

The results of the exploratory studies presented in this paper revealed several patterns. First, referents associated with both indefinite *this* in English and indefinite *so'n* in German are likely to be mentioned more often in the following discourse. This observation underlines the preferential discourse status occupied by referents marked in this way, compared to referents introduced by means of the simple indefinite article. Second, despite their high referential continuity, referents headed by *this* and *so'n* do not show a higher rate of pronominaliztion compared to their simple indefinite counterparts. The findings of both Exp1 and Exp2 underline the necessity to dissociate between the likelihood of subsequent mention of a referent and the likelihood of pronominalization (confirmation of recent findings on language production, e.g. [11], [10]), as they seem to be triggered by different factors. These two seemingly conflicting effects suggest that it might be helpful to revise such definitions of accessibility, activation, topicality, or discourse prominence, which equally weight the likelihood of re-mention of a referent and the type of subsequent anaphoric expression used for this purpose.

Acknowledgments. I am grateful to Klaus von Heusinger and Elsi Kaiser for helpful advice during the development of this research. I would also like to thank three anonymous reviewers for their insightful comments and suggestions, as well as António Branco, Iris Hendrickx, Ruslan Mitkov and Sobha Anna for organizing the DAARC 2011 conference and for editing the present volume. This research was supported by the German Science Foundation by a grant to the project C2: *Case and referential context*, as part of the Collaborative Research Centre 732 *Incremental Specification in Context* at the University of Stuttgart, Germany.

References

1. Ariel, M.: Referring and Accessibility. J. Linguistics 24, 65–87 (1988)
2. Arnold, J.: Reference form and discourse patterns. PhD dissertation, Stanford University. Dissertation Abstracts International 59, 2950 (1998)
3. Arnold, J., Griffin, Z.: The effect of additional characters on choice of referring expressions: Everyone counts. J. Memory and Language 56, 521–536 (2007)
4. Chiriacescu, S.: The presentative function of German so'n. In: Saramandu, N., Nevaci, M., Radu, C.I. (eds.) Lucrarile celui de-al Treilea Simpozion International de Lingvistica, pp. 345–356. Bucharest UP, Bucharest (2010)

5. Chiriacescu, S.: The discourse structuring potential of indefinite noun phrases. Special markers in Romanian, German and English. Ph.D. dissertation, University of Stuttgart (2011)
6. Chiriacescu, S., von Heusinger, K.: Discourse prominence and pe-marking in Romanian. The International Review of Pragmatics 2(2), 298–332 (2010)
7. Gernsbacher, M., Shroyer, S.: The cataphoric use of the indefinite 'this' in spoken narratives. J. Memory and Cognition 17, 536–540 (1989)
8. Givón, T.: Topic continuity in discourse: An introduction. In: Givón, T. (ed.) Topic Continuity in Discourse: A Quantitative Cross-Language Study, pp. 109–136. John Benjamins, Amsterdam (1983)
9. Haspelmath, M.: Indefinite pronouns: Oxford Studies in Typology and Linguistic Theory. Oxford University Press, Oxford (1997)
10. Kaiser, E.: Investigating the consequences of focus on the production and comprehension of referring expressions. The International Review of Pragmatics 2(2), 266–297 (2010)
11. Kehler, A., Kertz, L., Rohde, H., Elman, J.: Coherence and Coreference Revised. J. Semantics 25, 1–44 (2008)
12. Lyons, C.: Semantics. Cambridge University Press, Cambridge (1999)
13. Maclaran, R.: The Semantics and Pragmatics of the English Demonstratives. PhD dissertation, Cornell University (1982)
14. Prince, E.: Toward a taxonomy of given-new information. In: Cole, P. (ed.) Radical Pragmatics, pp. 223–256. Academic Press, New York (1981)
15. Von Heusinger, K.: Specificity, referentiality and discourse prominence: German indefinite demonstratives. In: Ingo, R. (ed.) Sinn & Bedeutung, vol. 15, pp. 9–30. Universaar – Saarland Unversity Press, Saarbrucken (2011)
16. Wright, S., Givón, T.: The pragmatics of indefinite reference: quantified text-based studies. J. Studies in Language 11, 1–33 (1987)

The Cataphoric Potential of Indefinites in German

Annika Deichsel and Klaus von Heusinger

Universität Stuttgart, Institut für Germanistik/Linguistik
Keplerstrasse 17, K2
70174 Stuttgart, Germany
{Annika.Deichsel,Klaus.vonHeusinger}@ling.uni-stuttgart.de

Abstract. Not only do indefinite noun phrases introduce new discourse referents, they also equip them with a cataphoric (or forward-looking) potential, i.e. with a certain degree of activation which is mirrored in discourse effects such as the frequency of anaphoric references back to the referent in the subsequent discourse. Comparing the two German indefinite determiners *ein* 'a(n)' and indefinite demonstrative *dieser* 'this', we claim that the degree of the cataphoric potential of an indefinite noun phrase (i) correlates with specificity and (ii) a second parameter independent of specificity.

Keywords: Discourse structure, referent tracking, referentiality, specificity, cataphoric potential.

1 Introduction

In this paper we present new empirical evidence based on two pilot studies and an original analysis with respect to the referential and discourse properties of the demonstrative determiner *dieser* 'this' in its indefinite interpretation in German and compare the results with the discourse properties of the ordinary indefinite article *ein* 'a(n)'. We show that indefinite *dieser*, in contrast to *ein*, behaves like a specific expression according to the standard tests for specificity. Indefinite *dieser* also shows a high cataphoric potential, which can be described by two measurable parameters (i) referential persistence and (ii) topic shift potential. The results of our first story continuation task suggest that specificity closely correlates with the discourse property of cataphoric potential, since indefinite *dieser* is specific and exhibits a higher degree of cataphoric potential than *ein*, which is in its prominent reading non-specific. Thus, we assume that specificity is one parameter which triggers an increase in cataphoric potential. In a follow up pilot study we separated specificity from the form of the indefinite expression, in order to test if the differences between *dieser* and *ein* with respect to the cataphoric potential can be explained by specificity alone.

In the first pilot study we assumed that indefinite *dieser* is always specific and that *ein* is prominently non-specific. In the second pilot study we constructed

I. Hendrickx et al. (Eds.): DAARC 2011, LNAI 7099, pp. 144–156, 2011.

contexts which forced the participants to understand both forms as either specific or non-specific. While it was unproblematic to create these contexts for the indefinite article *ein*, it was difficult to trigger non-specific readings for the indefinite demonstrative *dieser*. This design allowed us to distinguish between the influence of specificity and other additional parameters which have not been investigated so far. First results of this second story continuation task strongly suggest that (i) specificity is a crucial parameter determining the cataphoric potential of indefinite expressions and (ii) that it is not the only parameter. There must be additional parameters that underlie the high cataphoric potential of indefinite *dieser*, since it shows much higher values compared to the indefinite article, even if non-specific.

Section 2 gives an overview about the referential and discourse properties of indefinite *dieser*, presenting the results of the first story continuation study in its latter part. After a discussion of the results of the first pilot study in section 3, section 4 describes the follow-up pilot study. A summary of the overall results is given in section 5.

2 Indefinite Demonstrative *dieser*

The indefinite demonstrative *this* in English is intensively studied. There is a general consensus in the literature indefinite *this* (i) is a specific or referential indefinite determiner ([13,9]), passing the classic tests for indefiniteness and specificity ([5] (ii) introduces a discourse- and adresee-new referent into the discourse and (iii) is highly relevant for the discourse and referred to frequently in the subsequent discourse ([17]). ([9]:184) claims that it is felicitously used only, if its referent has an interesting or 'noteworthy' property.[13] argues that the function of indefinite *this* is to signal to the hearer that 'more information about the introduced referent is coming.'

(1) There is **this man who** lives upstairs from me **who** is driving me mad because he jumps rope at 2 a.m. every night. ([12]:85)

(2) ...A few years ago, there was **this hippie**, long-haired, slovenly... **He** confronted me... (Policeman; Terkel, 1974) ([13]:233)

We argue that the German equivalent expression indefinite *dieser* has very similar functions as English indefinite *this*, even though indefinite *dieser* is only rarely investigated in the literature. The discourse referent associated with the noun phrase preceded by *dieser* also seems to have the discourse function described in (iii) above. Example (3) shows, that it is odd to introduce a referent with indefinite *dieser* without mentioning it again in the subsequent context:

(3) Gestern im Kino hat mich **dieser Fremde** angesprochen.
'Yesterday in the movies this stranger talked to me.'
a. **Er** war sehr nett.
'He was very nice.'
b. ?? Dann bin ich nach Hause gegangen und habe ein Buch gelesen.
?? 'Then I went home and read a book.'

2.1 Referential Properties : Specificity of Indefinite *dieser*

As English indefinite *this*, indefinite *dieser* exhibits typical properties of specific indefinites, which can be tested by the classical tests for referential (4), scopal (5) and epistemic specificity (6) (see [16] for an overview):

(4) a. Eva will **diesen Film** über Eliade sehen.
'Eva wants to watch this movie about Eliade.'
b. Eva will **einen Film** über Eliade sehen.
'Eva wants to watch a movie about Eliade.'

(5) a. Jeder meiner Kollegen hat **dieses Buch** von Eliade gelesen
'Each of my colleagues read this book by Eliade.' [only 1 book]
b. Jeder meiner Kollegen hat **ein Buch** von Eliade gelesen
Each of my colleagues read a book by Eliade.' [several books possible]

(6) a. Peter gab das Buch **diesem Studenten**.
Peter gave the book to this student.
(i) ^{ok}Er heisst Hans und ist in meinem Englischseminar.
^{ok}His name is Hans and he is in my English class.
(ii) *Ich weiss nicht wer es ist.
*I don't know who it is.'
b. Peter gab das Buch **einem Studenten**.
'Peter gave the book to a student.
(i) ^{ok}Er heisst Hans und ist in meinem Englischseminar.
^{ok}His name is Hans and he is in my English class.
(ii) ^{ok}Ich weiss nicht wer es ist.
^{ok}I don't know who it is.'

The indefinite article *ein* in the complement of a verb of propositional attitudes (4) allows for a referential and a non-referential reading, whereas the use of indefinite *dieser* is only compatible with a referential reading (see for exceptions section 4). The indefinite article in (5) signals a preference for a narrow scope interpretation, whereas indefinite *dieser* always indicates wide scope. The indefinite article in (6) allows for both a specific and a non-specific reading, whereas indefinite *dieser* (disregarding the exceptions in section 4) only allows for the (epistemic) specific reading.

2.2 Pilot Study 1: Discourse Properties of Indefinite *dieser*

As exemplified in (1) and (2) above, the literature on English indefinite *this* claims that the referents introduced are of a greater importance with respect to the following discourse. The same seems to hold for German indefinite *dieser*. We offer experimental evidence that the referents of German indefinite *dieser* are highly relevant for the subsequent discourse after their introduction and we label this discourse property 'cataphoric potential' (*see* [4] and [3] for the related concept of *discourse structuring potential*).

Discourse-based studies [7,8,11,2] dealing with accessibility and discourse prominence already introduced several factors that can make a referent more accessible or prominent. However, these accounts are mainly concerned with the licensing of anaphora resolution. In order to make the cataphoric or forward-looking potential of the referents introduced with indefinite *dieser* a measurable concept we adopted the following two parameters following the definition in [4]: (i) *referential persistence* [7,1,6,2] or the number of anaphoric expressions which are used to refer back to the discourse referent and (ii) *topic shift potential* (modeled after Givóns topic continuity (1983)) or the probability with which a referent is mentioned again as a topic. Topics are defined as aboutness topics in the sense of [14] and[15]. For reasons of simplicity and traceability in the first study we equalized topics with grammatical subjects, since topics preferrably occur in syntactic subject position in German. This general preference was confirmed by the data of the pilot study in which we found a strong correlation between aboutness topics and subjects.

Assuming a correlation between specificity and the cataphoric potential, the following predictions concerning the discourse effects of German indefinite *dieser* and *ein* with respect to their cataphoric potential are made:

Prediction 1 (*referential persistence*): The referential persistence of the *dieser* marked referents will exceed the referential persistence of their counterparts marked with the indefinite article *ein*.

Prediction 2 (*topic shift poential*): In comparison to their *ein*-marked counterparts, *dieser*-marked referents will be more likely to become a topic in the subsequent discourse.

Methodology and Experimental Design. A small sentence continuation task (between-subject design) based on two- to four-sentence stories was designed, including two target stories and two distracting filler stories. The first one or two sentences in each test item set the context for the story and contained reference to the first person speaker *ich* ‘I’. The next sentence contained the target referent realized as an indefinite NP. The character introduced first (ich ‘I’) was the clearly established topic constituent of the story (mentioned at least once in subject position). We manipulated the realization form of the indefinite target referents in the target sentences (*dieser*-marked referents vs. *ein*-marked referents). Remember that the simple indefinite article *ein* generally allows for both a specific and a non-specific interpretation. (7) gives an example target story with both *dieser* and *ein*:

(7) Das Essen in dem Restaurant war wirklich total lecker, aber ziemlich teuer. Als ich nach fünf Gängen beim Dessert war, hab’ ich gesehen, wie **dieser/ein Mann** Sekt bestellte.
‘The food in the restaurant was really delicious, but pretty expensive. When I had dessert, after five courses, I saw how **this/a man** ordered champagne.’

20 native speakers of German participated, 10 participants for the *dieser*-condition and 10 participants for the *ein*-condition. The participants were asked

to read the given stimulus items and to write down five natural-sounding, logical continuation sentences. The respective 5 continuation sentences were coded with respect to the two parameters *referential persistence* and *topic shift potential* introduced in section 2.3. Referential persistence was measured by counting the anaphoric references by sentence and also as the sum of all anaphoric items up to S5 (cumulative). In order to account for the topic shift potential we checked if the *dieser*- or *ein*-marked referent became a topic in one of the subsequent 5 sentences. Whether this change was maintained in the subsequent discourse was of no relevance. In other words, we measured if and when a referent was taken up as a topic in the subsequent discourse for the first time after its introduction. Recall that in this pilot study we equalized 'topic' with 'subject' for reasons of simplicity.

Results. Figure 1 exemplifies the results for referential persistence of both indefinite forms in the test item in (7).

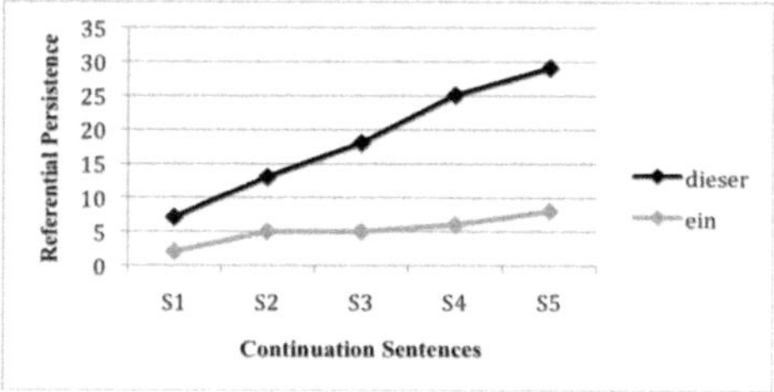

Fig. 1. Referential persistence (cumulative) of *dieser/ein* Mann in (7)

The sum of all items referring back to the indefinite in the five sentences provided by the 10 subjects is 29 for indefinite *dieser* and only 8 for the indefinite article *ein*. This clearly indicates a stark difference with respect to the discourse function between indefinite *dieser* and *ein*.

Figure 2 provides the results for the topic shift potential for the test item in (7). In this short fragment, the first person singular *ich* 'I' is established as the discourse topic and as an aboutness topic in the test item before the indefinite *dieser Mann* ('this man') introduces a new referent with a high cataphoric potential.

Figure 2 shows a remarkable difference in the topic shift potential between indefinites introduced by the indefinite article and those introduces by indefinite *dieser*: 80% of the 10 test persons shifted the discourse referent introduced with indefinite *dieser* to the topic at some point in the discourse after its introduction. For *ein*, this only happened in 40% of the cases, indicating a much lower topic shift potential.

In the test item in (7), with respect to both referential persistence and topic shift potential, the values for *dieser* are always higher compared to the values

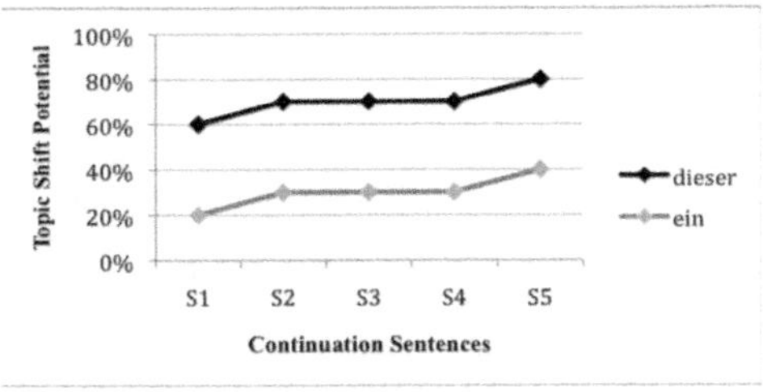

Fig. 2. Topic shift potential(cumulative) of *dieser/ein* Mann in (7)

for *ein*. This confirms the hypothesis that there is a strong correlation between the sentence semantics of the two determiners (specificity) and their discourse behavior in terms of cataphoric potential.

3 Discussion

The results of the story continuation task in section 2 clearly indicate that indefinite expressions have cataphoric potential and that indefinite *dieser* has a much higher cataphoric potential than the indefinite article *ein*. The results also allow the assumption of a correlation between the cataphoric potential and specificity. We can hypothesize that specificity is the underlying parameter that determines the cataphoric potential of indefinite expressions in a discourse. In order to provide more evidence for this hypothesis we designed a second story continuation task in which we cross-classified specificity and the (lexical) type of expression (indefinite *dies* vs. indefinite article *ein*).

In the first pilot study we assumed that indefinite *dieser* is always specific (as it is reported in the literature on English indefinite *this* ([13,5,9]). The indefinite article is ambiguous, with a preference for non-specific interpretations. The design of the first pilot study did not allow a distinction between the lexical form of the indefinite demonstrative *dieser* and the semantic feature [+ specific] that is attached to the form, presumably. Furthermore, for the indefinite article we were not able to clearly distinguish between specific or non-specific interpretations, thus weakening the hypothesis. Therefore, in the second pilot study we developed a design in which we forced either specific or non-specific readings for both indefinite *dieser* and *ein*, in order to be able to clearly differentiate specific and non-specific readings of *ein* and *dieser*. Our goal was a more detailed investigation of the presumed correlation of standard types of specificity with the cataphoric potential. Furthermore, we wanted to test if specificity can exhaustively explain the observed effects or if additional parameters might be at work as well.

4 Pilot Study 2: Discourse Effects of Specific Indefinite *dieser* vs. Specific *ein*

In order to provide more evidence for the hypothesis that specificity is a crucial factor determining the cataphoric potential of indefinites and in order to test if it is the only factor involved, we developed a further story continuation task similar to the one in section 2.3. In this follow-up pilot study we tried to separate specificity from the form of the indefinite expression and thus cross-classified specificity and the type of expression (indefinite *dieser* vs. indefinite article *ein*). In other words, we measured the discourse effects of the two indefinite determiners in either forced specific or forced non-specific readings in the test items (TI) containing the respective referents.

Table 1. Cross classification of parameters

Determiner / Specificity	+ specific	- specific
indef. dieser	TI1 - TI4	TI5 + TI6
ein	TI1 - TI4	TI5 + TI6

Test items 1 through 4 showed typical specificity contexts in form of forced wide scope readings under propositional attitude verbs (test item 1 and 2) exemplified in (8) and forced wide scope readings under semantic operators such as the universal quantifier (test item 3 and 4), exemplified in (9). The forced specific interpretations of the critical referents were guaranteed by direct anaphoric reference (realized by an object pronoun) to the critical referent in a subsequent sentence after its introduction [10] (Please note that the test items were presented all in plain bold and italics are only used in this article to emphasize the structure of the example):

(8) TI1: Peter will nächste Woche **eine/diese Spanierin** besuchen. Er hat sie letztes Jahr in Barcelona kennengelernt.
'Peter wants to marry **a/this Spaniard** next week. He met **her** last year in Barcelona.'

(9) TI3: Die Party gestern war wirklich sehr lustig. Jede Frau hat **einen/diesen Franzosen** angehimmelt. Alle haben **ihn** total umschwärmt.
'The party yesterday was really funny. Every woman adored **a/this French guy**. They all totally idolized him.'

Test item 5 and 6, on the other hand, were designed to force non-specific interpretations for both *ein* and *dieser*. The first sentence of each test item contained the critical referent, which was introduced under a propositional attitude verb (parallel to the [+specific] test items 1 and 2). Then, in order to force the desired non-specific readings, the critical referents were picked up again by an anaphoric pronoun under another operator, which is an instance of modal subordination. [10] shows that non-specific referents introduced in the complement of a modal verb can only be referred to again, if the anaphoric expression is in the complement of a modal verb as well, i.e. if the anaphoric expression is in the same mode as its antecedent (10a). He concludes that 'non-specific indefinites do not establish discourse referents when they appear in a complement of a modal verb,' and thus cannot be taken up by an anaphoric expression in the non-modal context, as in (10b):

(10) a. John wants to catch **a fish**. He would like to eat it for supper.
b. Do you see the fish over there?

The design of non-specific test items including *ein* was uproblematic: after their introduction the critical referents were mentioned again in the test items using *sollte* 'he should', which guaranteed the continuation of the modal mode and thus the non-specificity of the critical referents. The design of the analog examples for indefinite *dieser*, however, was a problem at first glance. There is a consensus in the literature that indefinite demonstratives, like indexicals, always refer rigidly to individuals in the actual world and are not affected by embedding ([9]: 189). This explains that they behave as if they were exclusively specific (see standard tests in section 2.2). From what we learned about indefinite *dieser* in section 2.2, we would expect the referents of indefinite *dieser* to refuse embedding under a modal operator.

However, there is a small group of contexts, in which the interpretation of indefinite demonstratives can be affected by embedding. Embedding is possible, if they are in the complement of a propositional attitude verb (11). These non-specific readings for indefinite demonstratives are clearly marked, however perfectly acceptable in German as well. Thus, designing test items in which the non-specific *dieser* was introduced under a propositional attitude verb and then taken up modally embedded, we were able to create the desired non-specific readings for indefinite *dieser*.

(11) John dreamt that he was in this Eskimo restaurant. ([13]:241)

Dieser, in these contexts, does not pass the standard tests for specificity (in terms of exclusive wide-scope behavior, see section 2.2). In one interpretation of (11) the speaker is clearly not intending to talk about a particular Eskimo restaurant that exists in the world of utterance and (11) doesnt even entail that the speaker believes that Eskimo restaurants do exist at all. Using propositional attitude verbs in test items 5 and 6 thus enabled us to design the desired test items for the non specific condition for *dieser*. An example of a test item for *dieser* and ein in the non-specific reading is given below in (12): the critical referent is introduced under a propositional attitude verb (sie hofft 'she hopes') and then taken up modally embedded, continuing the mode in which the referent was introduced in the first place.

(12) TI 5: Jenny ist immer noch Single. Sie hofft darauf, dass irgendwann **ein/dieser Märchenprinz** vorbei kommt. **Er** sollte gutaussehend und charmant sein.

'Jenny is still single. She hopes to meet **a/this fairytale prince** at one point. **He** should be good looking and charming.'

4.1 Methodology, Experimental Design

As in the first pilot study, the participants (p=28) were asked to read test items which, again, were small stories (6 overall and 4 distracting filler stories) containing the target referents. The realization form of the target referents was manipulated and varied between *ein* and *dieser*-marked referents in either forced specific (test items 1 4) or forced non-specific (test item 5 6) readings. In the specific readings, test items 1 and 2 included propositional attitude verbs and test item 3 and 4 used the universal quantifier.

The target referents were exclusively human direct objects. The participants were asked to read the test items and to provide 6 natural-sounding continuation sentences. This time, inter-subject variation between the participants was used.

An example response of one participant in pilot study 2 for *dieser* in its non-specific reading is given in (13). Note that the critical referent is continued in the same mode in which it was introduced in the test item. In S1 and S5 the referent is under a modal verb (*soll, würde*), and in S6 under the modal adverb *am besten* 'it would be best'.

(13) TI1: Jenny ist immer noch Single. Sie *hofft* darauf, dass irgendwann **dieser Märchenprinz**$_1$ vorbei kommt. **Er**$_1$ sollte gutaussehend und charmant sein.
TI1: 'Jenny is still single. She *hopes* to meet **this fairytale prince**$_1$ at one point. **He**$_1$ *should* be good looking and charming.'

S1: Am besten soll **er**$_1$ auch noch reich sein.
'**He**$_1$ should be rich as well.'
S2: Die hat vielleicht Vorstellungen.
'She has lots of fantasies.'
S3: Und anstatt sich mal auf die Suche zu machen, hockt sie nur zu Hause.
'And she always just sits at home, instead of looking for somebody.'
S4: Sie geht ja auch nie weg, in Discos oder so.
'And she never goes out, to clubs or the like.'
S5: Als würde **der**$_1$ auf einmal vor ihrer Tür stehen.
'As if **he**$_1$ stood in front of her door one day.'
S6: Am besten hat **er** $_1$ noch einen Schimmel. Haha.
'It would be best if **he**$_1$ had a white horse as well. Haha.'

The 6 continuation sentences given by the participants for each test items were coded with respect to referential persistence and topic shift potential. In this paper, however, we are only able to report the results with respect to referential persistence.

4.2 Results

Figure 3 repeats the results of pilot study 1 for referential persistence and shows the results for referential persistence of both indefinite *dieser* and *ein* in both specific (test item 1-4) and non-specific (test item 5+6) readings in pilot study 2. The numbers represent the mean values per sentence with which the critical referents were picked up after their introduction. That is, the total numbers for referential persistence, e.g. 29 for *dieser* in pilot study 1, were divided by the number of participants (10 in pilot study 1) and by the number of sentences provided per person (5 in pilot study 1). Thus, the value 29 for *dieser* in pilot study 1 is mirrored in the value 0,58 in the figure below. That is, *dieser* in pilot study 1, was mentioned again 0,58 times per sentence on an average.

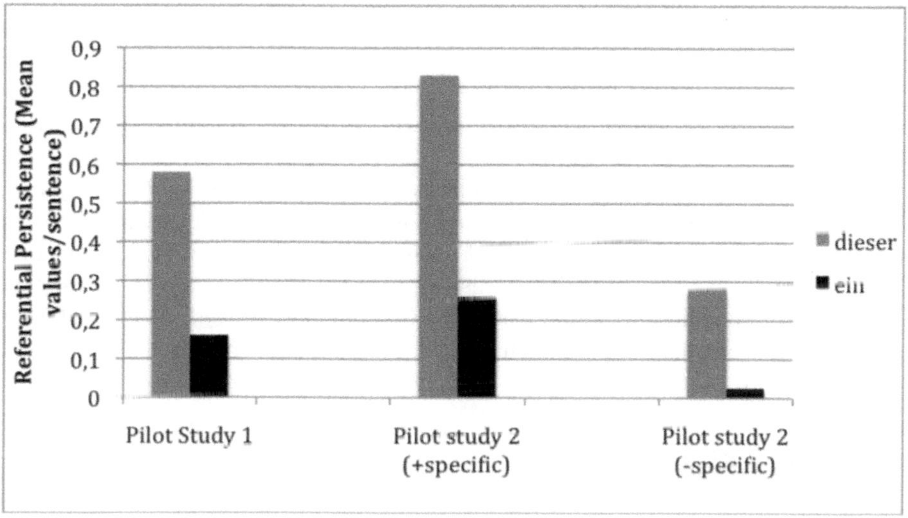

Fig. 3. Referential persistence of *dieser* and *ein*: mean values per sentence in pilot study 1 and 2

Pilot study 2 has three main results, which are summarized below:

1. Comparing the results of pilot study 1 with the results of the [+specific] cases in pilot study 2, we find that in both pilot studies the values for *dieser* show a much stronger preference to be referred to again in the subsequent discourse, compared to the values for *ein*. As figure 3 depicts, the values in pilot study 2 are higher for both *dieser* (0,82) and *ein* (0,28), compared to pilot study 1 (*dieser* 0,58, *ein* 0,16). This increase of the values in the [+specific] condition in pilot study 2, however, was expected. Remember that the critical referents were referred to again one more time by an object pronoun in the test items in

pilot study 2 already. This was not the case in pilot study 1. Thus, the critical referents were of greater salience in the test items in pilot study 2, what can explain the general tendency of the participants to pick up both referents (*ein* and *dieser*) more often in the [+specific] cases in pilot study 2.

2. Comparing the values for *dieser* and *ein* within the either [+specific] or [-specific] conditions in pilot study 2, we find that *dieser* still receives higher values compared to *ein*. In the [+specific] readings *dieser* is referred to again 0,82 times on an average per sentence, whereas *ein* only receives the value 0,26. The same holds for the [-specific] readings where *dieser* reaches 0,28 and *ein* only 0,025. In both the [+specific] and the [-specific] readings *dieser* receives higher values for referential persistence than *ein*. That is, independent of specificity, the cataphoric potential of *dieser* in terms of referential persistence is much higher compared to the one of *ein*, even in the non-specific readings. This means that some additional parameter besides specificity must be a determining factor for the cataphoric potential of indefinite expressions as well.

3. Comparing between the [+specific] and the [-specific] conditions within each lexical form of pilot study 2, we see that the values for referential persistence of specific *dieser* (0,82) and non-specific *dieser* (0,28) in pilot study 2 differ as well. Specific indefinite *dieser* is much more likely to be referred to again in the subsequent discourse than non-specific indefinite *dieser*. The same holds for specific *ein* (0,26) and non-specific *ein* (0,025): specific *ein* is much more likely to be referred to in the subsequent discourse than non-specific *ein*. This difference between specific and non-specific readings of both *dieser* and *ein* strongly suggests that specificity is a determining factor with respect to the force of the expressions cataphoric potential in terms of referential persistence.

5 Conclusions

Asking a general question about the means available for referents to provide information with respect to the upcoming discourse structure we investigated the indefinite demonstrative determiner *dieser* and the indefinite article *ein* in German. After showing that *dieser*, as far as its sentence semantics are concerned, usually behaves like a specific expression we came up with quantifiable means to prove that indefinite *dieser* introduces new discourse referents and equips them with a higher degree of cataphoric potential compared to *ein*. The cataphoric potential was measured as (i) referential persistence and (ii) topic shift potential. The results of our first story continuation study showed that indefinite *dieser* has a higher cataphoric potential compared to *ein*. This suggested that specificity closely correlates with the discourse property of cataphoric potential of indefinites. An interim conclusion was that specificity can account for the differences in cataphoric potential between indefinite *dieser* and *ein*. The results of a follow-up study supported the findings of the first pilot study, confirming that specificity is a determining factor increasing the cataphoric potential of indefinites. But the results of the second study also showed that specificity can not be the only parameter underlying the cataphoric potential, since we still found differences with respect to the cataphoric potential of *ein* and *dieser* within unambiguously [+specific] and [-specific] interpretations. Thus, the results allow the assumption that the cataphoric potential of indefinites also highly depends on additional factors which most probably might be related to the indexical nature of demonstratives.

Acknowledgements. This research is supported by the German Science Foundation by a grant to the project C4, as a part of the Collaborative Research Center 732 Incremental Specification in Context at the University of Stuttgart. We are grateful to Sofiana Chiriacescu, Paul Dekker, Cornelia Ebert, Laurence Horn, Elsi Kaiser, Craige Roberts, Britta Stolterfoht and Henk Zeevat for helpful comments.

References

1. Ariel, M.: Referring and Accessibility. J. Linguistics 24, 65–87 (1988)
2. Arnold, J.: How Speakers Refer: The Role of Accessibility. Language and Linguistic Compass 4, 187–203 (2010)
3. Chiriacescu, S.: The Discourse Structuring Potential of Indefinite Noun Phrases. Special Markers in Romanian, German and English. Doctoral Dissertation. University of Stuttgart (2011)
4. Chiriacescu, S., von Heusinger, K.: Discourse Prominence and Pe-Marking in Romanian. International Review of Pragmatics 2(2), 298–332 (2010)
5. Fodor, J., Sag, I.: Referential and Quantificational Indefinites. Linguistics and Philosophy 5, 355–398 (1982)
6. Gernsbacher, M., Shroyer, S.: The Cataphoric Use of the Indefinite 'this' in Spoken Narratives. Memory and Cognition 17, 536–540 (1989)
7. Givón, T.: Topic Continuity in Discourse: An Introduction. In: Givón, T. (ed.) Topic Continuity in Discourse. A Quantitative Cross-Language Study. John Benjamins, Amsterdam (1983)
8. Gundel, J., Hedberg, N., Zacharski, R.: Cognitive Status and the Form of Referring Expressions in Discourse. Language 69, 274–307 (1993)
9. Ionin, T.: This is Definitely Specific: Specificity and Definiteness in Article Systems. Natural Language Semantics 14, 175–234 (2006)
10. Karttunen, L.: Discourse Referents. In: 1969 Conference on Computational Linguistics. Sång-Säby, Sweden, 1–38, `http://portal.acm.org/citation.cfm?id=990403.990490` Reprinted in. J. McCawley (ed.) Syntax and Semantics 7: Notes from the Linguistic Underground, pp. 363–385. Academic Press, New York (1969/1976)
11. Kehler, A., Kertz, L., Rohde, H., Elman, J.: Coherence and Coreference Revised. J. Semantics 25, 1–44 (2008)
12. Maclaren, R.: The Semantics and Pragmatics of the English Demonstratives. Doctoral Dissertation. Cornell University (1982)

13. Prince, E.: On the Inferencing of Indefinite-this NPs. In: Josh, A., Webber, B., Sag, I. (eds.) Elements of Discourse Understanding, pp. 231–250. CUP, Cambridge (1981)
14. Reinhart, T.: Pragmatics and Linguistics: An Analysis of Sentence Topics. Philosophica 27(1), 53–93 (1981)
15. Roberts, C.: Topics. In: von Heusinger, K., Maienborn, C., Portner, P. (eds.) Semantics: An International Handbook of Natural Language Meaning, vol. 2, pp. 1909–1935. De Gruyter, Berlin (2011)
16. Von Heusinger, K.: Specificity. In: von Heusinger, K., Maienborn, C., Portner, P. (eds.) HSK Semantics. An International Handbook of Natural Language Meaning, vol. 2, pp. 1025–1058. De Gruyter, Berlin (2011)
17. Wright, S., Givón, T.: The Pragmatics of Indefinite Reference: Quantified Text-Based Studies. Studies in Language 11(1), 1–33 (1987)

Semantic and Structural Constraints on the Resolution of Ambiguous Personal Pronouns - A Psycholinguistic Study

Miriam Ellert and Anke Holler

Courant Research Centre "Text Structures", University of Göttingen, Germany*
{miriam.ellert,anke.holler}@phil.uni-goettingen.de

Abstract. We present a series of on- and off-line experiments to investigate the influence of semantic and structural constraints on the resolution of subject pronouns in German, thereby revealing inconsistencies of previous studies. On the basis of factors like (in-)animacy, the presence/absence of different types of connectors and clausal structure (coordination versus subordination) we show in which way structural and semantic information interact in inter- and intra-sentential anaphor resolution.

Keywords: pronoun resolution, animacy, connectives, discourse processing, visual world eye-tracking, referent assignment, sentence completion.

1 Introduction

When speakers and hearers engage in discourse, they need to keep track of the entities which have been evoked and map subsequent information onto them. Pronouns are frequently used when the speaker wishes to maintain reference to a previously mentioned discourse entity. However, when there is more than one potential antecedent available (matching with gender and number), the question arises as to how hearers determine which antecedent the speaker had in mind. A number of constraints have been claimed to influence pronoun resolution preferences, such as order of mention (first-mentioned entities being preferred) [17], grammatical role (subjects over objects) [15,14], and topicality (topics over non-topics) [23,9]. All of these factors have been shown to influence the salience level of the potential antecedents, thereby making one antecedent more or less available for pronoun resolution. According to theories of reference [2,19,24], the more activated a discourse entity is in the mind of the interlocutor, the less lexical information needs to be encoded on the referential expression, i.e. when speakers make use of personal pronouns, they are very likely to refer to a previously mentioned highly salient discourse entity. Thus in (1)[1], the personal pronoun

* Funded by the German Initiative of Excellence.

[1] Example taken from [33].

I. Hendrickx et al. (Eds.): DAARC 2011, LNAI 7099, pp. 157–170, 2011.

(pp) should preferentially be resolved towards *the waiter*, since it is the first-mentioned entity, the syntactic subject and topical. In German, there exists the special situation that a second pronominal form could be used: a d-pronoun (dp). Although d-pronouns do not encode more lexical information than personal pronouns, they are sought to be fuller forms in terms of their prosodic weight [2], and therefore co-refer to less salient entities (to *the detective* in (1)).

(1) Der Kellner$_i$ erkennt den Detektiv$_j$, als das Bier umgekippt wird.
Er$_i$/Der$_j$ ist offensichtlich sehr fleißig.
The waiter$_i$ recognizes the detective$_j$ as the beer is tipped over.
He (pp$_i$/dp$_j$) is clearly very hard working.

While previous psycholinguistic studies in German were able to repeatedly show that d-pronouns are resolved in the predicted direction (NP2-preference) [9,33], the predicted NP1-preference for personal pronouns was not consistently found: some studies found an NP1-preference [10,20], others did not [9,33].

The difference in results might have been obtained due to differences in the experimental designs (e.g. on- and off-line tasks) and stimulus materials used (inter- vs. intra-sentential resolution), or due to the fact that some influencing factors were not taken into account; for example in SVO sentence structures, the types of verbs or whether connectives were used or not may have had an influence on the resolution preferences and should have therefore been controlled for. Moreover, all of the above studies focused on the use of animate antecedents and it may be asked whether these results also generalize to inanimate antecedents. Therefore, in our study we systematically tackled these issues and asked in which ways these semantic and structural factors would act as constraints regarding pronoun resolution preferences. In the current study we addressed three questions:

1. Does the inherent semantic factor animacy have an influence on pronoun resolution? And if yes, does it affect the resolution of different pronominal forms such as personal and d-pronouns? (Experiments 1a and 1b)
2. Are resolution preferences for German personal pronouns affected by the type of connector used? (Experiment 2)
3. Does the clausal structure in which NP1 and NP2 are presented influence the resolution of personal pronouns? (Experiment 3)

In order to investigate these issues, we set up a number of on- and off-line experiments which will be presented in the following sections.

2 Semantic Constraint or Cognitive Principle: Animacy

[28] differentiated the semantic factor animacy from other factors, such as grammatical role and order of mention, in that it encodes inherent accessibility by its intrinsic semantic properties compared to derived accessibility which is encoded temporarily by the linguistic or extra-linguistic context. Research on word order and sentence processing has shown that animacy is a highly ranked cue

in language comprehension. For example, the well-established animate-first effect reflects a preference for animates to occur in agent-first utterances while inanimates are more frequently preferred to occur in patient-first utterances such as passivizations [28,32,21,12]. Furthermore, [25] could show that the well-established processing preference for subject over object relative clauses which had previously been found in Dutch and German for animate entities disappeared when the object of the relative clause was inanimate[2].

Since the above studies were able to show that animacy is an important cue in sentence processing, it is assumable that it would also affect pronoun resolution. [16] addressed this question in an English language production study. They used a sentence completion task which showed an antecedent sentence like *The rowers/boats overtook the swimmers/yachts in the end. Clearly,...* comprising either two animate (AA), or two inanimate (II) antecedents, or two antecedents of mixed animacy (AI, IA), and measured the occurrence of personal pronouns when participants were asked to refer to the syntactic subject. Participants used personal pronouns more frequently when the syntactic subject was animate than inanimate, regardless of the animacy level of the syntactic object (AI, AA >IA, II). These results are very interesting with regard to our study, since they show that even in the conditions where animacy does not disambiguate between the antecedents (AA, II), personal pronouns occur more frequently with animate antecedents.

The question is whether animacy affects the resolution of different pronominal forms equally, i.e. one could assume that animacy is a general cognitive principle and therefore has a principle role in processing which is also reflected in pronoun resolution. Then, we would assume that it should affect the resolution of personal pronouns as well as the resolution of d-pronouns. If animacy effects vary across pronominal forms, then we would assume a linguistic component underlying the effect. The current study addressed the animacy issue by using animate (AA) and inanimate items (II) and presenting the stimuli via an on-line visual-world eye-tracking task [13,29] and an off-line referent-assignment task. The antecedents were embedded in comparative constructions to avoid effects of case and verb causality and it was asked whether personal and d-pronouns would be resolved towards NP1 or NP2, and whether the results would be affected by the animacy level of the antecedents.

2.1 Experiment 1a: Visual-World Eye-Tracking

Method. Twenty-eight German native speakers participated in the experiment (mean age=23; SD=3). All had normal or corrected to normal vision. The participants were paid for their participation. Participants' eye movements were recorded with an SR Research EYELINK II eye tracker. Twenty-four experimental items were created: 12 AA, 12 II. The first sentence introduced NP1 and NP2 in a comparative construction. The second sentence started either with a

[2] Note that in the animate object condition both entities were of the same kind of animacy, while in the inanimate object condition the entities were of different animacy levels.

personal or a d-pronoun, followed by a third wrap-up sentence, cf. (2) for an example of the stimulus material. A German native speaker read the items out loud and they were digitally recorded to computer.

The 24 experimental items were mixed with 48 filler items. The order of presentation was pseudo-randomized and two experimental versions were created following a latin-square distribution. The stimuli were divided into two experimental blocks to allow for a short break in between and the order of presentation was counterbalanced across participants. The experimental display showed the two target pictures (*cupboard, table*) in either top left or right position and a non-related distractor (e.g. *sofa*) in down central position. At the beginning of each trial we implemented a 1000 ms preview before the first sound file started playing. After the first sound file a fixation cross was shown in the middle of the screen for 1500 ms before the second sound file started playing. This was done in order to assure that all the fixations entering the analysis were due to the pronoun and not to spill over effects from the first sound file.

(2) Der Schrank ist schwerer als der Tisch. Er_i/Der_j stammt aus einem Möbelgeschäft in Belgien. Das Sofa soll nächste Woche geliefert werden.
The cupboard is heavier than the table. He (pp_i/dp_j) *originates from a furniture store in Belgium. The sofa is supposed to be delivered next week.*

Results. We calculated linear mixed-effect models on the eye-tracking data according to [5] using R's lme4 package [7]. The analysis was run on the fixations effectuated at pronoun onset (0 ms) until 2000 ms after pronoun onset. This time span was divided into 10 time windows of 200 ms and the data was averaged across participants and conditions. The outcome variable which was the proportion of looks towards a picture was transformed into empirical logits [6] . A stepwise approach to model building was used, applying a forward elimination method, which ensures that only the minimum number of predictors accounting for the variance in the data enter the model.

Table 1. Overview of the goodness-of-fit of the mixed models for the 10 time windows (Intercept = condition: d-pronoun, mention: 1st, animacy: animate)[3]

Model	**Formulas in R**	**Time windows**
Simple model	lmer(looks∼condition+mention+(1|pp)+(1|item))	1-3 (0-600 ms)
Interaction model	lmer(looks∼condition*mention+(1|pp)+(1|item))	5-6 (800-1200 ms) 9-10(1600-2000 ms)
Animacy model	lmer(looks∼condition*mention*animacy+(1|pp)+(1|item))	4 (600-800 ms) 7-8 (1200-1600 ms)

[3] Due to space limitations, we restrain ourselves to report the statistically significant results. The interested reader is very much welcome to contact the authors for the exact values.

The fixed-effects analysis showed a marginally significant interaction between order of mention and animacy in time window 4. In time windows 6 and 7, the two-way interaction 'mention x condition' and the two main effects order of mention and condition became (marginally) significant indicating that the pronouns were resolved differently; overall there were more looks for the personal pronoun than for the d-pronoun, and there was an overall NP2-preference. In time windows 7 and 8, the three-way interaction 'condition x mention x animacy', and the two-way interactions of 'mention x animacy' and 'condition x animacy' were either marginally significant or significant. In addition, in window 8 there was a significant main effect of animacy. The beta coefficient suggested that there were more looks for AA than for II. In general, the significant interactions with animacy showed that this factor had an influence on the resolution effects. To break down the interactions individual analyses were conducted for AA and II which revealed an overall NP1-preference for the personal pronoun. Interestingly, this preference emerged quite early in AA (window 4) compared to II (window 8). For the d-pronoun, we found an overall NP2-preference. The emergence of the effects was earlier for II (window 4) compared to AA (window 6); however, when we collapsed AA and II and conducted the individual analyses for the two types of pronouns, the overall NP2-preference for d-pronouns emerged in window 5 while for the personal pronoun the NP1-effect began to be significant in window 8. Therefore, we would argue that there does not exist a timing difference in the emergence of the NP2-effect for d-pronouns, while for the personal pronoun there is with AA having the NP1-effect appear quite early compared to the late effect in II.

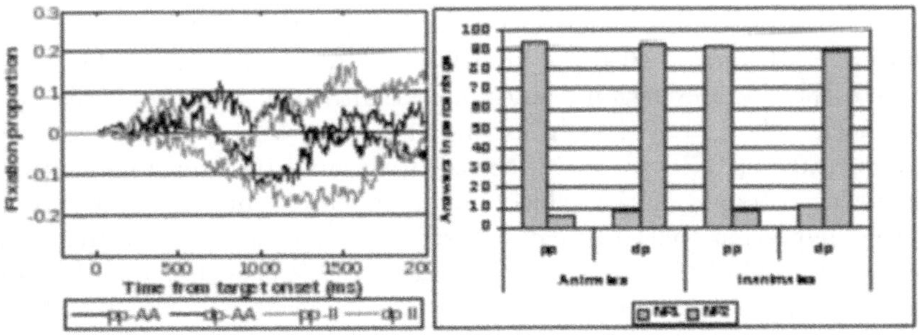

Fig. 1. Animacy. Left: Experiment 1a (Eye-tracking NP1-advantage scores: proportion of looks to NP1 minus proportion of looks to NP2). Right: Experiment 1b (Referent-assignment).

2.2 Experiment 1b: Referent-Assignment Task

Method. Twenty native speakers of German participated in the study. They were teachers at the Goethe Gymnasium Karlsruhe in Germany. We used the same experimental items as in Experiment 1a. The items were written out and the pronouns appeared in bold letters. The participants were asked to circle the part of the sentence that the word in bold letters was referring to. As for the eye-tracking task two experimental versions were created. Thirty-six items from the set of fillers of the eye-tracking task were chosen, so that the participants received a total of 60 items. The filler items consisted of pronouns of various kinds (personal and demonstrative pronouns, feminine, neuter, plural) and were unambiguous.

Results. We conducted a three-way loglinear analysis on the off-line data, entering referential choice (NP1, NP2), pronoun type (pp, dp) and animacy (AA, II) as predictors, and chose a backward elimination method. The analysis produced a final model that retained but the 'choice x pronoun' two-way interaction and its main effects. The likelihood ratio of this model was χ^2 (4) = 1.4919, p= .83. This indicated that the two-way interaction 'choice x pronoun' was significant, χ^2 (1) = 391.741, p<.001***. Animacy did thus not have an effect on the distribution of referential choice. For personal pronouns there was a clear NP1-preference (93%); for the d-pronoun, a clear NP2-preference (91%).

Discussion. The first experimental study was designed to test whether the animacy level of the antecedents would have an effect on the resolution preferences of personal and d-pronouns. The off-line data showed that animacy did not affect the final interpretation preferences. We found a highly significant NP1-preference for the personal pronoun and a highly significant NP2-preference for the d-pronoun. These preferences were also found in the eye-tracking task, still there was a difference between AA and II which affected the timing of the results. In AA the NP1-preference appeared quite early (at 600 ms) compared to II where it appeared only at 1400 ms to be significant. D-pronouns seemed not to be as sensitive towards this factor, considering that the NP2-preference emerged at 600 ms in II and at 1000 ms in AA which was not considerably earlier or later than the overall effect in the collapsed data (800 ms). As to the duration of the effects, there was a longer lasting NP2 effect in II (600-1800 ms) than in AA (1000-1200 ms). However, this sensitivity cannot be interpreted since we do not know what longer lasting effects might indicate. Our results are not in line with the suggestion that d-pronouns prefer animate antecedents regardless of the animacy level of the competitor antecedent, because they qualify better as subsequent topics [8]. Our pattern of results is rather in line with the claim that d-pronouns are marked for a non-topical co-reference function, whereas personal pronouns are unmarked and therefore more sensitive to contextual cues such as animacy [9,1]. Furthermore, had animacy been a mere cognitive principle not specific to pronoun resolution, we would not have expected to find this resolution difference across pronouns. For personal pronouns, disambiguation was facilitated in AA indicating a preference for animate over inanimate antecedents. To further investigate this issue in the future mixed items of the type AI and IA would be needed. Interestingly, we would not have been able to find these subtle differences had we only used the off-line referent assignment task. This suggests that although ultimately participants come to a final choice, the relative level of ease/difficulty with which they arrive at this choice, may be influenced by such disambiguating cues as animacy.

3 Semantic or Structural Constraints: Connectives

Another factor which might have an effect on pronoun resolution is whether the pronoun refers to an antecedent which has been presented inter- or intra-sententially, cf. [22]. Intra-sentential pronoun resolution has been tested by linking the antecedent clause to the pronominal clause via a connective, such as *but* or *while*. While some of the above outlined German psycholinguistic studies systematically used a connective [20] or not [33], others did not control for this factor [10]. According to [18] pronoun resolution may be affected by the type of connector used. Using a sentence completion task, they found that in English the personal pronoun was preferentially resolved towards NP1 when following the connective *but*. However, when following *because*, the resolution preferences depended on the implicit causality of the verb (*frighten*→NP1, *fear*→NP2). However, by changing the type of connective used, the structure of the second clause was also changed, i.e. main clause vs. subordinate clause. As [26] showed in a sentence completion experiment on pronoun resolution in English following different types of connectors (*however, although, then, when*), the amount of interpretation preferences towards NP1 was affected by the type of connective (temporary vs. contrastive adverbial) and even more so by the type of structure that was introduced by the connective. When the pronoun was introduced in a subordinate structure by the contrastive connector *although*, it was preferentially resolved towards NP1 (although less strong than with the main clause adverbial *however*); interestingly after the temporary connector *when* this preference switched into an NP2-preference. Importantly, the sentence materials only comprised verbs assigning the agent role to NP1, and the patient role to NP2 (such as *hit*). Thus, had the connectors been sensitive towards the verb causality information, then they should have been biased towards NP1; this argument even strengthens the observed effect for subordinate structures. However, as [26] points out, the semantics of the connector *when* might have varied a lot from the semantics of the connector *then*, since when may evoke a causal reading (and not only a temporary one). In a second experiment she therefore enlarged the set of connectors which stemmed from various semantic categories to see whether she could replicate the structural constraints effect. Although subordinate connectors decreased the NP1-preference for the personal pronoun (slightly below 50%) compared to main clause connectors (about 85%), they also did not evoke an NP2-preference. This result may be taken as evidence that structural constraints did influence the interpretation, but were modulated by the type of connective used.

Thus, on the one hand there is indication that the semantics of the connectors used have an impact on pronoun resolution preferences; on the other hand there is evidence that the structural constraint introduced by the connector is even a stronger predictor. Since these studies were conducted in English, it is unclear whether they follow a universal principle or whether the influence of these factors may be subject to cross-linguistic variation. With regard to production studies in the second language literature, it is known that especially the use of connectives varies between native speakers of English and native speakers of German [11]. This indicates that connectives might be processed differently across languages, and therefore might also have a different influence on the resolution of pronouns.

Furthermore, German connectives introducing a subordinate structure result in a change of verb position. For example, the connector *because* fits three different translations in German, e.g. *denn*, *da* and *weil*. While *denn* introduces a main clause, *da* subordinates the clause structure, and *weil* can be used in both constructions (*cf.* 4 and 5). Thus, in German there is a word order change marking the type of clause structure on the surface. In the above outlined studies, the connectives always preceded the pronominal clause whose structure was manipulated by a connective. Thus both antecedents were presented within the same clause, only differentiated by their position/grammatical function. However, with regard to theories of discourse structure [3,4], it may be asked whether placing NP1 and NP2 in different clauses would have an influence on the interpretation of a subsequent personal pronoun, due to a change in the salience level of NP2. According to the Right Frontier Constraint [27], an antecedent at the right frontier of a discourse unit is more salient and available for subsequent co-reference with a pronoun. Therefore, when NP2 is part of a coordinated structure, this should result in an NP2-preference, while a subordinated NP2 should favour an NP1-preference. This issue was addressed in our study with the aim to find out how syntactic structure and discourse structure might interact in the resolution of ambiguous pronouns.

3.1 Experiment 2: The Semantic of Connectives

The current sentence completion task was designed to test whether the use of different types of connectives (no connector, additive, contrastive, causal) would influence the resolution preferences. We concentrated on the resolution preferences for personal pronouns only, since they are claimed to be more sensitive towards contextual cues than d-pronouns, and we wanted to maximize the possibility to find a difference across conditions.

Method. Twenty-four native speakers of German participated in the study. They were students at the University of Göttingen and were paid for their participation (mean age=23; SD=3). Twenty-four experimental items of type in (3) were constructed. The modal verb *wanted* was implemented, because it biases for NP1-readings [11] to control for effects of verb causality. The second main clause either started with the target segment, either with the personal pronoun, or with a connective before it.

(3) Der Polizist wollte mit dem Brieftrger Radio hören
The policeman wanted to listen to the radio with the mailman

Er.../	und er.../	aber er.../	denn er...
He.../	*and he.../*	*but he.../*	*because he.../*

Two sets of twenty-four filler items were constructed[4]. We constructed four experimental lists following a latin-square distribution. The experiment was programmed as a web experiment [https://www.soscisurvey.de/]. The order of stimulus presentation was randomized. Participants were instructed to read the beginnings of some mini stories and to complete them by typing in their answers.

Results. The sentence completions were judged by three independent raters to either refer to NP1 or to NP2[5]. We accessed the inter-rater reliability by calculating Fleiss' Kappa which was acceptable with $\kappa = 0.4625$. The relatively low Kappa value was not judged to be a problem, since the results obtained were very clear (Fig.2). The judgments perfectly converged on 86% of the answers ($p_i=1$), in all of the other cases one rater differed in her rating ($p_i=.33$). In these latter cases, the answers of the two judges who agreed in their ratings entered the analysis (*76 cases in total:* 19 *He*, 7 *and he*, 24 *but he*, 26 *because he*). We conducted a two-way loglinear analysis on the off-line data, entering referential choice (NP1, NP2) and condition (no connector, additive, contrastive, causal) as predictors, and chose a backward elimination method. The analysis produced a final model that retained but the main effect of referential choice with a likelihood ratio of χ^2 (6) = 2.1162, p= .91. The type of connective did thus not have an effect on the distribution of referential choice. The main effect of referential choice was highly significant, χ^2 (1) = 478.401, p<.001***, due to a highly significant NP1-preference for the personal pronoun.

Discussion. The above study tested the influence of different kinds of connectors on the resolution preferences for personal pronouns. In line with the results of study 1, there was an overall preference for the personal pronoun to be resolved towards NP1. This preference did not differ across conditions; thus the semantics of the connectives did not affect the resolution preferences. Interestingly with regard to earlier sentence completion experiments which found an influence of connector type on the resolution of English personal pronouns [18,26] our results did not show such an influence. Considering that we were quite restrictive when constructing our materials, and therefore used a modal verb to control for any implicit causality biases, this criterion might have been so strict that it overruled other linguistic cues such as the semantics of the connectives. Moreover, the studies of [18] and [26]used connectors which differed not only in their semantics, but also in the clause structure they introduced (main clause vs. subordinate) which resulted in different interpretation patterns. The results showed a relatively robust NP1-preference across main clause connectors

[4] One filler set comprised the experimental stimuli of Experiment 3a. The set presented proper names instead of full NP-antecedents and the sentences followed a different sentence structure, and were thus considered to well mask the other experimental set.

[5] One erroneously constructed item resulted in an unambiguous reading. Four more answers needed to be eliminated, because they were not plausible continuations of the sentence beginnings resulting in a sample of 548 sentence completions which entered the analysis.

which is in line with what we found. The semantics of the connectives affected pronoun resolution after subordinate connectors differently [26]. Since we did not use subordinate connectors in our experiment 2, we cannot draw any firm conclusions on this issue, but it indicates the need to address this question using different types of subordinate connectors in future studies.

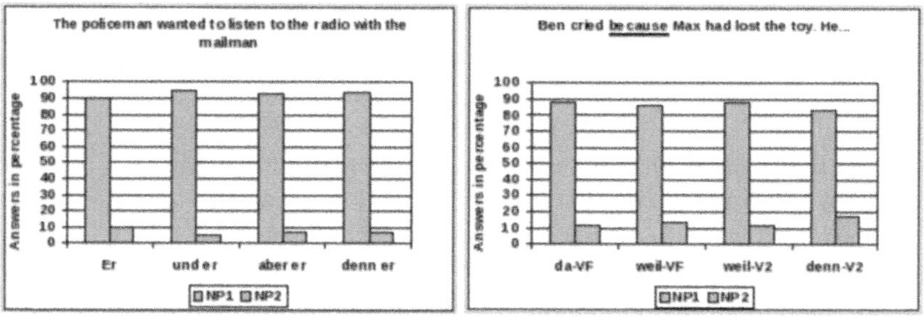

Fig. 2. Left:Experiment 2, Semantics of Connectives Right:Experiment 3, Clause Structure

3.2 Experiment 3: Clausal Structure

The current sentence completion experiment was designed to test whether the clausal structure in which NP2 was presented (subordination, coordination) would affect the interpretation preference of a subsequent subject pronoun as proposed by models of discourse structure such as the Right Frontier Constraint (RFC) account [27]. This account predicts that coordination may override the NP1-preference for personal pronouns, since it presents NP2 as the antecedent at the right frontier of the discourse unit and thus makes it more salient.

Method. We constructed 24 experimental items presenting NP1 in a first main clause, and NP2 either in a coordinated or a subordinated clause. The second sentence started with a personal pronoun. We used three different causal connectors (*da*, *weil*, *denn*) all of which can be translated with the English connector *because*. In the first two conditions (4), the connectors introduced a verb final structure (subordination), while in the other two conditions (5) a verb-second structure was used coordinating both clauses. Note, that the verb-second *weil* structure is a marked structure in spoken German. We implemented it to explore whether it would give rise to the same interpretational pattern as the verb-final *weil* construction being driven by the type of connector, or whether it was closer to *denn* due to the clausal structure it was placed in. The same experimental versions were used as in experiment 2.

(4) Ben weinte, da/weil Max das Spielzeug verloren hatte. Er... (VF)
(5) Ben weinte, weil/denn Max hatte das Spielzeug verloren. Er... (V2)
Ben cried because Max had lost the toy. He...

Results. The same judges as in Experiment 2 rated the set of answers[6]. We accessed the inter-rater reliability by calculating Fleiss' Kappa which was very high with κ= 0.8144. The judgments perfectly converged on 93% of the answers (p_i=1), in all of the other cases one rater differed in her rating (p_i=.33). In these latter cases, the answers of the two judges who agreed in their ratings entered the analysis (41 cases in total: 2 *da*-VF, 13 *weil*-VF, 12 *weil*-V2, 14 *denn*-V2). We conducted a two-way loglinear analysis on the off-line data, entering referential choice (NP1, NP2) and structure (coordination, subordination) as predictors, and chose a backward elimination method. The analysis produced a final model that retained but the main effect of referential choice with a likelihood ratio of χ^2 (2) = .3695, p= .83. The type of structure did thus not have an effect on the distribution of referential choice. The main effect of referential choice was highly significant, χ^2 (1) = 336.204, p<.001***, due to a highly significant NP1-preference for the personal pronoun.

Discussion. Experiment 3 addressed the question of whether the clausal structural in which NP2 was presented influenced the resolution of a subsequent personal pronoun. We did not find such an effect. The personal pronoun was consistently interpreted as co-referring to NP1. The pattern of results was thus in line with the patterns which had been found in experiment 1 and 2. However, they were not in line with the predictions made by the RFC [27] which suggested an NP1-preference for the personal pronoun after subordination and an NP2-preference following a coordinated structure. We can think of two reasons why this was the case. First the RFC account was formulated with regard to larger discourse units. Our conception was that if such structural constraints affected resolution processes in discourse it should also well be observable in very small discourse units. However, maybe our sentence materials were too short to elicit such discourse constraints. If this was the case, the study should be repeated using larger chunks of discourse. Another possibility is that subordination and coordination may be understood as a syntactic concept, as we operationalized it here by verb position, or as a discourse-semantic principle. Text can be structured in the way that e.g. narration gives rise to a coordinated structure while explanation gives rise to a subordinated discourse structure [3,4]. While our materials were perfectly able to draw a difference concerning subordination and coordination with regard to syntax, the connectors might not have been sufficient to introduce these concepts in terms of discourse-semantic structure. One possible way to find out might be to manipulate the second clause so that it either has a narrative or an explanatory discourse structure. Furthermore, while we manipulated the clause structure in which NP2 was presented, we kept the clause structure in which NP1 was presented equal: it was always presented in a main clause. In future studies it would be interesting to manipulate the clause structure of NP1 by positioning a connective sentence-initially as in *Since Max had lost the toy, Ben cried. He...* and to investigate, whether this would make NP2 more salient and thus more available for pronoun resolution.

[6] Six answers needed to be eliminated, because they were not plausible continuations of the sentence beginnings, resulting in a sample of 570 sentence completions.

4 General Discussion

The work presented here investigated in which ways semantic and structural factors such as the animacy of the antecedent candidates, the type of connector used preceding the pronoun, and the clause structure in which NP2 is presented influence pronoun resolution preferences. Across experiments we repeatedly found personal pronouns to favor NP1 co-reference over NP2 co-reference. The first experiment additionally used a second type of pronominal form: a d-pronoun, and directly compared the resolution preferences across pronouns. For the d-pronoun there was a very robust NP2-preference which replicated earlier findings [9,33]. However, earlier studies differed with regard to the resolution preferences found for personal pronouns [9,33,10,20], which were claimed not to be as robust. Our experiments show that at least with regard to the factors which were under investigation and with regard to the well-controlled linguistic environment we provided, the NP1-interpretation preference for the personal pronoun is quite robust.[7]

References

1. Ahrenholz, B.: Verweise mit Demonstrativa Im Gesprochenen Deutsch. In: Grammatik, Zweitspracherwerb und Deutsch als Fremdsprache. Walter De Gruyter, Berlin (2007)
2. Ariel, M.: Accessing NP antecedents. Routledge, London (1990)
3. Asher, N., Lascarides, A.: Logics of Conversation. Cambridge University Press, Cambridge (2003)
4. Asher, N., Vieu, L.: Subordinating and coordinating discourse relations. Lingua 115, 591–610 (2005)
5. Baayen, R.H., Davidson, D.J., Bates, D.M.: Mixed-effects modeling with crossed random effects for subjects and items. J. Memory and Language 59, 390–412 (2008)
6. Barr, D.J.: Analyzing 'visual world' eyetracking data using multilevel logistic regression. J. Memory and Language 59, 457–474 (2008)
7. Bates, D.M., Sarkar,D.: lme4: Linear mixed-effects models using S4 classes, version 0.999375-27 (2007), `http://www.r-project.org`
8. Bittner, D.: Influence of animacy and grammatical role on production and comprehension of intersentential pronouns in German L1-acquisition1. Paper Presented at the Conference on Intersentential Pronominal Reference in Child and Adult Language (2007)
9. Bosch, P., Umbach, C.: Reference determination for demonstrative pronouns. Paper Presented at the Conference on Intersentential Pronominal Reference in Child and Adult Language (2007)

[7] We gratefully acknowledge Johanna Klages, Dirk Buschbom, Susanna Auberlen, Stefanie Rößler, Judith Schlenter, and Christine Göb at the University of Göttingen, and Nina Zuurveen, Marcus van Ackeren, Johanna Tewes and Tilman Harpe at the MPI for Psycholinguistics for their help with stimulus preparation, data collection and sentence completion ratings, and Holger Mitterer and Eva Reinisch for their Perl and MATLAB scripts. Thanks to the MPI for Psycholinguistics where the data of experiment 1a were collected.

10. Bouma, G., Hopp, H.: Coreference Preferences for Personal Pronouns in German. Paper Presented at the Conference on Intersentential Pronominal Reference in Child and Adult Language (2007)
11. Carroll, M., Rodeutscher, A., Lambert, M., Van Stutterheim, C.: Subordination in narratives and macrostructural planning: A comparative point of view. In: Fabricius-Hansen, C., Ramm, W. (eds.) 'Subordination' Versus 'Coordination' in Sentence and Text, pp. 161–184. John Benjamins (2008)
12. Clifton Jr., C., Traxler, M.J., Mohamed, M.T., Williams, R.S., Morris, R.K., Rayner, K.: The use of thematic role information in parsing: Syntactic processing autonomy revisited. J. Memory and Language 49, 317–334 (2003)
13. Cooper, R.M.: The control of eye fixation by the meaning of spoken language: A new methodology for the real-time investigation of speech perception, memory and language processing. Cognitive Psychology 6, 84–107 (1974)
14. Crawley, R., Stevenson, R., Kleinman, D.: The use of heuristic strategies in the interpretation of pronouns. J. Psycholinguistic Research 4, 245–264 (1990)
15. Frederiksen, J.: Understanding anaphora: Rules used by readers in assigning pronominal referents. Discourse Processes 4, 323–347 (1981)
16. Fukumura, K., Van Gompel, R.P.G.: The effects of animacy in the choice of referring expressions. In: Language and Cognitive Processes, October 13 (2010)
17. Gernsbacher, M.A.: Mechanisms that improve referential access. Cognition 32, 99–156 (1989)
18. Grober, E.H., Beardsley, W., Caramazza, A.: Parallel function strategy in pronoun assignment. Cognition 6, 117–133 (1978)
19. Gundel, J.K., Hedberg, N., Zacharski, R.: Cognitive status and the form of referring expressions in discourse. Language and Cognitive Processes 69, 274–307 (1993)
20. Hemforth, B., Konieczny, L., Scheepers, C., Colonna, S., Schimke, S., Pynte, J.: Language specific preferences in anaphor resolution: Exposure or Gricean maxims? In: Proceedings of the 32nd Annual Conference of the Cognitive Science Society, Portland, USA (August 2010)
21. Igoa, J.M.: The relationship between conceptualization and formulation processes in sentence production: some evidence from Spanish. In: Carreiras, M., Garca-Albea, J.E., Sebastin-Galls, N. (eds.) Language Processing in Spanish, pp. 305–351. Lawrence Erlbaum Associates, Mahwah (1996)
22. Kehler, A.: Coherence, Reference, and the Theory of Grammar. CSLI Publications, Standford (2002)
23. Lambrecht, K.: Information Structure and Sentence Form: Topic, Focus, and the Mental Representations of Discourse Referents, Cambridge UK (1994)
24. Levinson, S.C.: Pragmatic reduction of the binding conditions revisited. J. Linguistics 27, 107–161 (1991)
25. Mak, W.M., Vonk, W., Schriefers, H.: The influence of animacy on relative clause processing. J. Memory and Language 47, 50–68 (2002)
26. Miltsakaki, E.: The syntax-discourse interface: Effects of the main-subordinate distinction on attention structure. University of Pennsylvania, Pennsylvania (2003)
27. Polanyi, L.: A formal model of the structure of discourse. J. Pragmatics 12, 601–638 (1988)
28. Prat-Sala, M., Branigan, H.P.: Discourse Constraints on Syntactic Processing in Language Production: A Cross-linguistic Study in English and Spanish. J. Memory and Language 42, 168–182 (2000)

29. Tanenhaus, M.K., Spivey-Knowlton, M.J., Eberhard, K.M., Sedivy, J.C.: Integration of visual and linguistic information in spoken language comprehension. Science 268(5217), 1632–1634 (1995)
30. Traxler, M.J., Morris, R.K., Seely, R.E.: Processing subject and object relative clauses: Evidence from eye movements. J. Memory and Language 47, 69–90 (2002)
31. Trueswell, J., Tanenhaus, M.K., Garnsey, S.: Semantic influences on parsing: Use of thematic role information in syntactic ambiguity resolution. J. Memory and Language 33, 285–318 (1994)
32. Van Nice, K.Y., Dietrich, R.: Task-sensitivity of animacy effects: Evidence from German picture descriptions. Linguistics 41(5), 825–849 (2003)
33. Wilson, F.: Processing at the syntax-discourse interface in second language acquisition. University of Edinburgh, Edinburgh (2009)

Exploring the Lexical and Acoustic Consequences of Referential Predictability

Elsi Kaiser, David Cheng-Huan Li, and Edward Holsinger

Department of Linguistics, University of Southern California
Los Angeles, CA 90089, USA
{emkaiser,lidc,holsinge}@usc.edu

Abstract. Findings from various domains suggest that predictability is an important component of language processing. We report psycholinguistic research suggesting that predictability also influences referential processing, in the form of reduced acoustic durations for predictable referents. However, we do not find evidence that predictability directly influences likelihood of pronominalization, contrary to some prior claims. Instead, our data indicate that the use and interpretation of pronouns is influenced by thematic role, independently of which referent is most predictable, i.e., most likely to be mentioned next. We suggest that likelihood-of-mention is influenced by the mapping between syntactic and thematic roles. Our results highlight the benefits of exploring both lexical and acoustic aspects of referential production.

Keywords: psycholinguistics, reference resolution, anaphora, predictability, acoustic reduction.

1 Introduction

A growing body of research indicates that the language processing system is sensitive to predictability. In the domain of phonology, for example, words are produced with shorter durations and greater phonological reduction when they are predictable on the basis of preceding words/collocational frequencies ([4,10]). Predictability effects have also been explored in areas such as syntax ([8,16]) and language change ([9]).

We report two experiments that investigate the role of predictability in reference-tracking, focusing especially on the relation between (i) how an entity is referred to and (ii) how likely it is to be mentioned, i.e., how predictable it is.

Given the importance of predictability in many models of human language processing, it may seem surprising that in the domain of reference-tracking, there is as of yet no consensus regarding the role of predictability. One view is that referents' predictability – likelihood of being mentioned subsequently – is closely connected to the choice of referring expression: Reduced forms (e.g. pronouns) are preferentially used for highly predictable, expected referents (e.g. [1,6]).

In contrast, others claim that likelihood-of-mention is separate from choice of referring expression. For example, Fukumura & van Gompel [5] argue that

I. Hendrickx et al. (Eds.): DAARC 2011, LNAI 7099, pp. 171–183, 2011.

likelihood-of-mention is influenced by semantic factors, and that referring expression choice is influenced by accessibility/structural prominence, with pronouns preferring syntactically-prominent referents/subjects. In related work, Kehler, Kertz, Rohde & Elman's [14] Bayesian approach to pronoun comprehension and production makes it possible to separate likelihood-of-mention from likelihood-of-prominalization.

$$\mathrm{P}(\textit{referent}|\textit{pronoun}) = \frac{\mathrm{P}(\textit{pronoun}|\textit{referent})\ \mathrm{P}(\textit{referent})}{\mathrm{P}(\textit{pronoun})}$$

Fig. 1. Kehler et al.'s Bayesian approach

According to this approach, comprehenders have expectations about who is likely to be mentioned next in a discourse. Kehler et al. suggest that when considering pronoun interpretation patterns, represented by (P(*referent*| *pronoun*)) – given a pronoun, what is the probability that it refers to a particular referent – it is useful to treat interpretation biases as being composed of two expectations: (i) the probability that a particular referent will be mentioned subsequently (P(*referent*)) (see also [2]) and (ii) the probability that a particular referent will be referred to with a pronoun (P(*pronoun*| *referent*)). Pronoun interpretation is of course also sensitive to the overall probability of using a pronoun, P(*pronoun*). Thus, from the perspective of the comprehender, pronoun resolution involves P(*referent*| *pronoun*), i.e., given a pronoun, what is the probability that it refers to a particular referent x?

Crucially, according to this approach, likelihood-of-mention (P(*referent*)) can be separated from likelihood of producing a pronoun (P(*pronoun*| *referent*)) and does not necessarily map directly to pronoun interpretation.

Further evidence pointing to a dissociation between likelihood-of-mention and pronominalization comes from Kaiser's [11] data on it-clefts (e.g. *It was Mary that Kate tickled*). In an open-ended production task after subject clefts, participants were most likely to pronominalize reference to the immediately preceding subject (i.e., P(*pronoun*| *subject*) was relatively high), but this character was not overall the most likely referent to be mentioned next. Although we will not be framing the experiments in this paper in specifically Bayesian terms, the approach sketched out above helps to show how likelihood-of-mention and pronominalization can be separated. This differs from the Expectancy Hypothesis [1], which suggests that the expectancy /predictability of different entities is closely tied to speakers' choice of referring expression, with more attenuated forms used for more expected/predictable referents.

In sum, existing research on the relationship between likelihood-of-mention (how predictable, how expected a particular referent is at a certain point in the discourse, which can be formalized as P(*referent*) in Kehler's terms) and likelihood-of-pronominalization – both in terms of how likely speakers are to use pronouns (e.g. P(*pronoun*| *referent*)) and how likely hearers are to resolve pronouns in a particular way (P(*referent*| *pronoun*)) – has led to divergent claims.

2 Overview of Experiments

To shed light on the debate regarding the relation between predictability and referential form, we explored effects of likelihood-of-mention in two different dimensions: (i) on the production and choice of referring expression and (ii) the acoustic duration of referring expressions. As a starting point, we investigated *pronoun interpretation*: When given a pronoun, how do people interpret it (Experiment 1)? Then, in Experiment 2 we investigated how pronoun interpretation compares to *pronoun production*, i.e., in a production task, when do people opt to use pronouns rather than names or other referring expressions? Crucially, we also probed which referents participants choose to talk about, thereby obtaining a measure of how predictable different referents are.

With this methodology, we obtain two kinds of information about pronominalization that allow us to probe the relation between pronominalization and likelihood-of-mention: (i) *Comprehension*: When faced with a pronoun, does a person tend to interpret it as referring to the most predictable referent? and (ii) *Production*: When producing pronouns, do people produce pronouns mostly when referring to the most predictable referent? In addition, the production task (Experiment 2) allows us to test for potential effects of acoustic reduction.

In this paper, we use the terms predictability and likelihood-of-mention to refer to both speakers and comprehenders. Comprehenders have probabilistic expectations about who will be mentioned next ([14,2]), and thus, from the comprehenders' perspective, referents vary in how predictable / expected they are. Crucially, following [17,14], we regard comprehenders as "savvy anticipators" who have forward-looking expectations about who the speaker will talk about next and with what kind referring expression (see Fig.1). These expectations are shaped by prior context and continuously updated over the course of a discourse on the basis of new linguistic input (see also [2]). Broadly speaking, according to this view, under normal circumstances the comprehender's expectations about which referents are most predictable should largely mirror the speaker's expectations (see Fig.1).

3 Experiment 1: Prompt Pronoun

3.1 Participants, Materials and Design

Twenty-four native English speakers from the University of Southern California community participated. Participants heard auditorily-presented sentences (ex.1) with agent-patient verbs (e.g.AGENT *kicked* PATIENT, AGENT *tickled* PATIENT) over headphones, while viewing scenes depicting the two mentioned characters and other objects. The two characters always had the same gender (two women or two men). We used four male and four female characters throughout the study (female: *Lisa, Kate, Mary, Anne;* male: *Peter, Greg, John, Mike*). At the start of the experiment, participants completed a familiarization procedure to learn which name maps onto which character. However, because we did not want to induce a memory burden or induce potential misunderstandings, the name of each character was also included on the displays, as shown in Fig.2. On critical items, the two characters were located on the left and right sides of the display, with other things between them (Fig.2). The left/right location of subjects and objects was counterbalanced. We also counterbalanced how often each character appeared on the left and on the right, and in subject position and object position.

(1a) Mary slapped Lisa at the zoo. As a result she...
(1b) Lisa was slapped by Mary at the zoo. As a result she...

Fig. 2. Sample image

The critical sentences were in the active or the passive voice, and were followed by a sentence fragment consisting of a connective and a pronoun (ex.1). The participants' task was to produce natural-sounding continuations using the sentence fragment. This task can be regarded as a combination of comprehension and production, as participants need to understand the critical sentence and – crucially for our purposes – need to interpret the pronoun in the sentence fragment before they can provide a continuation (see [2,17] for discussion of this task).

All critical sentences ended in a location expression (e.g. *at the museum, on the beach*) which was related to the objects between the two characters. This was included because participants' eye-movements were recorded during this task, and the location expression acted as a look-away, encouraging participants to look away from both characters before they hear the pronoun. (Eye-movements are not reported here.)

Because coherence relations between sentences influence discourse flow (e.g., [14,13,3]), we used the causal 'as a result' connective, to ensure consistency in the coherence relations that participants construct.[1] More specifically, causal connectives after agent-patient verbs are known to focus the patient thematic role (see e.g. [15]). Thus, we used 'as a result' to create a situation in which there is a bias towards the patient, at least in the active voice. The behavior

[1] Experiments 1 and 2 also included 'then' connectives, which are ambiguous between a temporal interpretation (*Peter came home. Then he ate dinner*) and a causal interpretation (*Peter kicked Andy. Then Andy started to cry*). Preliminary analyses suggest that when used causally, 'then' resembles 'as a result'. However, due to the ambiguity of 'then' and the resulting unbalanced data points, in this paper we focus on 'as a result' only, for both experiments.

of subject pronouns after a passive clause and a causal connective is not yet well-understood, and thus we wanted to test whether the predicted patient bias persists in passives. The study included 24 targets and 36 fillers. In targets, we manipulated active vs. passive voice, and whether the connective was 'as a result' or 'then' (see footnote 1). We used a Latin-Square design to construct four lists. Reverse lists were also constructed to control for trial order.

3.2 Coding

All continuations were double-coded by two coders working independently. Coders noted whether the prompt pronoun was used to refer to the preceding subject, the preceding object, or whether its antecedent was unclear. We use the term 'subject' to refer to the grammatical subject of the critical sentence, i.e., the agent in actives and the patient in passives. We use the term 'object' to refer to the direct object in actives (the semantic patient) and the object of the by-phrase (the semantic agent) in passives.

Each coder went through the data independently. Coders were instructed to be conservative and to avoid over-interpretation, i.e., to err on the side of choosing 'unclear' if there was not enough information available to determine the intended antecedent. Subsequently, any discrepancies between the coders were resolved through discussion. If the two coders did not agree on a referent (i.e. if a discrepancy could not be resolved), the pronoun was coded as 'unclear'. In the end, 25% of pronouns in the 'result' conditions that are reported here were coded as having unclear/ambiguous antecedents; these were excluded from subsequent analyses. This kind of coding procedure is similar to [14,2,11,17]. Examples of participants' continuations and how they were coded are provided in ex(2).

(2a) Peter was scratched by Greg at the car wash. As a result, he ... got mad and made Greg pay for the car wash. [referent of pronoun = subject]

(2b) Kate was punched by Lisa at the restaurant. As a result, she ... got a bruise on her arm ... [referent of pronoun = subject]

(2c) Lisa pushed Anne on the beach. As a result, she ... hurt her leg and got angry at Lisa. [referent of pronoun = object]

(2d) Kate hit Mary at school. As a result, she ... got angry at Kate. [referent of pronoun = object]

(2e) John punched Peter at the museum. As a result, he ... accidentally broke a vase. [referent of pronoun = unclear]

3.3 Results and Discussion

As can be seen in Figure 3, participants mostly interpreted the pronoun prompt as referring to the character that is the patient in the prompt sentence, i.e., the object in active voice and the subject in passive voice. In the active conditions, the object preference is significantly higher than chance (t1(23)=2.34, p<.05, t2(23)=2.98, p<.01) and in the passive conditions, the subject preference is significantly higher than chance (t1(23)=6.72, p<.001, t2(23)=9.28, p<.001). (In these analyses, we are looking only at the binary choice between subject continuations and object continuations, and thus chance was estimated to be 0.5.)

Figure 3 also suggests that the bias to interpret the pronoun as referring to the preceding patient is stronger in passives than in actives. To test this, we computed a 'patient advantage score' for both passives and actives, by subtracting the proportion of non-patient continuations from the proportion of patient continuations both by subjects and by items. Paired t-tests show that sentences in the active voice do indeed result in a weaker patient preference than sentences in the passive voice (t1(23)=-2.03, p=.054, t2(23)=-2.97, p<.01). We suggest that the 'patient boost' exhibited by passives may be due to the patient being promoted to a non-canonical subject position.

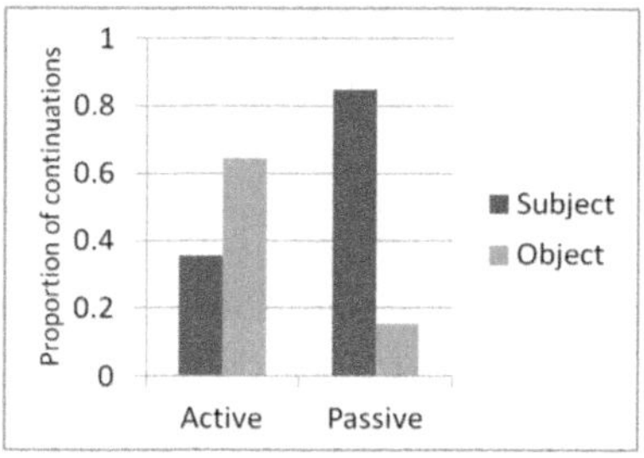

Fig. 3. How frequently did people use the prompt pronoun to refer to the preceding subject vs. the preceding object? (Experiment 1)

Overall, we find a clear effect of thematic role on pronoun interpretation: When comprehenders encounter a gender-ambiguous pronoun, they tend to interpret it as referring to the preceding patient. This preference arises both with patients in object position (actives) and patients in subject position (passives). Interestingly, we do not find a main effect of syntactic position/subjecthood, contrary to Fukumura & van Gompel's [5] findings with Stimulus-Experiencer and Experiencer-Stimulus verbs.

4 Experiment 2: No Prompt Pronoun

4.1 Participants, Materials and Design, Coding

Experiment 2 had the same design as Experiment 1, except that no pronoun prompt was provided: the sound files were truncated at the end of the connective. The stimuli were otherwise identical to Experiment 1. Thus, participants were now free to continue the sentence in a more open-ended way and could use a range of referring expressions. Experiment 2 allows us to test (i) which referent participants are mostly likely to talk about, and thereby obtain a measure of predictability/likelihood-of-mention, and (ii) what kind of referring expressions participants choose when referring to different antecedents. Because participants had to produce the referring expression themselves, we can also measure their durations to test for potential effects of acoustic reduction. Twenty-four new participants took part in Experiment 2.

Two coders worked through the data independently, working in the same way as described for Experiment 1. They noted what kind of referring expression participants used (e.g. pronoun, name, full noun phrase) and what it referred to (subject, object, unclear, another referent). Participants produced pronouns on about 11% of all trials,[2] and out of these, 27% were coded as having unclear/ambiguous antecedents. These unclear trials are excluded from subsequent analyses.

Ex.(3) shows examples of different continuations and how they were coded. In addition to the forms and coreferential relations in the continuations, the acoustic durations of the names produced by the participants were measured.

(3a) Kate hit Mary at school. As a result ... Mary did not want to be friends with Kate anymore. [coded as form=name, referent=object]

(3b) Mike pushed Peter at the airport. As a result ... security took them both and talked to them. [coded as form=noun, referent=other]

(3c) Lisa punched Kate at the restaurant. As a result ... they were banned from the restaurant for being overly dramatic. [coded as form=plural pronoun, referent=subject & object]

(3d) Greg scratched Peter at the car wash. As a result ... he had marks on his arm for a week. [coded as form=pronoun, referent=object]

(3e) Mary tapped Anne in the forest. As a result ... she woke up a bear and they had to run away. [coded as form=pronoun, referent=unclear]

4.2 Results and Discussion: Who Is Mentioned and How

We first report which entities are most likely to be mentioned and with what kind of referring expressions. Then, we turn to the acoustic durations of names

[2] 11% is relatively low, and we often obtain higher rates of pronoun production in comparable written tasks where participants continue sentences without a visual scene, which suggests the low rate may be task-related. However, as we will see below, although the rate of pronouns in Exp.2 is low, the trials where people did produce pronouns show patterns that are strikingly similar to the interpretation of pronouns in Exp.1 (cf. Fig.3, Fig.4). This is a positive finding, because it shows that although the task may have led to an overall decrease in the proportion of pronouns produced, it crucially did not distort the underlying patterns.

produced by participants, to see whether predictability is associated with acoustic reduction.

Overall, participants produced a variety of continuation types.[3] When we look at only those trials where participants chose to start their continuation with a pronoun (Figure 4), the patterns look very similar to Experiment 1 (Figure 3). In other words, we again find indications of an overall *patient preference*, which is stronger with passives. (Due to the low number of observations, no statistics are reported.) In other words, when participants chose to produce a pronoun, this mostly occurred when they were talking about the patient of the preceding sentence.

Let us now look more broadly at which referent participants are more likely to continue with, independent of the referring expression that is used. These results will give us a measure of which referents are most predictable, most likely to be mentioned next, in the different conditions. Here, a very different pattern emerges. As can be seen in Figure 5, the patient is not consistently the entity with the highest likelihood-of-mention:

In *active conditions*, most continuations do indeed start with the preceding object/patient, and the proportion of subject continuations is significantly lower than chance ($t1(23)=-6.33$, $p<.001$, $t2(23)=-8.82$, $p<.001$). Thus, after an active sentence followed by a causal connective, the patient has a high likelihood-of-mention.

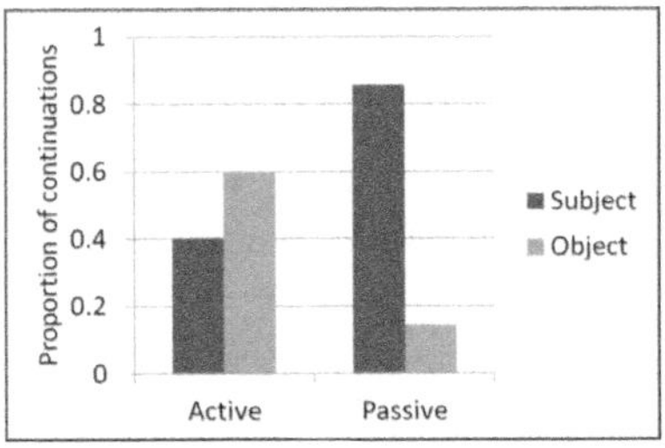

Fig. 4. On trials where participants chose to produce a pronoun, what did the pronoun refer to? (Experiment 2)

However, in the *passive conditions*, continuations were evenly split between the patient (the promoted subject) and the agent (demoted to the by-phrase), as can be seen in Figure 5 on the next page. The proportion of subject continuations does not differ significantly from chance ($t1(23)=.68$, $p>.5$, $t2(23)=.74$, $p>.4$). (In these analyses, as in Experiment 1, we only looked at those trials where people continued with either the subject or the object. i.e., we are focusing on the binary choice between subject vs. object, and thus chance was estimated to be 0.5.)

[3] We focus on trials where the participants start by referring to the preceding subject or object. Continuations that start with other entities (e.g. the restaurant manager) or refer to both subject and object (e.g. they) are excluded, as are continuations where it was unclear whether people were referring to the subject or the object.

As a whole, we see that in passives, the patient and the agent are equally predictable, equally likely to be mentioned in subsequent discourse: Neither is a clear winner. Thus, the passive results reveal a striking dissociation between likelihood-of-mention and likelihood-of-pronominalization: Patients are the most likely to be pronominalized, but not the most likely to be mentioned next.

It is worth noting that the difference in the likelihood-of-mention patterns exhibited by actives and passives emerges from our results, i.e., it was not specifically manipulated as an independent variable. We regard this as a strength of our design, as it means that the predictability differences exhibited by agents and patients depending on voice emerged naturally and were not pre-specified by the experimental design.

Similar to Experiment 1, we also computed patient advantage scores by subjects and by items. Paired t-tests show – not surprisingly, given the patterns visible in Figure 5 – that sentences in the active voice now have in a stronger patient preference than sentences in the passive voice ($t1(23)=3.65$, $p<.005$, $t2(23)=6.04$, $p<.0001$).

This pattern can also be described in terms of there being relatively more agent continuations in the passives than in the actives: Passives fail to show the overwhelming patient preference that we see in actives. In the next section, we consider the reasons for the boost in the rate of agent continuations with passives.

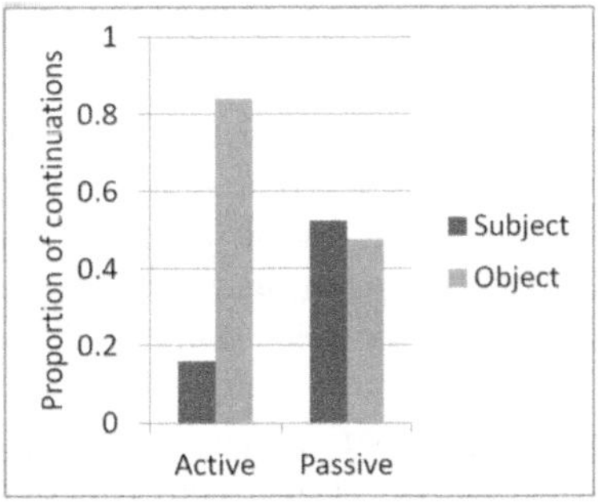

Fig. 5. How frequently did people start their continuations by reference to the preceding subject vs. the preceding object (regardless of form)? (Experiment 2)

4.3 Why Do Actives and Passives Differ with Respect to Likelihood-of-Mention?

We saw in the preceding section that (i) active agent-patient verbs followed by a causal connective create an expectation that the patient will be mentioned next, but (ii) passive agent-patient verb render both the agent and the patient equally expected/predictable. Another way of putting this is to say that the passives boost the rate of agent continuations. An important question is why this difference arises.

One possibility is that the active/passive asymmetry can be derived from a patient-bias combined with linear recency effects: In active sentences, thematic role and linear recency coincide (the object is a patient, i.e., focused by the causal connective, and also linearly the most recent argument), whereas in passive sentences, thematic role and recency favor different arguments (the grammatical subject and the object in the by-phrase, respectively). Could this be the reason why passives do not result in a clear expectation for one referent over the other?

We would like to suggest that the answer is no: We argue that the asymmetrical behavior of actives and passives cannot be reduced to linear recency. Evidence for this claim comes from other experiments, parallel to Experiments 1 and 2, that we conducted (see [12]) with stimulus-experiencer verbs (e.g. annoy, irritate). With stimulus-experiencer verbs, a causal connective is known to focus attention on the experiencer (e.g. *Peter irritated John and as a result John stomped out of the room*, [17,18]). Crucially, we found that with this verb class, actives and passives pattern in the same way: Participants preferred to start their continuations by talking about the experiencer, and this effect was not influenced by linear recency.

In light of these findings, instead of blaming the active/passive difference exhibited by agent-patient verbs on linear recency, we hypothesize that it stems from the thematic structure of agent-patient verbs. More specifically, agents are commonly regarded as semantically more prominent than patients (e.g. [7] and many others) and thus passivization of an agent-patient verb ends up demoting a semantically prominent argument (the agent) into a syntactically low-prominence position (the by-phrase of the passive). Thus, passivized agent-patient verbs can be regarded as suffering from a syntax-semantics mismatch. (Crucially, no such mismatch occurs when stimulus-experiencer verbs are passivized: the stimulus ends up in the by-phrase, but the thematic role of stimulus is commonly viewed as less prominent than the role of experiencer, and thus passivized stimulus-experiencer verbs do not suffer from a syntax-semantics mismatch).

In sum, when it comes to agent-patient verbs, we suggest that the asymmetrical behavior of actives and passives stems from the syntax-semantics mismatch that arises when semantically-prominent arguments – agents – are placed in a syntactically low-prominence position, the by-phrase.

However, it is worth noting that our findings regarding the dissociation between likelihood-of-mention and likelihood-of-pronominalization do not hinge on this question of why actives and passives differ. While the question of why they differ in this way is an important question in its own right, what is crucial for our claims regarding the relationship between likelihood-of-mention and likelihood-of-prominalization is simply that actives and passives do differ in terms of which argument is most likely to be mentioned subsequently, and that these likelihood patterns do not match the pronominalization patterns.

4.4 Results and Discussion: Acoustic Duration of Names

Given the dissociation between likelihood-of-mention and likelihood-of- pronominalization, does this mean that predictability plays no role in reference-tracking? Or might we find predictability effects in another dimension?

In an initial exploration of this question, we looked at the duration of names that participants produced in subject position in Experiment 2 (e.g. the second occurrence of 'Lisa' (underlined) in *Mary slapped Lisa at the zoo. As a result Lisa stormed off angrily*). We compared names produced in the active condition, where the object of the prompt-sentence has a high likelihood of subsequent mention (i.e. it's the expected referent), and names produced in the passive condition, where there is no clearly expected referent, since continuations were split between subject and object (Fig. 5). All of the analyzed names were in subject position, following the connective 'As a result.' The key difference is simply whether the preceding sentence was active or passive. This allows us to investigate whether predictability influences duration of proper names. The durations of the names (from the onset of each name to the offset of each name) were measured by a phonetically-trained annotator using Praat (Boersma & Weenink, *praat.org*). Datapoints whose duration was more than 4 standard deviations from the mean were excluded from analysis (1.6% of the data).

Analyses of duration show that names in subject position are shorter (283ms) after active sentences than names in subject position (320ms) after passive sentences (Figure 6). This finding is marginal by subjects and significant by items ($t1(22)=-1.8$, $p=.0858$, $t2(23)=-2.335$, $p<.03$).[4]

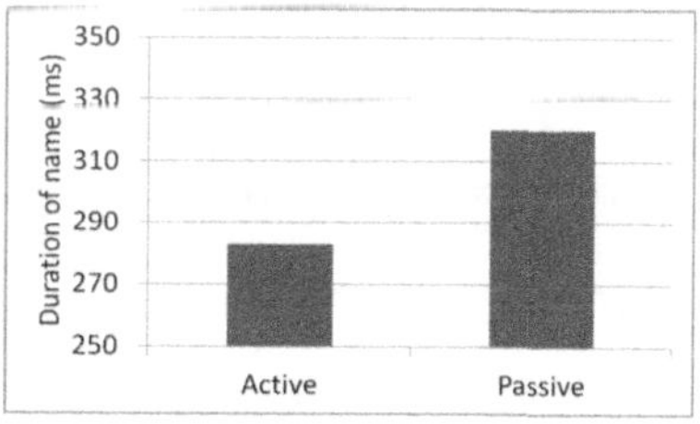

Fig. 6. Duration of names in subject position after actives and passives

Recall that in all conditions, the relevant name had been mentioned in the immediately preceding sentence. Thus, this effect cannot be attributed to whether the name was given or new information: all names were discourse-old/given. Additionally, all names occurred in both conditions and in each condition as both the agent and patient in different trials, and thus these results are not easily attributable to inherent differences in the names themselves.

In sum, we found that when participants produced names, the duration of the names showed effects of predictability. Although further work and more analyses

[4] The by-subjects analysis has 23 participants, because one person did not start with any names.

are needed to assess the validity of our preliminary findings, we would like to suggest that effects of likelihood-of-mention/predictability do exist in the domain of reference-tracking, although they do not appear to influence referring-expression choice. An intriguing question for future work concerns the prosodic realization of the names, in particular the presence/absence of pitch accents. We plan to conduct further analyses to explore this issue, as it could provide additional evidence for effects of predictability in the domain of reference-tracking.

5 Conclusions

Findings from a range of domains suggest that predictability is an important aspect of human language processing. Our findings suggest that predictability can also influence referential processing, in the form of reduced acoustic durations for predictable referents. However, we do not find evidence that predictability is directly linked to the likelihood of pronominalization, contrary to what some researchers have claimed. Instead, our findings reveal that – at least in the contexts we tested – the use and interpretation of pronouns is influenced by thematic role (e.g. agent vs. patient), independently of which referent is most predictable (i.e., most likely to be mentioned next). On the basis of our divergent findings for actives and passives, we also suggest that referents' likelihood-of-mention is influenced by an interplay of syntactic and semantic factors, in particular the mapping between syntactic roles and thematic roles. As a whole, our results highlight the benefits of exploring not only lexical but also acoustic aspects of referential production.

Acknowledgments. This work was partially funded by NIH grant R01HD061457 to E. Kaiser. Many thanks to Jackie Kim, Monica Do and Heidi Mettler for assistance with data analysis and coding. We also thank three anonymous reviewers for their useful comments and feedback. An earlier version of this project was presented at the *Workshop on the Production of Referring Expressions* (PRE-CogSci 2011).

References

1. Arnold, J.: Reference production: Production-internal and addressee-oriented processes. Language and Cognitive Processes 23, 495–527 (2008)
2. Arnold, J.: The Effect of Thematic Roles on Pronoun Use and Frequency of Reference Continuation. Discourse Processes 31(2), 137–162 (2001)
3. Asher, N., Lascarides, A.: Logics of Conversation. Cambridge University Press (2003)
4. Bell, A., et al.: Effects of disfluencies, predictability, and utterance position on word form variation in English conversation. J. Acoustic Society of America. 113, 1001–1024 (2003)
5. Fukumura, K., van Gompel, R.: Choosing anaphoric expressions: Do people take into account likelihood of reference? J. Memory and Language 62, 52–66 (2010)

6. Givón, T.: Mind, Code and Context: Essays in Pragmatics. Lawrence Erlbaum (1989)
7. Grimshaw, J.: Argument Structure. MIT Press, Cambridge (1990)
8. Hale, J.: A Probabilistic Earley Parser as a Psycholinguistic Model. In: NACCL, vol. 2, pp. 159–166 (2001)
9. Hume, E., Mailhot, F.: The role of entropy and surprisal in phonologization and language change. In: Yu, A. (ed.) Origins of Sound Patterns, University Press (to appear)
10. Jurafsky, D., Bell, A., Gregory, M., Raymond, W.: Probabilistic relations between words. Frequency and the Emergence of Linguistic Structure, pp. 229–254. John Benjamins (2001)
11. Kaiser, E.: Investigating the Consequences of Focus on the Production and Comprehension of Referring Expressions. International Review of Pragmatics 2, 266–297 (2010)
12. Kaiser, E., Holsinger, E., Li, D.: Who next? Consequences of syntax-semantics mismatches for likelihood of mention. In: CUNY Conference on Human Sentence Processing, Stanford (2011)
13. Kehler, A.: Coherence, Reference, and the Theory of Grammar. CSLI Publications (2002)
14. Kehler, A., Kertz, L., Rohde, H., Elman, J.: Coherence and coreference revisited. J. Semantics 25, 1–44 (2008)
15. Kertz, L., Kehler, A., Elman, J.: Evaluating a Coherence-Based Model of Pronoun Interpretation. In: Workshop on Ambiguity in Anaphora, Malaga, Spain (2006)
16. Levy, R.: Expectation-based syntactic comprehension. Cognition 106, 1126–1177 (2008)
17. Rohde, H.: Coherence-Driven Effects in Sentence and Discourse Processing. Ph.D., UC San Diego (2008)
18. Stevenson, R., Crawley, R., Kleinman, D.: Thematic roles, focusing and the representation of events. Language and Cognitive Processes 9, 519–548 (1994)

Clitics in Spanish Agrammatic Aphasia: A Study of the Production of Unaccusative, Reflexive and Object Clitics

Sara Sanchez–Alonso[1], Silvia Martinez–Ferreriro[2], and Roelien Bastiaanse[3]

[1] Yale University, USA
[2] Univ Pompeu Fabra, Spain
[3] Univ of Groningen, The Netherlands
sara.sanchez-alonso@yale.edu
silvia.martinez@upf.edu
y.r.m.bastiaanse@rug.nl

Abstract. Cross-linguistic research on language pathologies has shown that production of clitic pronominals is problematic for patients with aphasia. The current contribution provides the first data on production of the unaccusative/middle clitic SE and considers how pronominal interpretation influences verb production. Two morphologically similar constructions are studied: unaccusative and refexive sentences. Results are compared with production of direct object clitics. The data show that transitive sentences with DO clitics are harder to produce than unaccusative, reflexive and transitive (will full DPs in object position) constructions. These findings are explained by the increase in difficulty that processing of DO clitics involves: discourse linking and clitic placement. Finally, reflexive verbs were not more difficult to produce than transitive sentences. The current study therefore supports the analysis of reflexives as structurally similar to unergative entries.

Keywords: Spanish, agrammatism, clitic, unaccusative, reflexive, sentence production.

1 Introduction

The term 'agrammatism' refers to a grammatical disorder characterized by non-fluent output and relatively intact comprehension. Agrammatic speakers present poor grammar with omission and substitution of function words (both grammatical morphemes and free standing words) and frequent use of uninflected verbs. In particular, omission of pronominals in agrammatic speakers have been reported in several studies cross-linguistically (in Dutch, [8]; In Greek, [22]; in Italian [6,12,14], in Spanish [13]). In Romance languages, research in Italian show that non-brain damaged speakers produce less pronouns than agrammatic speakers [20] In particular, Martinez Ferreiro [13] observed a disocciation between reflexive and direct object clitics in Spanish Broca's aphasics.

I. Hendrickx et al. (Eds.): DAARC 2011, LNAI 7099, pp. 184–197, 2011.

Difficulties encountered by aphasic speakers in production of pronominals have been linked to a lack of processing resources and particularly to the integration of different linguistic modules, which require a higher processing load ([1,2,4]). However, to this date, it is still unknown to what extent brain-damaged speakers encounter difficulties within the range of clitics in Romance and how the establishment of a pronominal-antecedent relationship determines clitic production.

In the current study, we investigate production of three different types of clitics in Spanish, which differ in how they establish reference, that is, how they select their antecedent. It provides the first data on production of the unaccusative SE in Spanish and considers how pronominal-antecedent resolution influences production. Two types of SE anaphors (unaccusative SE and reflexive SE) are studied and compared to production of direct object clitics.

In the following sections, an overview of the pronominal system in Spanish is provided. This will be followed by a description of pronominals and their underlying syntactic structure. Then, relevant studies in agrammatism are discussed and finally the syntax-discourse model will be presented in order to explain current results in production of pronominals.

1.1 Clitics through Their Syntactic Representation

Kayne [11] divided personal pronouns into two main categories: strong and clitic. Two main syntactic properties characterize clitics. They cannot be stressed and they cannot appear in isolation. In written form, clitics can be adjoined to the verb either enclitically (1), as in the case of the imperative or non-finite forms, or proclitically (2), for the rest of verb forms.

(1) Recógelo.
pick-IT *up*.
'Pick it up'.

(2) Lo recogerá.
IT *will pick up*.
'[He/she][1] will pick it up'.

The majority of clitics bear features of gender, number and person. They also carry case feature, and thus they are further subdivided into different syntactic categories, such as reflexive or unaccusative clitics. For the purposes of the current study, we will concentrate on three main clitic types: unaccusative, reflexive and direct object clitics.

1.2 SE Anaphors: Unaccusative and Reflexive Clitics

On the basis of Reinhart [16], unaccusative (3) and reflexive (4) clitics are SE anaphors which function as purely "syntactic placeholders" that satisfy the predicate's arity requirements. The author further claims that the clitic SE in Romance languages is the residue of the thematic role, and agrees with Burzio [5] in that it signals the derivation of unaccusative entries from transitive ones.

[1] Spanish is a pro drop language, thus the subject is often omitted.

(3) El vaso se rompió.
the glass $SE_{cl.unacc.}$ *broke.*
'The glass broke'.

(4) La niña se lavó.
the girl $SE_{cl.refl.}$ *washed.*
'The girl washed herself'.

In the current study, we focus on a particular group of unaccusative verbs, those that have a transitive counterpart and that are commonly known as "verbs with alternating transitivity". In these cases, the unaccusative SE appears with verbs such as 'open' or 'break' that involve the predicate CAUSE and two arguments: the causer argument and the passive participant (the *patient* or *theme*) that undergoes the change. These verbs describe an event that is under the control of an external cause, which brings about the event. The external cause corresponds to the external argument of unaccusatives and it might be of different nature: agents, instruments or natural forces (e.g. the girl/ball/earthquake broke the window). In other words, a window breaks because of an external event, and not solely due to the internal properties of the window. The external cause can be left unspecified, but even then our knowledge of the world indicates that the event could not have happened without the existence of an external cause.

As for reflexive constructions, a preliminary analysis of the data on production of reflexive verbs and verbs with alternating transitivity in brain -damaged speakers [21] have provided evidence for the analysis of reflexives as unergative entries [9,17,18,19]. Under this approach, reflexive constructions are the outcome of suppression of the internal argument through reduction. In particular, Reinhart [16] argues that role-reduction applies to the internal theta role and the argument that survives reductions needs to be externally realized. Thus, the non clitic DP is the external argument and, no movement operation is required. The reflexive clitic is considered a marker of this reduction process, which operates in the lexicon on transitive entries to produce reflexive verbs.

1.3 Direct Object Pronouns

Kayne [11] provided one of the most influential studies on the syntactic structure of direct object (DO) clitics. He claims that DO clitics surface in their final position through a movement transformation known as Clitic Placement (Cl-Pl). He further argues that clitics are an extension of the strong pronominal forms, which in turn are generated as an expansion of NPs. Thus sentence (5) in French is derived from deep structure (6).

(5) Marie nous connaît (Kayne, 1975:73).
Marie NOUScl.acc.2nd knows.
'Marie knows us'.

(6) Marie connaît nous (Kayne, 1975:74).
Marie connaît NOUSpron.acc.2nd.

Cl-Pl should be applied in (5), moving the pronoun to the left of the verb, resulting in (6). In order to account for the lack of contrastive stress and the fact that clitics cannot occur in the absence of a verb, Kayne further argues that the pronoun and the verb are closely bound together, yielding the sequence clitic + verb, which is dominated by the node V[2].

1.4 Clitic Production in Agrammatic Aphasia

A number of cross-linguistic studies have focused on problems encountered by agrammatic speakers during production of pronominals [8,22]. Of particular importance for the current study are data in Romance languages, which have shown that agrammatic participants produce fewer pronominal clitics than non-brain damaged subjects [6,12,14]. Particularly, Rossi [20] noted that agrammatic speakers of Italian produce fewer reflexive, direct object and indirect object clitics than non-brain-damaged individuals. There are few studies in Spanish that specifically deal with the analysis of clitic production. Some evidence is found in a study by Reznik et al. (1995) on a River Plate Spanish speaker, in which the authors observed that 56.14% of clitics were omitted. More recently, Martinez-Ferreiro [13] observed a significant dissociation between object and reflexive clitics in several varieties of Ibero-Romance (Spanish, Catalan and Galician). The author reports that reflexive forms were correctly produced around 85% of the time, whereas object clitics posed more difficulties in the three languages under study, with 3 participants not reaching 10% of correctness.

Although the source of the difficulties in production of clitic pronouns is to this date unclear, Avrutin's [1] work on pronominal interpretation in children and individuals with Broca's aphasia offers an explanation on the underlying cause of these difficulties. Following Reinhart's [15] work on analyses of pronominals as bound variables and referring expressions, Avrutin argues that agrammatic speakers have problems in pronoun interpretation and particularly in establishing pronoun reference. His ideas were further elaborated into the Syntax-Discourse Model ([1,2,4,15,23] which postulates two different levels of representation, syntax an discourse) and a set of rules which serves as a connection between the two levels. It takes Heim's [10] discourse model as a basis, and describes a well-formed information unit as consisting of a frame and a heading. The frame contains referential properties and is introduced by a functional category; whereas the heading provides the content information through a lexical category. Crucially, pronominals violate these conditions because they introduce empty frames, and require a heading in order to be fully interpretable. Consequently, they are referentially dependent on their antecedents. The authors argue that the process of establishing a dependency between the pronominal

[2] In spite of the superficial similarities between DO clitics and SE-constructions, Kayne (1975) convincingly showed that the movement transformation assumed for the first cannot account for the particular properties of the second. This has been assumed for all approaches to clitics since then, and therefore it is not further discussed in this paper.

and its antecedent to create a well-formed unit is at the heart of the difficulties encountered by agrammatic speakers in comprehension of pronominals.

In particular, Avrutin [1] claims that reflexives, or SE anaphors in general, are so-called 'locally bound' and their interpretation requires co-indexation with the subject. As a result, a dependency between the anaphor and its antecedent is established at the level of syntax [4] which suffices to create a corresponding well-formed unit. Hence, only knowledge of syntactic principles[3] which is speaker internal, is required. The author considers this operation to be mainly automatic, which accounts for the perfect performance observed in children and agrammatic speakers in sentences with reflexives. In contrast, DO clitics are not bound within the sentence, but require implementation of discourse-related principles, through a 'discourse linking' operation. For example, in the sentence 'the boy_i is washing $himself_i$', the pronoun 'himself' is interpreted as a variable that is bound in syntax, and thus 'himself' and 'the boy' refer to the same entity. In the sentence '*the boy_i washes him_i', the indices cannot be the same because of Principle B [7], which states that pronouns must be locally free. Burkhardt [4] argues that the potential antecedent is identified on the basis of morphological feature matching and discourse prominence. Hence, the only grammatical representation of this sentence is the one where 'him' refers to someone outside the sentence and an extrasentential link should be made. This process is known as 'discourse linked'[4]. A crucial difference between the unaccusative and the reflexive SE is that in reflexive constructions, the clitic is a coargument with its antecedent, and therefore its interpretation can be accounted for by syntactic operations alone. Nonetheless, the unaccusative SE is not a coargument with its antecedent, and therefore its interpretation cannot be explained by syntactic operations alone. In fact, only if the speaker employs his/her knowledge of the world would s/he be able to establish the correct interpretation.

Avrutin further argues that discourse linking (henceforth D-linking) calls for a higher processing load than local binding because it requires making inferences about other speakers' representations of discourse. Accordingly, the deficits observed in individuals with Broca's aphasia can be explained in terms of difficulties implementing discourse-related operations. Thus, in contrast to the clitic SE in reflexive constructions, every clitic pronoun, whether it is in production or comprehension, needs to be D-linked.

Although the Syntax-Discourse model is mainly focused on comprehension of pronominals, its predictions can be applied, to some extent, to production. A relevant difference is that, during production, the individuals and event units must exist before the syntactic structure is assembled. Nonetheless, the frame provided by the pronominal still serves as the connection between narrow syntax and discourse. Hence, as for production of DO pronouns, the heading is still

---

[3] Only knowledge of Binding Principles [7] is necessary:
-Principles A: reflexives must be locally bound
-Principles B: pronouns must be locally free.,

[4] Discourse-linking has been found to be relevant for other construtions, such as Wh-questions [1] or reference to the past [3].

supplied from the preceding discourse and even though the event already exists, the speaker should establish a relationship between the event and the clitic. Similarly, in the case of the unaccusative SE, the speaker must employ his/her knowledge of the external world (e.g. the wind made the glass fall and consequently it broke) and translate it into syntactic symbols. This process implies that the speaker has to establish a clear connection between their knowledge of the external word and the clitic. Furthermore, the speaker has to ensure that both the hearer shares his/her external knowledge. In other words, the speaker is integrating discourse and syntax levels in order to transmit his/her message. Consequently, the supposed additional processing load needed for interpretation of DO clitics and unaccusative SE allows us to predict that more difficulties will arise in agrammatic speech in both production and comprehension.

2 Method

2.1 Participants

Eleven Spanish agrammatic speakers (five females and six males; mean age: 49 years, mean education: 20 years) were tested. All participants were between 23-263 months post-onset of a single left hemisphere stroke (one participant had bilateral damage) at the time of the study; all were right-handed, had normal (or corrected to normal) hearing and vision, and had at least a high school education. None of the participants had a history of drug or alcohol abuse, hospitalization for psychiatric disorders, speech/language disorders, or learning disabilities before the stroke that could have influenced the test results.

Participants were classified as Broca's aphasic individuals based on a Spanish version of the Boston Aphasia Examination (Goodglass and Kaplan, 1972) and confirmed by the speech therapist. All participants showed classic Broca's aphasia: non-fluent and telegraphic speech production and relatively intact comprehension. None of the individuals had articulatory impairments that might have interfered with the test results. Eleven native speakers of Spanish matched in gender, age and education (six females and five males, mean age: 45 years, mean education: 20 years) with no language or speech impairment history served as the control group.

2.2 Materials

A total of 16 action verbs with alternating transitivity were selected for a sentence completion task. Each verb was used twice, once in the transitive and once in the unaccusative condition. Transitive forms were used to elicit both DO clitics and full DPs in object position. Furthermore, eight reflexive verbs were selected for comparison across clitic types. For each item, color photographs were created. The verb (infinitive form) depicting the action was printed above every pair of photographs to avoid word finding problems. An example of a test item is shown in Figure 1.

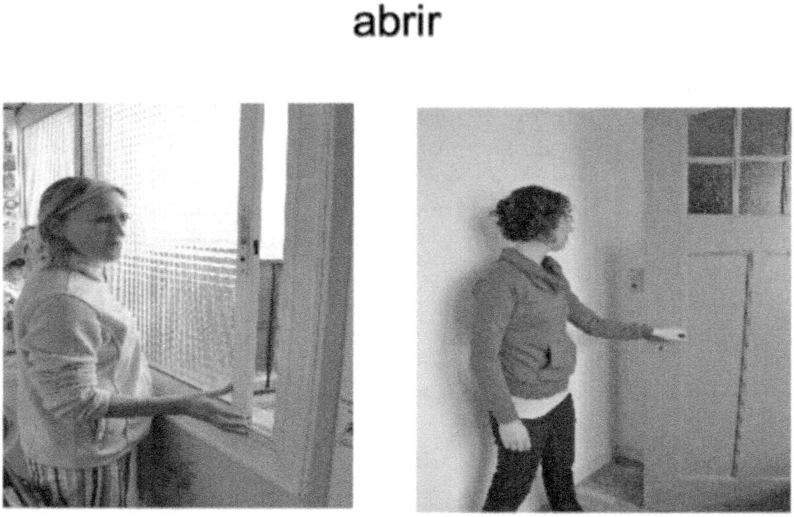

Fig. 1. *Qu hace la chica?* What is the girl doing?

2.3 Procedure

A sentence completion test consisting of 32 items was developed. Only verbs with alternating transitivity and reflexive verbs were used as items. The task presented to each participant consisted of the following photographs: Eight items elicited an unaccusative sentence (e.g. *la puerta* SE *abre*, 'the door opens'); eight items elicited a transitive sentence, for which no clitic was expected in the answer (e.g. *la niña abre la puerta*, 'the girl opens the door'); eight different items were used to elicit a transitive sentence, for which a DO clitic in object position was expected (e.g. *la niña* LA *abre* 'the girl opens it'); and eight items were used to elicit reflexive sentences (e.g. *la niña* SE *lava*, 'the girl washes herself'. Items were randomized and presented one at a time to elicit the target sentence.

For every pair of photographs, the experimenter named the objects and individuals in the photograph to ensure proper recognition. Then, she asked a question of the type *qué hace la niña?* 'what is the girl doing?'. The subject of the next sentence was given, and the participant had to complete the sentence with the same verb and the required clitic/full DP. Participants were asked to listen carefully to the experimenter as she read the item aloud, and they had to complete the last sentence read with the given verb and a similar construction. Depending on the condition, the question asked by the experimenter was slightly modified in order to elicit the target clitic/full DP. An example of each condition is found in (7-10).

(7) Transitive condition (full DP expected):
qué hace la niña?
'What is the girl doing?'

Target answer:
La niña abre la puerta.
'The girl opens the door'.

(8) Unaccusative condition (SE clitic expected):
qué sucede con la puerta?
'What happens to the door?'
Target answer:
La puerta se abre.
'The door opens'.

(9) Transitive condition (DO clitic expected):
qué hace la nia con la puerta
'What is the girl doing to the door?'
Target answer:
La niña la abre.
'The girl opens it'.

(10) Reflexive condition (SE clitic expected):
qué hace la niña?
'What is the girl doing?'
Target answer:
La niña se lava.
'The girl washes herself'.

Practice trials for each condition were provided and repeated when necessary to ensure that participants understood the task. On the request of the participant, items were repeated once. No time limits were imposed.

2.4 Scoring

All responses were tape-recorded, transcribed and analyzed. A response was considered to be correct if it contained the required verb and clitic/full DP, and if the clitic/full DP was in the required position. Any verb form produced was counted as a correct response (e.g. *romper el espejo* 'to break the mirror', or *va a apagar la vela* '[she] is going to blow the candle', were counted as correct). In the DO-clitic condition, some verbs were produced in the infinitive form, which requires enclisis of the pronoun (e.g. *secarlo* 'to dry it'). This use of the pronoun was counted as correct because the main purpose was to study production of clitics and full DPs. Both quantitative and qualitative analyses were completed. For the quantitative analysis, correct responses were tallied. For the qualitative comparison, an error analysis was carried out. Errors were defined post *hoc* based on the most frequent errors occurring. These included (a) clitic omissions (e.g. the participant only produced the verb), and (b) clitic substitutions (i.e. substitution by a different clitic/full DP). Grammatical responses were also analyzed for deviations from the target sentences. The main deviations were classified into five categories: different tense form, different gender/number (in the target clitic), synonymous verb, unrelated verb and use of a different full DP.

2.5 Data Analysis

Percentages of correctly produced sentences involving all four conditions were calculated for each participant. Group means were computed for each sentence type. Due to the relatively small group of participants, differences between sentence types were analyzed using the Wilcoxon and Mann-Withney nonparametric tests. Percentages of error types and deviations from target sentences were also calculated for each sentence type.

3 Results

3.1 Quantitative Analysis

Non-brain-damaged (NBD) participants as a group performed significantly better on the test than agrammatic participants in three out of the four conditions: DO clitics (Mann-Withney, z= -3.447, p= .001), unaccusatives (Mann-Withney, z= -2.547, p= .011) and reflexives (Mann-Withney, z= 2.148, p= .032). Performance between the two groups was not significantly different in production of transitives will full DPs in object position (henceforth 'transitive condition') (Mann-Whitney, z= -.269, p= .788). The analysis reported an accuracy score in this condition of 75.18 % for NBD participants, whereas speakers with agrammatism achieved an accuracy score of 69.73 %. A closer analysis of the data reveals that this low score in the NBD participants is due to the nature of the task. Participants were presented with two photographs and the persons and objects in the photographs were named by the experimenter in order to provide the participant with a reference. Since this reference was provided, control participants used DO clitics instead of full DPs in 19% of the responses in the transitive condition, whereas omission of the clitic only occurred in 5% of the responses. These responses were all counted as incorrect. In contrast, aphasic participants omitted the full DP in 20% of the responses, whereas only 2% accounted for substitutions by a DO clitic. Therefore, it was decided to analyze the data with the inclusion of substitutions of full DPs by DO clitics as correct answers in both groups. The new analysis, however, did not show a clear significant difference in production of transitives between the aphasic participants and the control group either (Mann-Withney, z= -1.715, p= .086). Knowing this, we leave the data of the control group and focus on the agrammatic data.

Overall, production by agrammatic speakers showed a different pattern from the control group, with 43% of correct responses. The analysis of the agrammatic data shows that reflexives are better preserved than clitics in the other conditions (DO clitics and unaccusatives), and that they are just as difficult to produce as the transitive sentences with full DPs. DO clitics are the clitics that account for the highest number of errors.

The number of incorrect responses in the DO-clitic condition was significantly higher than that found in the three other conditions: the reflexive condition (Wilcoxon, z= -2.947, p= .003), the transitive condition (Wilcoxon, z= -2.937, p= .003) and the unaccusative condition (Wilxocon, z= -1.963, p= .05). Second, unaccusatives were significantly harder to produce than reflexives (Wilcoxon, z= -2.366, p= 0.018), and transitives with full DPs (Wilcoxon, z= -2.240, p= .025). Finally, regarding the transitive and reflexive conditions, the difference between the two of them was not significant (Wilcoxon, z= -.135, p= .893).

In sum, the agrammatic data demonstrate that production of transitives with full DPs and with reflexive verbs was relatively spared. Transitive sentences that require production of DO clitics and unaccusative constructions posed more constraints for agrammatic speakers, and in particular, DO clitics registered a higher number of errors.

3.2 Qualitative Analysis

The qualitative analysis focused on the types of errors observed in the four conditions. First, the main error types across conditions were compared. Then, the contributions of the error types to each condition separately were calculated. Finally, a qualitative analysis of main deviations in grammatical responses was conducted in order to study relevant differences between the responses given by the participants and the target answers.

Participants produced ungrammatical sentences in 57% of the total responses. The most frequent error observed when aphasic individuals produced ungrammatical sentences were omissions: omissions of full DPs and clitics in object position. Omissions accounted for 71% of all ungrammatical responses, most of them (38% of all omissions) occurred in the unaccusative condition. The remaining 29% ungrammatical responses were related to substitution of the clitic or full DP.

In the DO-clitic condition, the main error type was substitution of the clitic by a full DP in base position, followed by omission of the clitic. A closer analysis of the data revealed a difference between these two types of errors: Omissions mainly occurred in aphasic speakers scoring lower in the total number of correct sentences, whereas substitution of the DO clitic was mostly found in participants with a higher number of correct responses.

In the case of the unaccusative sentences, the main error type was omission of the clitic SE. There was only one case in which the participant produces a DO clitic instead of a SE clitic (i.e. instead of the target answer *la leche* SE *calienta*, 'the milk warms up'; the speaker produced *calentándola* 'warming it up').

As for the transitive condition with full DPs, errors were mainly object omissions. The DP was substituted by a DO clitic by three aphasic participants, all of them scoring high in the total number of correct responses. Regarding reflexives, the only error type was clitic omission.

Finally, an analysis of constituent order in production revealed no word order deviations in any of the four conditions. A comparison of the mean percentage of all response types (including correct responses) is provided in Figure 2.

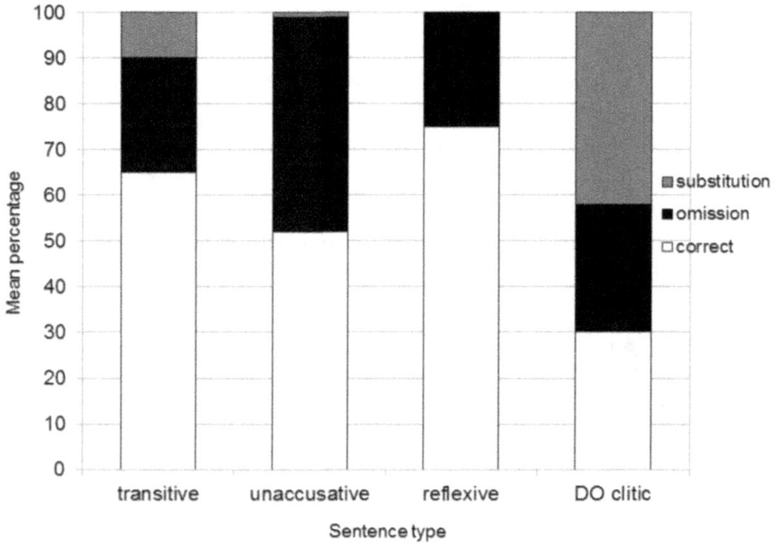

Fig. 2. Mean percentage of total production by sentence and response type

In sum, producing sentences in the DO-clitic condition was significantly more difficult than in the unaccusative, reflexive and transitive conditions; the main error types in this condition being omission of the clitic and substitution by a full DP. Furthermore, unaccusative constructions were also significantly more difficult than reflexives; when participants made an error, it was mainly due to omission of the clitic.

4 Discussion

Our first question focused on the similarities between two SE anaphors: unaccusative SE and reflexive SE. Although the two clitics share a number of similarities e.g. they cannot be stressed, they cannot stand alone, and especially, they carry a minimal number of features, speakers were more impaired in production of the unaccusative SE. The question then is what complicates production. We argue that the main difference between the two SE anaphors lies in their interpretation. In the case of the reflexive SE, interpretation of the clitic takes place at the syntax level because the clitic is in a coargumenthood relationship with its antecedent, i.e. Both of them are arguments of the same predicate. In contrast, the unaccusative SE serves as a residue of the external argument and indicates the existence of an external element which causes the "change". It serves, therefore, as a link between narrow syntax and the knowledge of the internal world or discourse level. In order to establish the correct interpretation, the speaker should be able to integrate both levels in order to achieve a correct interpretation. S/he should also be able to make inferences about the listener's knowledge of the external world.

Secondly, due to the similarities in pronoun interpretation, our second objective was to compare production of the unaccusative SE and the direct object clitics. On the basis of the Syntax-Discourse model [1], [2], [4], [15], [23] both clitics should call for a higher processing load than the reflexive SE because they require integration of two different linguistic modules. As expected, both of them were impaired in agrammatic speech and in particular production of direct object clitics registered the highest number of errors. This difference in production might be due to their feature composition since DO pronouns have a full feature composition (i.e. number, gender, person and case). Indeed, an analysis of the errors and deviations from target sentences shows that production of clitic features (gender and number) is difficult for agrammatic speakers. This error type was already identified by Rossi [20] in Italian. The author argues that feature load poses problems for aphasic speakers. If related features are not correctly checked, the clitic will bear the wrong gender/number. The present study indicates that participants made errors with gender and number. In fact, some speakers even produced several variants of the same clitic before they provided the correct number and gender. Further research is needed to clarify the difficulties that feature checking pose for some agrammatic speakers.

There is an additional error which shows that, in line with previous findings on clitic production in Spanish [13] and Italian [20], DO clitics are predominantly substituted by full DPs. In some cases, agrammatic speakers omit the clitic, and thus avoid the D-linking process, but the result is an ungrammatical sentence. However, by substituting the clitic with a full DP, speakers are able to produce a grammatical answer which accurately describes the picture. And, what is more important, they escape the d-linking operation. In contrast, in the unaccusative construction, the main error was clitic omission. In these constructions, there is no equivalent structure in Spanish that allows the agrammatic speakers to escape the additional processing of accessing the discourse level and, at the same time, produce a grammatical sentence that describes the photograph. Therefore, they are left with only one strategy: omission of the clitic. This explains the high number of omission errors in the unaccusatives, as compared to DO clitics. Interestingly, DO clitics were predominantly omitted by participants with a low number of total correct responses, whereas those scoring higher in the number of correct responses tend to substitute the DO clitic. This dissociation in the type of error indicates that mildly agrammatic individuals show a higher sensitivity to argument structure and, therefore, they are faster in implementing new strategies, and processing new information, although the syntactic operations at stake still pose the same problems.

References

1. Avrutin, S.: Development of the syntax-discourse interface. Kluwer, Boston (1999)
2. Avrutin, S.: Weak syntax. In: Grodzinsky, Y., Amunts, K. (eds.), Broca's region, pp. 49-62. Oxford: Oxford University Press (2006)
3. Bastiaanse, R., Bamyaci, E., Hsu, C.J, Lee, T., Duman, Y., Thompson, C.K.: Time reference in agrammatic aphasia: A cross-linguistic study, 652-673, (2011)
4. Burkhardt, P.: The Syntax-Discourse Interface: Representing and Interpreting Dependency. John Benjamins Publishing Company, Amsterdam/Philadelphia (2005)
5. Burzio, L.: Italian syntax: A government-binding approach. Reidel, Dordrecht (1986)
6. Chinellato, P.: Disturbi di sintassi nell'afasia fluente: un'analisi linguistica dell'agrammatismo italiano e dialettale. PhD thesis, University of Padova (2004)
7. Chomsky, N.: Lectures on government and binding. Foris Publications, Dordrecht (1981)
8. Drijbooms, E., & Bastiaanse: Production of pronouns and reflexives by agrammatic French-Dutch bilingual speakers. Paper presented at Science of Aphasia XII, Barcelona, September 1-5 (2011)
9. Grimshaw, J.: On the lexical representation of Romance reflexive clitics. In: Bresnan, J., (Ed.) The mental representation of grammatical relations. MIT Press, Cambridge, MA, pp. 87-146 (1982)
10. Heim, I.: The Semantics of Definitie and Indefinite Noun Phrases. Ph.D. thesis, University of Massacusetss, Amherst (1982)
11. Kayne, R.: French syntax: The transformational cycle. MIT Press, Cambridge, MA (1975)
12. Lonzi, L., Luzzatti, C.: Relevance of adverb distribution for the analysis of sentence representation in agrammatic patients. Brain and Language, 45, 306-317 (1993)
13. Martinez Ferreiro, S.: Title. PhD Thesis, Autonomous University of Barcelona (2010)
14. Miceli, G., Mazzucchi, A.: Agrammatism in Italian: Two case studies. In: Menn, L., Obler, L., (eds.), Agrammatic aphasia: a cross linguistic narrative sourcebook, pp. 717–757. Benjamin, Amsterdam (1990)
15. Piñango, M.M and Burkhardt, P.: Pronominal Interpretation and the Syntax-Discourse Interface: Real-time Comprehension and Neurological Properties. In: Branco, A., McEnery, T. and Mitkov, R. (eds.) Anaphora Processing: linguistic, cognitive and computational modelling. Amsterdam/Philadelphia: John Benjamins Publishing Company, 221–238 (2005)
16. Reinhart, T.: The Theta system: syntactic realization of verbal concepts. OTS Working Papers in Linguistics, Utrecht (2000)
17. Reinhart, T.: Syntactic Effects of Lexical Operations: Reflexives and UiL. OTS Working Papers in Linguistics, Utrecht (1997)
18. Reinhart, T., Siloni, T.: Against the Unaccusative Analysis of reflexives. In: Alexiadou, A., Anagnostopoulou, E., Everaert, M., (eds.), The Unaccusativity Puzzle. Oxford University Press, Oxford (1999)
19. Reinhart, T.: Coreference and bound anaphora: A restatement of the anaphora question. Linguistics and Philosophy, 6, 4788 (1983)

20. Rossi, E.: Clitic production in Italian agrammatism. PhD thesis, University of Groningen (2007)
21. Sanchez Alonso, S., Martinez Ferreiro, S, Bastiaanse, R.: Production of verbs with alternating transitivity in Spanish agrammatic speakers (in press)
22. Stavrakaki S. and Kouvava S.: Functional categories in agrammatism: Evidence from Greek. Brain and Language 86,129-141 (2003)
23. Vasi, N., Avrutin, S., E., Ruigendijk: Interpretation of pronouns in VP-ellipsis constructions in Dutch Broca's and Wernicke's aphasia. Brain and Language 96(2), 191-206 (2006)

Author Index

GPSR Compliance

The European Union's (EU) General Product Safety Regulation (GPSR) is a set of rules that requires consumer products to be safe and our obligations to ensure this.

If you have any concerns about our products, you can contact us on ProductSafety@springernature.com

In case Publisher is established outside the EU, the EU authorized representative is:

Springer Nature Customer Service Center GmbH
Europaplatz 3
69115 Heidelberg, Germany

Batch number: 10844619

Printed by Printforce, the Netherlands